EDITOR
WILLIS F. OVERTON
Temple University

EDITORIAL ASSISTANT
DANIELLE L. HORVATH
Temple University

CONSULTING EDITORS FOR THE MONOGRAPHS (2001)

RHYTHMS OF DIALOGUE IN INFANCY: COORDINATED TIMING IN DEVELOPMENT

Joseph Jaffe
Beatrice Beebe
Stanley Feldstein
Cynthia L. Crown
Michael D. Jasnow

WITH COMMENTARIES BY
Philippe Rochat
Daniel N. Stern

Willis F. Overton
Series Editor

MONOGRAPHS OF THE SOCIETY FOR RESEARCH IN CHILD DEVELOPMENT
Serial No. 265, Vol. 66, No. 2, 2001

Boston, Massachusetts   Oxford, United Kingdom

RHYTHMS OF DIALOGUE IN INFANCY: COORDINATED TIMING IN DEVELOPMENT

CONTENTS

COMMENTARIES

ABSTRACT

Jaffe, Joseph; Beebe, Beatrice; Feldstein, Stanley; Crown, Cynthia L.;
and Jasnow, Michael D. Rhythms of Dialogue in Infancy. *Monographs
of the Society for Research in Child Development*, 2001, **66** (2, Serial No.
265).

Although theories of early social development emphasize the advantage of mother-infant rhythmic coupling and bidirectional coordination,
empirical demonstrations remain sparse. We therefore test the hypothesis
that vocal rhythm coordination at age 4 months predicts attachment and
cognition at age 12 months. Partner and site novelty were studied by
recording mother-infant, stranger-infant, and mother-stranger face-to-
face interactions in both home and laboratory sites for 88 4-month-old
infants, for a total of 410 recordings. An automated dialogic coding scheme,
appropriate to the nonperiodic rhythms of our data, implemented a systems concept of every action as jointly produced by both partners. Adult-
infant coordination at age 4 months indeed predicted both outcomes at
age 12 months, but midrange degree of mother-infant and stranger-
infant coordination was optimal for attachment (Strange Situation), whereas
high ("tight") stranger-infant coordination in the lab was optimal for cognition (Bayley Scales). Thus, high coordination can index more *or* less
optimal outcomes, as a function of outcome measure, partner, and site.
Bidirectional coordination patterns were salient in both attachment and
cognition predictions. Comparison of mother-infant and stranger-infant
interactions was particularly informative, suggesting the dynamics of infants' early differentiation from mothers. Stranger and infant showed different patterns of vocal rhythm activity level, were more bidirectional,
accounted for 8 times more variance in Bayley scores, predicted attachment just as well as mother and infant, and revealed more varied contingency structures and a wider range of attachment outcomes. To explain
why vocal timing measures at age 4 months predict outcomes at age 12
months, our dialogue model was construed as containing procedures for

regulating the pragmatics of *proto-conversation*. The timing patterns of the 4-month-olds were seen as *procedural* or *performance* knowledge, and as precursors of various kinesic patterns in the outcomes of 12-month-olds. Thus, our work further defines a fundamental dyadic timing matrix—a system that guides the trajectory of relatedness, informing all relational theories of development.

I. INTRODUCTION

Relating to another person is a shared process. As partners communicate, they adapt moment-by-moment by coordinating verbal and nonverbal rhythmic patterns, such as on-off cycles of vocalizing and pausing, or of looking and looking away. Lashley (1954) argued that rhythmic structure is fundamental because most of our motor behaviors are rhythmically organized. The simplest rhythms are strictly regular (periodic). But the rhythms of human communicative behavior are in general irregular or nonperiodic, as shown by Jaffe and Feldstein (1970), with later confirmations by Jaffe, Stern, and Peery (1973), Cohn and Tronick (1988), Feldman, Greenbaum, Yirmiya, and Mayes (1996), and Warner (1988). Rhythm thus requires a more general definition. In this monograph, *rhythm* is defined as a recurrent nonrandom temporal patterning that may or may not be strictly regular.

Interaction rhythms possess temporal structures essential for effective communication. We experience some interaction rhythms, perhaps those with which we resonate, as "good vibes," whereas others are experienced as disturbing. Because a partner's rhythm is assessed in reference to one's own, Byers (1976) suggested that we continuously assess an interpersonal rhythmic relationship, a form of coordination. We define *coordination* most generally as interpersonal contingency, such that each partner's behavior can be predicted from that of the other. The coordination of interpersonal timing involves the prediction of each partner's timing pattern from that of the other.

This capacity for rhythmic coordination is essential to cognition and bonding. In cognitive development, repeating rhythmic accents permit prediction and anticipation of the pattern of accented elements, facilitating efficient information processing, memory, and the representation of interpersonal events. In social interactions, rhythm itself provides ongoing information necessary to predict and coordinate with one's partner, so that each can anticipate how the other will proceed (Warner, 1992). Because rhythmic patterns facilitate information processing and interpersonal

1

prediction, they provide the infant with a structure for forming temporal expectancies that organize both social and cognitive experience.

Although theoretical models of infant social development in the past two decades have used these concepts to emphasize the key role of reciprocal interaction and rhythmic coordination, empirical study of these constructs in relation to developmental outcomes has remained sparse. By the mid-1980s, researchers employing a variety of approaches deemed reciprocal interaction and rhythmic coordination critical to the social development of infants. Yet, apart from a small number of provocative studies (e.g., Bakeman & Brown, 1980; Feldman et al., 1996; Isabella & Belsky, 1991; Lewis & Feiring, 1989; Malatesta, Culver, Tesman, & Shepard, 1989), few researchers have specifically attempted to predict infant social outcomes. In this study we therefore evaluate the contribution of experiences with vocal rhythm coordination at age 4 months to the emergence at age 12 months of two central measures of infant development: attachment (Ainsworth Strange Situation) and cognition (Bayley Scales). By age 4 months mother and infant have a well-established history, and this age is standard for assessment of face-to-face mother-infant interaction. Age 12 months was chosen as the first point at which mother-infant attachment could be assessed by the Ainsworth Strange Situation.

The meaning of *coordination,* both in early mother-infant interactions as well as its implications for infant developmental outcomes, remains controversial. Studies of adults initially articulated this debate, and three competing hypotheses emerged relating degree of coordination to quality of relatedness. Chapple (1970) regarded high coordination as *optimal* for communication. Gottman (1979) suggested that high coordination indexes communicative *distress.* Warner, Malloy, Schneider, Knoth, and Wilder (1987) proposed an optimal midrange model in which *both* high and low degrees of coordination are negatively experienced. At the time that we began this project, in the late 1980s, Cohn and Elmore (1988) called for further infant research to determine whether there is an optimal range of coordination, as a function of type of interaction, context, and developmental outcome. Despite scattered evidence suggesting that higher coordination may be disadvantageous, this question remains unresolved.

A related debate concerns the definition and significance of *bidirectional* coordination, both in early mother-infant interactions, as well as in the evolving trajectory of infant developmental outcomes. The central definitional paper, that of Cohn and Tronick (1988), defined bidirectional coordination as an *across-group* rather than a *within-dyad* phenomenon. But the very concept of bidirectional coordination implies that each partner is adjusting his or her own behavior to that of the other. We explore both definitions of bidirectional coordination in describing adult-infant interactions at age 4 months, as well as in predicting outcomes. The

2

existence of bidirectional mother-infant coordination (across-group) has been well established in the last two decades, and it has generally been assumed to be a positive feature of interactions. But, again, little research has specifically investigated its link to developmental outcomes such as bonding or cognition. Further empirical study of bidirectional coordination and its relation to developmental outcomes is important in order to test a central tenet of modern systems views of development that bidirectional coordinations between components of the system (such as infant and parent) provide one critical "engine" of development (e.g., Gottlieb, Wahlsten, & Lickliter, 1998; Lerner, 1998; Lewkowicz, 2000; Overton, 1998).

A *dyadic systems* view of communication frames our study of rhythms of dialogue. We wanted to concretize the ideas of Sullivan (1940), Winnicott (1965), and others who held that, psychologically, the individual does not exist independent of his or her relationships. In a dyadic systems view, any action of an individual is jointly defined by the behavior of both partners. We therefore use a *dyadic* coding in which vocal states are jointly defined by both partners (both vocalizing, both silent, or one or the other partner vocalizing alone). However, within our systems approach, we want to be able to define the component individuals as well as the dyad. When either partner vocalizes while the other remains silent, it is clear who is the speaker and who is the listener. But in simultaneous speech and simultaneous silence, who is the speaker and who the listener? And who is interrupting in simultaneous speech? Based on a simple turn-taking rule stipulating that whoever vocalizes unilaterally gains the turn, Jaffe and Feldstein (1970) classified every vocal state as occurring within one or the other partner's turn, thus generating a system of coding relevant to both the dyad and the individuals within it. In this system, dialogue consists of a slower turn rhythm as speaker and listener exchange roles, as well as a faster vocalization-pause rhythm within each person's turn. Jaffe and Feldstein further elaborated their model of adult dialogue by including not only vocalizations, pauses, and turns, but also *switching pauses* at the point of the turn exchange, and two types of simultaneous speech. They also built an automated instrument to measure sounds and silence durations directly from each speaker's microphone.

The Jaffe-Feldstein approach was used in many studies of adult-adult spontaneous face-to-face communication, focusing on the coordination of vocal rhythms between partners. When speakers coordinate rhythmic patterns such as sound-silence or look-look away, they are in fact exchanging important information regarding the perceived warmth, similarity, and empathy of their interaction. Further research on adult communication has continued to show that matching and coordinating the timing of communicative behaviors facilitates interpersonal attraction, empathy, and social relatedness. In the mid-1970s a series of initial investigations by our group, which at that time included Daniel Stern, showed the value of a rhythmic approach to mother-infant gaze, vocalization, and facial interactions. Welkowitz, Cariffe, and Feldstein (1976) also used this approach to examine peer interactions in children. But not until the 1980s did our group show that the complete Jaffe-Feldstein approach was feasible for adult-infant vocal interaction.

In this monograph we extend the study of adult dialogic vocal rhythms to those between infants and adults. Launched in the late 1980s, it is the first large-scale application of this method to infancy. We investigate the possibility that, similar to adult-adult studies, infant-adult coordination in the first year may reflect the *quality* of interaction.

But why would coordination of rhythms at age 4 months predict infant development at age 12 months? Most generally, the infant's perception of temporal patterns is a foundation for processing both social and cognitive information, and for constructing expectancies of exchanges with the partner and the environment. More specifically, analogous to the adult finding that vocal rhythm coordination is an index of features such as warmth or empathy, we hypothesize that patterns of vocal rhythm coordination of adults and 4-month-old infants carry fundamental qualities of the social interaction, and thus predict the trajectory of social/cognitive development. But what particular timing processes might link vocal rhythm coordination to attachment and cognitive outcomes? We view the units of our dialogic model—which include mother and infant turn-taking, activity level, joining and being joined, yielding and interrupting—as procedures for regulating the timing pragmatics of dialogue. We understand these vocal patterns at age 4 months as a form of procedural representation or performance knowledge, analogous to and precursors of various kinesic patterns in the outcomes of 12-month-olds. In both the Bayley and the Strange Situation, the infant must also manage attention, take turns, regulate activity level, join, interrupt, and track. We draw an analogy between the 4-month-old infant's management of vocal action, joint action, and turn-taking, and the way the 12-month-old infant attends, joins, ignores, or tracks the mother in the Strange Situation reunion, or the way the infant tracks the experimenter and takes his or her turn manipulating objects in the Bayley test. Thus the same interpersonal timing patterns may have similar functions at the two ages.

Although a good deal is already known about the general topic of the coordination of mother-infant interaction at age 4 months, we still lack a full understanding of *how* vocal rhythms coordinate. There is currently no unifying theory of the interpersonal coordination of *nonperiodic* rhythms. Whereas most approaches in the literature address rhythm coordination using the assumption that rhythms are periodic, our approach is to discover modes of coordination from the behavioral organization of the nonperiodic rhythms themselves. Our rhythmic approach explores the proposal that the *patterns* of sound and silence provide additional information about the organization of communication not evident in the separate components of sound and silence. For example, is it the beat (defined here as the mean duration of the vocalization-plus-pause cycle) that is correlated between partners? Such correlation is often termed *entrainment* and is generally assumed to be the central rhythmic process (Warner, 1988; Winfree, 1975). Or is it the level of activity (the mean ratio of vocalization to pause durations) within cycles that partners track? As one partner adjusts durations of sounds and silences to those of the other, is the adjustment one of positive correlation, so that as one partner lengthens durations, the other does likewise? Or is the adjustment one of negative correlation, so that as one partner lengthens, the other shortens duration?

Despite its acknowledged importance for early social development, an infant's experience of a stranger, as compared to his or her mother, is a relatively unexplored topic in the study of early face-to-face interactions. We are interested in whether vocal rhythm and timing coordination might be differential relational features at this early age, thus providing one way of defining the infant's first differentiation from the original mother-infant dyadic matrix. Furthermore, because the challenge of novelty can amplify aspects of a system's organization, we conjecture that the dimension of *familiar-novel* will clarify the meaning of vocal rhythm coordination and its role in infant development. Novelty of partner and site is thus introduced by comparing mother-infant and stranger-infant vocal interactions, both at home and in the laboratory. To contrast the adult-infant data, we also examine adult-adult (mother-stranger) vocal interactions at both sites. Thus the system under study is broader than the mother-infant interaction: It includes the stranger-infant interaction, each at two different sites.

Novelty is known to be important in both social and cognitive development in infancy. In the infant's social development, for example, Bowlby (1969) emphasized the importance of the dimension of *familiar-strange* in the infant's appraisal of the environment, and in the development of the attachment system. In adult-adult interactions, Crown (1991) showed that unfamiliar partners coordinate their vocal interactions to a greater degree than do familiar ones. We investigate whether novelty of partner or site will increase degree of vocal coordination in infant-adult interactions, similar to Crown's (1991) findings for adults. Regarding the infant's cognitive development, response to novelty is central to infant cognition and the concept of intelligence at all ages (Berg & Sternberg, 1985; Fagan, 1982). We expect that our doubly novel context of infant in the laboratory with the stranger will be most powerful in predicting the infant's cognitive outcome.

The study thus has five goals: (a) a description of the *durations* of vocal rhythms of infants and adults, based on the Jaffe-Feldstein model of adult conversational timing, as well as the possible modes or methods of interpersonal coupling of these rhythmic patterns; (b) a description of the *coordination* and *bidirectional coordination* of these vocal rhythms, which goes beyond the durations of events to interpersonal contingencies, as well as the possible modes or methods of such coordination; (c) an evaluation of the significance of adult–4-month-old-infant vocal rhythm coordination for two well-known constructs of infant development at age 12 months, attachment and cognition; (d) an exploration of the role of familiar versus novel partner and site contexts within each of the first three goals; and finally (e) demonstration of the value of an inexpensive, precise, automated vocal timing instrument for large N infancy studies, which bypasses the usual labor-intensive coding methods for face-to-face mother-infant interaction research. Although the design of the study is well defined, the project is also in an important sense exploratory. It is the first large infancy study to address vocal dialogues with the Jaffe-Feldstein approach, to include the systematic evaluation of the impact of novel partner and site, and to link the coordination of vocal rhythms to developmental outcomes.

Hypotheses

The main hypothesis of the study is that variations in degree of vocal rhythm coordination between 4-month-old infants and adults predict attachment and cognition in 12-month-olds. A secondary component of this hypothesis is that bidirectional (reciprocal) coordinations predict measures in 12-month-olds. The analyses of the role of partner and site novelty at age 4 months (stranger-infant as compared to mother-infant, laboratory as compared to home) are primarily exploratory, investigating the general proposal that vocal rhythm and timing coordination are differential relational features, providing one way of defining the infant's first differentiation from mother as he or she interacts with a stranger, in a strange place. More specifically, however, guided by findings from studies of adults we hypothesize that coordination is greater between unacquainted partners. Also, guided by infant cognition findings, we hypothesize that infant response to double novelty (stranger in the laboratory) will be most informative about cognitive development.

Outline of Chapters

The literature review is organized into three sections. First we review the timing of mother-infant dialogues, focusing on those microanalytic studies that document timing coordination, irrespective of modality. We note those studies that have addressed the role of novelty in timing co-ordination, although they are few. Then we describe the dyadic systems view of communication that informs our work, and the Jaffe-Feldstein model of vocal rhythm as one such dyadic systems view. We briefly describe the procedural representation of dialogic timing to set the stage for the proposal that prediction of outcomes at age 12 months vocal rhythm coordination at age 4 months can be attributed to common timing methods that may have similar functions at the two ages. The final section, the prediction of age 1-year outcomes, reviews the literature predicting the Ainsworth attachment test and the Bayley Scales from earlier interactions. The Method chapter (chapter III) describes the design of the study, the automated vocal analyses, the definitions of vocal rhythms, the outcome measures, and the data analytic procedures, particularly the evaluation of coordination by time-series regression analysis. The results are organized into three chapters. Chapters IV and V ask a parallel set of questions, first for the vocal state *duration* data, and then for the *coordination* of these durations, regarding the role of partner and site novelty, and modes of rhythmic coordination. In chapter VI, the Ainsworth Strange Situation and Bayley Scales at age 12 months are predicted from the degree of coordination of vocal state durations at age 4 months. The final chapter discusses the results in terms of modes of rhythmic coordination, the role of novelty of partner and site in coordination at age 4 months, the prediction of attachment and cognition outcomes from 4-month-olds' coordination, and the procedural representation of dialogic timing pragmatics, which links 4-month-olds' coordination with outcomes at age 12 months.

II. LITERATURE REVIEW

THE TIMING OF MOTHER-INFANT DIALOGUES

In the 1970s, Jaffe and Feldstein's research program on adult dialogic timing changed its focus from verbal to preverbal interactions. Stern and his colleagues' suggestion that "the modality of stimulation may prove a less crucial feature of human behavior for an infant than the temporal patterning of that stimulation" (Stern, Beebe, Jaffe, & Bennett, 1977, p. 192; see also Jaffe, Stern, & Peery, 1973) led us to the view that the dialogic timing system is far more general and fundamental than its manifestation in either adult or child conversations. From this perspective, vocalization and kinesics are parts of a larger communicative "package" that may be organized by a common rhythmic time base. For example, mother-infant vocal rhythms are highly correlated with those of looking, head movement, and gesture (Beebe & Gerstman, 1980; Stern et al., 1977). As such, speech rhythm is one easily quantified index of the rich communicative package that mothers and infants display and coordinate in face-to-face communication.

Our exclusive focus on how partners coordinate the vocal timing aspect of this package depends on the infant's general sensitivity to temporal information. At birth and even in the fetus, infants perceive time and estimate durations of events (DeCasper & Carstens, 1980; DeCasper & Fifer, 1980). Newborns also discriminate speech rhythms of different cultures (Ramus, Hauser, Miller, Morris, & Mehler, 2000). Lewkowicz (1989) noted that the discrimination of duration is one of the most basic functions of the auditory system. Numerous studies document the infant's capacity to perceive temporal information in various modalities, based on experimental studies of soothing (Brackbill, 1975; Korner, & Thoman, 1972), rhythm perception (Demaney, McKenzie, & Vurpillot, 1977), temporal heart-rate conditioning (Allen, Walker, Symonds, & Marcell, 1977), discrimination of temporal synchrony between auditory and visual stimuli (Bahrick & Watson, 1985; Lawson, 1980; Spelke & Cortelyou, 1981), and studies of temporal conditioning (Abrahamson, Brackbill, Carpenter, &

Fitzgerald, 1970). In a recent review of the literature on infant perception of temporal information, Lewkowicz (2000) concluded that within the first month of life infants can discriminate unimodal auditory duration changes of 20 ms and perceive synchrony; by age 4–5 months infants can discriminate duration, rate, and rhythm. At age 4 months vocal timing taps a system in which the infant is fully competent (like sucking or gaze), and thus it provides an excellent route to investigating infant communication. Furthermore, sensitivity to timing necessarily involves sensitivity to affective and cognitive information (Bloom, 1993; Lewkowicz, 1989).

Theoretical Rationales

Key researchers in the 1970s and 1980s appreciated the critical importance of the coordination of mother-infant timing and rhythms, and considered it central to mother-infant bonding. But most research consisted of existence proofs of interpersonal coordination, without examination of replicability and generalizability. Moreover, despite the centrality of the theory that rhythmic coordination and interpersonal contingencies are central to infant development, specific developmental consequences of such coordinations were rarely assessed (for notable exceptions see Feldman et al., 1996; Isabella & Belsky, 1991; Lewis & Feiring, 1989; and Malatesta et al., 1989). Thus, this monograph fills a critical gap in the literature, namely, the empirical correlation of variations in rhythmic coordination with infant outcomes, in a reasonably large number of subjects, using a method of demonstrated replicability.

Before the burgeoning of empirical infant research, Spitz (1963) introduced the concept of *mother-infant dialogue* and argued that reciprocal action exchanges between mother and infant were crucial to establish a sense of being responded to and a sense of identity. In acquiring a dialogue, the infant learns that he or she can affect the partner, with expectable consequences. Work in this area increased in the early 1970s, and many researchers, using different procedures and modalities, characterized interaction between mother and infant as a conversation, dialogue, or proto-conversation (Als, 1975; Anderson, Vietze, & Dokecki, 1977; Bateson, 1975; Beebe, Stern, & Jaffe, 1979; Brazelton, Kozlowski, & Main, 1974; Condon, 1979; Field, 1978; Goldberg, 1977; Kaye, 1982; Papousek & Papousek, 1979; Spitz, 1963; Stern, 1974; Stern et al., 1977; Tronick, 1980). The term *dialogue* emerges as a broad metaphor that potentially included all modalities, including, for example, even sucking (Kaye & Wells, 1980).

Stern (1974) placed the study of mother-infant dialogue into the larger context of its importance for interpersonal object relations and attachment: "By providing a more fine-grained view of the instant-by-instant interactive events which make up the mother-infant relationship, we may

9

be in a better position to modify and expand current working theories on the nature of developing object relations or attachments" (p. 402). Further, Stern, Beebe, Jaffe, and Bennett (1977) pointed to the critical importance of timing and rhythm in the early mother-infant interaction, arguing that a detailed knowledge of the sequential structure and temporal patterning of mother-infant behaviors is essential, and that "these will be the actual events which organize many of the infant's crucial developmental achievements" (p. 178), including forming bonds of attachment, acquiring experience with the effect of his own social behaviors, and experience with the self-regulation of his own states of arousal and affect. The Beebe, Lachmann, and Jaffe team built on Stern's proposal and explicated the relevance of empirical studies of mother-infant dialogue for the presymbolic origins of self and object representations (Beebe, Jaffe, & Lachmann, 1992; Beebe & Lachmann, 1994; Beebe, Lachmann, & Jaffe, 1997; see also Lichtenberg, 1989; Stern, 1985). The present study is a further elaboration of the basic position that fine-grained empirical analyses are necessary to further our understanding of the role of the coordinated dialogic rhythms for infant development.

Many researchers concur on the critical importance of timing. Trevarthen (1979, 1993) argued that it is fundamental to interpersonal coordination, accomplished through the entrainment of rhythms, based on the matching of time, form, and intensity of communicative gestures and expressions, across modalities. Sander (1977) proposed that the domain of time is critical to conceptualizing the coordination of infant and mother, suggesting that biorhythmicity and phase control provide the (noncausal) mechanisms or methods of this coordination. Schaffer (1977) similarly noted that the temporal integration of the two partners' responses seems to be the critical variable in "successful" mother-infant interactions. Brazelton et al. (1974) argued that the interdependency of rhythms is at the root of the attachment between mother and infant. Bullowa (1979) also suggested that, for the preverbal infant, the state of being in communication is defined by sharing the same rhythm. She contended that the sharing of temporal patterns, experienced on literally thousands of occasions between infant and caretaker, lays the basis for the development of empathy in the child. Byers (1976) also asserted that the temporal patterning of interaction is the basis for human communication, suggesting that "We can . . . imagine a human or animal world that is communicationally related through the sharing of time forms in multiple levels of behavioral organization" (p. 160). A decade later, Fogel (1988) similarly argued that mother-infant face-to-face interaction studies differ from other studies of social interaction because issues of sequence and cyclicity are at the forefront, time is used as an explicit variable, and the role of timing in the process of mutual regulation is a central concern. At this time,

Cohn and Tronick (1988) made a pivotal contribution in their documentation that coordination between mothers and infants is bidirectional, based on a temporal organization that is probabilistic (stochastic) rather than periodic.

Work With Adults Influenced Our Methods and Questions

Our research on vocal timing originated in the 1950s, as an attempt to quantify the psychotherapy process. The story begins with a study (suggested by Miller, 1954) that patients and psychotherapists relate by improving predictions of each other's word usage. Although Feldstein and Jaffe (1963) could not confirm this hypothesis, they did use the technique as a measure of social distance. Feldstein's (1962) interest in speech dysfluencies as an anxiety measure led to the design of the Automated Vocal Transaction Analyzer (AVTA) (Cassotta, Feldstein, & Jaffe, 1967). This freed us from tedious transcription and counting of words and facilitated the study of conversational speech timing as an approach to the quantification of nonverbal behavior (Jaffe & Feldstein, 1970).

But in the 1950s, there was no easy way to record or measure nonverbal communication. Movie film could be studied frame by frame by numbering the frames sequentially (see Beebe & Stern, 1977; Beebe et al., 1979; Stern, 1971), but videotape and computers were still uncommon. Thus, the field of nonverbal behavior research (kinesics) was both theoretically and technologically years behind psycholinguistic analysis of computer-readable audio transcripts (Jaffe, 1962). And even when videotape was available, we had no automated system. Gaze coding was done by hand, originally using running paper tape (Stern, 1974).

The move from labor-intensive coding of kinesics to automated analysis of vocalization is the most fundamental way that the studies of adults influenced our infant studies, providing a method that freed researchers from the painstaking work of microanalysis of kinesic behavior from videotapes. Although not all questions can be addressed through the vocal modality, especially those dealing with facial affect and gaze, automated interaction chronometry addresses the temporal structure of dialogue, which is conceptually applicable to any modality if an appropriate transducer exists.

Four themes from work on adult dialogic timing have influenced our approach: a focus on the temporal structure of interactive sound and silence, the bidirectional coordination of rhythms, the relation of dialogic timing to affect and bonding, and the impact of a novel partner on dialogic timing. One strength of applying the Jaffe-Feldstein adult dialogue model to the study of preverbal dialogues is that, irrespective of whether the sounds are words, sounds such as "ummm" or "huh," or preverbal sounds, this approach provides a model of the timing rules of the social use of language (pragmatics), cutting across its preverbal and verbal stages, and across modalities. In this model, dialogue consists of a slower turn rhythm as speaker and listener exchange roles, as well as a faster vocalization-pause rhythm within each person's turn. A simple turn-taking rule stipulates that whoever vocalizes unilaterally gains the turn. Switching pauses occur at the point of the turn exchange, and simultaneous speech is also coded. Because patterns of gaze seemed as important as patterns of vocalization for both mother-infant and mature face-to-face conversations, we began in the 1970s to study vocal and gaze dialogues with this model. Thus, for three decades we have researched rhythms of dialogue in infancy in an effort to define both similarities and differences in the timing structure between adult-adult and adult-infant dialogue.

A second central theme in the studies of adults is the finding of a strong tendency for speakers to "match" (correlate) the average durations of pauses, and that this mutual pacing is "referable to a bilateral adjustment . . ." (Jaffe, 1962; Jaffe & Feldstein, 1970, p. 4; see also Cappella, 1981, 1996; Chapple, 1970; Feldstein & Welkowitz, 1978; Matarazzo & Weins, 1972; Warner, 1988). As important as this theme of bilateral adjustment is, the language is more bidirectional than the actual statistical results. As Jaffe and Feldstein (1970) noted, their measure of rhythm matching (vocal congruence) ". . . is computed over many dyads and is not concerned with the moment-to-moment tracking of each participant by the other *within* a particular conversation" (p. 46). Nevertheless, the concept of *bidirectional adjustment* or *influence* was used to describe these findings and was idealized as a positive dimension of interactions.

A third central theme in the adult work is that the mutual pacing of conversations is related to the communication of mood, the phenomenon of *empathy*, interpersonal attraction, and the breakdown of effective dialogue (Feldstein & Welkowitz, 1978; Welkowitz & Feldstein, 1970). But, as noted above, most of the work on *infant* vocal dialogues has proceeded without reference to obvious outcome measures of mood or affect, of successful versus disrupted interactions, or security/insecurity of bonding.

A fourth theme in the studies of adults is the role of familiarity versus novelty of partner. Several studies suggest that interactions between strangers are more coordinated, or more tightly organized, than those between acquainted pairs. Hedge, Everitt, and Frith (1978) showed that a person's temporal patterns of gazing and vocalizing become more tightly organized, with fewer dimensions, in conversations with strangers, as compared to friends. Crown (1991) showed that degree of vocal coordination is greater between unacquainted, as compared to acquainted, dyads. Cappella (1996) showed that interpersonal attraction is associated with higher vocal coordination when partners are unacquainted strangers than when intimate, replicating Crown. Although not concerned with a novel partner, Gottman's (1979) finding that higher coordination is associated with distressed, rather than nondistressed, marital pairs can be seen as analogous.

Thus the first two themes, the temporal structure of dialogue and the bidirectional coordination of rhythms, have been pursued with energy in work on face-to-face infant interaction. But the third theme, how the mutual pacing of dialogue relates to bonding, and the fourth, the impact of familiar versus novel partner on temporal coordination, have been neglected in the work on infant vocal dialogues. All four themes are central to this monograph.

Early Work on Preverbal Dialogues

This overview of early work on dialogues in infancy includes current methods and findings. However, because the focus is on dialogic timing, a large literature on "motherese" (an adaptation of adult speech when it is infant-directed) is omitted. Although 4-month-old infants vocalize only about 10–15% of the time, this participation has been sufficient to demonstrate vocal coordination in many studies. To facilitate this review, it is useful to consider Lewkowicz's (1989) distinctions among (a) temporal features such as duration or rhythm, (b) (interpersonal) temporal relationships, such as synchrony or contingency, and (c) anticipation on the basis of temporal regularity (expectancies). Some studies use a strictly *durational* approach, examining the temporal structure of on-off durations per se; correlational studies of interpersonal matching of durations are included in this type. Others use some form of contingency analysis to examine the *sequential constraint* between durations of the respective partners, which fits our definition of interpersonal contingency or coordination. In the 1970s various forms of analyses of sequential probabilities were in use; not until the mid-1980s were the time-series techniques for assessing coordination widely available.

Aspects of the Jaffe-Feldstein (1970) adult dialogue model of temporal coordination have been applied to studies of mother-infant interaction in neonates (Bakeman & Brown, 1977); to gaze and kinesic interactions at age 4 months (Beebe et al., 1979; Beebe, Jaffe, Feldstein, Mays, & Alson, 1985; Crown et al., 1988; Stern, 1974; Stern et al., 1977); to the exploration of the mathematical structure of mother-infant gaze (Jaffe et al., 1973b); to vocal interactions at ages 4 months (Beebe, Alson, Jaffe, Feldstein, & Crown, 1988) and 9 months (Jasnow & Feldstein, 1986); and to the examination of session-to-session consistency within and among dyads (Zelner, 1982).

Jaffe, Stern, and Peery (1973) showed that a Markovian model of contingencies of on-off cycles, from ¼ s to the next, is common to both

13

adult verbal conversation and infant-adult gaze patterns. They speculated that this short-range constraint is a "universal formal property of dyadic communication . . . detectable in infant gazing long before the onset of speech" (p. 327).

Using a completely durational approach, Stern (1977; Stern et al., 1977) demonstrated that timing structure transcends modality in maternal behavior, with remarkable similarities across repeated vocal or kinesic rhythmic actions, in a *burst-pause* format, at a fairly regular rate, with minor fluctuations around an average tempo. These repeating action patterns with minor variations are ideally suited to create expectancies, avoid habituation, maintain the infant's attention, and create subtle nuances for the infant's affective experience. The co-creation by mother and infant of relatively stable expectancies is a critical accomplishment of early social relatedness, cognition, and acculturation (Bruner, 1975; Haith, Hazan, & Goodman, 1988; Lewis & Goldberg, 1969).

Stern and Gibbon (1979), also using a completely durational approach, showed that the ratio of the mean to the standard deviation remains constant (a scalar timing process) in durations of maternal vocal and kinesic behavior, where the content of behavior is repetitive. They speculated that the infant must also employ scalar timing processes for decoding temporal information. Recently pursuing this model, Zlochower and Cohn (1996) showed that depressed mothers and infants fail to show scalar timing, whereas control dyads do.

The early studies of this research team show startling similarities between time patterns of vocal and kinesic events in infancy and the temporal patterns of sound and silence during adult conversation. A critical similarity is an alternating turn structure. Bloom (1993) suggested that the title of Jaffe and Feldstein's (1970) book, *Rhythms of Dialogue,* is prophetic for vocal exchanges with infants (citing Beebe & Jaffe, 1992; Jasnow & Feldstein, 1986; and Stern et al., 1975): "Before they begin to say words, they can already participate in the rhythms of dialogue" (p. 101). Many other researchers have described turn-taking patterns (e.g., Anderson et al., 1977; Collis, 1979; Mayer & Tronick, 1985; Papousek, Papousek, & Bornstein, 1985).

Adults in conversation tend to speak one at a time. Turn taking is the fundamental temporal structure of dialogue, and switching pauses mark the boundaries of the turn exchange. The switching pause is initiated by one partner, who falls silent, and is terminated by the other, who begins speaking, thus taking the turn. In both adult conversation and mother-infant interaction, switching pause durations between partners show a positive correlation, or match (Beebe et al., 1988; Beebe et al., 1985; Jaffe, 1962; Jasnow & Feldstein, 1986). This positive correlation suggests that the exchange is being regulated similarly: Each partner pauses for a similar duration before taking a turn. Mothers and 4-month-old infants also show precise matching (correlation) of kinesic rhythmic cycles during alternating behavioral sequences (Beebe et al., 1979). On the basis of these studies we proposed that the matching of temporal patterns of behavior implies a (noncausal) timing mechanism or method (such as a biological clock) that can be adjusted to the partner, and that aspects of a dialogic structure are already in evidence prior to speech onset, and regulated in a manner that is similar to adult conversation (Beebe et al., 1985, 1988). Welkowitz et al. (1976) found that matching of switching pauses occurred earlier than matching of pauses in preschool children.

Although the most common temporal regulation of the turn exchange is the switching pause, a second method of switching the turn is a quasi-simultaneous coactive switch. Here the person who interrupts, or chimes in, takes the turn. This mode of turn switch has been found to occur under conditions of high arousal, positive or negative (Beebe et al., 1979; Stern et al., 1975). In adults a coactive turn switch tends to occur during arguing, lovemaking, gossiping, or time pressure. As an example of high negative arousal, Feldstein (1998) found that coronary-prone adults use more interruptive simultaneous speech, and that this pattern is associated with hostility. Although adults rarely use the coactive mode, it is predominant in preverbal vocal and kinesic 4-month-olds' dialogues, decreasing by age 9 months (Jasnow & Feldstein, 1986).

Stern (1977) demonstrated that even when the infant does not vocally respond, in her own vocal timing the mother behaves as if the infant had. Using a durational approach, his simulation model suggests that ". . . after speaking the mother waits the average adult dialogue pause length (0.6 s). She then remains silent for the duration of an imagined infant vocal response (0.43 s), and then again waits the average adult dialogue pause length (0.6 s) before speaking again" (p. 16).

Other studies also have shown temporal coordination between mother and infant vocalizations in terms of both interpersonal contingencies, as well as strictly durational approaches to the timing of onsets of behavior (Anderson et al., 1977; Stern, 1971; Stern et al., 1975; Stevenson, Verhoeve, Roach, & Leavitt, 1986). Bateson (1971, 1975) was one of the first to describe a pattern of alternating vocal exchanges as "proto-conversation," and to suggest that the infant's behavior reflects an innate emotional foundation for making emotional bonds. Trevarthen (1979, 1993), also a pioneer in this area, described the infant as born with the capacity to use the behaviors of the partner in "conversational" negotiation of emotions. Based on microanalysis of film, he described sequences in which the infant moved mouth, hands, and eyes in rhythmic coupling with the adult, particularly in a turn-taking format. Both Bateson and Trevarthen used a strictly durational approach.

15

Fogel (1977) examined the temporal organization of face-to-face interaction within single mother-infant dyads between the 1st and 4th months of life, also using a durational approach. Both kinesic and vocal acts were grouped into repeating patterns with a similar beat from the initiation of one action to the initiation of the next. Temporal organization thus serves to package the behaviors of mother and infant.

This early work debated whether these preverbal dialogues were truly bidirectional, such that each partner contributes to the regulation of the exchange (e.g., Anderson et al., 1977; Bakeman & Brown, 1977; Kaye & Wells, 1980; Langhorst & Fogel, 1982; Stern, 1971; Stern et al., 1975; Stevenson et al., 1986), or whether a unidirectional model, in which the parent makes the primary contribution to the regulation pattern, is more accurate (e.g., Kaye, 1982; Messer & Vietze, 1988; Schaffer, 1977; Thomas & Martin, 1976). This debate is refined by the introduction of time-series analysis, noted in a later section.

The Role of Novelty in Adult-Infant Vocal Dialogues

Unlike the studies of adults, little research examines the role of novelty of site or partner in vocal dialogues in infancy. Regarding site, studies generally use samples either at home or in the laboratory. However, Lewedag, Oller, and Lunch (1994) studied vocalization patterns of 4- to 5-month-old infants across home and laboratory environments and found that infants vocalize more than twice as much at home, compared to the laboratory. Belsky (1980) compared maternal behavior in home and laboratory settings of 12-month-old infants. Despite moderate levels of consistency, mothers showed significantly more attention, vocalization, and responsiveness to infants in the laboratory.

Regarding novelty of partner, Delack (1976) found that, in the 1st year of life, infants alter their vocalization patterns as a function of partner: Vocalization quantity is lower with a stranger than with mother. Roe, McClure, and Roe (1982) found that 3-month-old infants who respond with higher vocal output to mother than stranger have higher verbal-cognitive scores at ages 3, 5, and 12 years. Again, these studies examine infant vocalization rather than infant-adult vocal dialogue. Studying vocalizations and smiles, Bigelow (1998) (discussed in more detail later) found infants to be more contingently responsive to their mothers than to strangers. Only when the stranger's own level of contingent responsiveness is similar to that of the infant's mother does the infant respond to the stranger with the same level of contingency as that used with the mother. In studies of gaze, rather than vocalization, Masi and Scott (1983) found that infants look more at mothers than strangers; Sherrod (1979) and Kurzweill (1988) found the opposite; whereas Ellsworth, Muir, and Hains (1993) found no differences. These studies are sufficiently different in method that they are difficult to compare.

Studies of adults indicate that degree of coordination increases with novelty, particularly novelty represented by an unfamiliar partner. Crown (1991) and Cappella (1996) suggested that, with an unfamiliar partner, coordination increases in an effort to make the interaction more predictable. With a familiar partner, such high levels of interpersonal predictability do not seem necessary. Comparable studies of infants are lacking. If infants were to show results similar to those of adults, it would help to clarify the meaning of coordination in infancy. However, the one study in the infant literature addressing this question, that of Bigelow (1998), suggested an entirely different hypothesis: that infants respond more contingently to a familiar partner, and to an unfamiliar partner who nevertheless responds with a familiar degree of coordination.

Current Methods and Findings: The Introduction of Time-Series Analysis

Despite the large body of literature documenting many patterns of coordination in the first 6 months of life, few investigators have tried to replicate their own or others' findings. No generally accepted statistical paradigm emerged until the introduction of time-series analysis into the behavioral sciences in the early 1980s. Earlier time-series techniques, such as Markovian and other contingency models of sequential probabilities, addressed direction of coordination, but they did not in general control for autocorrelation, a key feature of time-series techniques. Time-series approaches take into account *both* how the person responds to his own behavior (autocorrelation) and how each person responds to the partner's behavior (cross-correlation) (Gottman, 1981; Gottman & Ringland, 1981; Thomas & Martin, 1976). Metaphorically, autocorrelation can be conceptualized as the predictability of each partner's current behavior from the entire series of his own past behaviors, over the course of a session. The time-series approach to interpersonal contingencies does not yield causality, but rather prediction. The analysis remains one of *correlation*. Using lag-correlation, it yields separate indices of whether either partner's behaviors are coordinated with those of the other. In bidirectional regulation, each partner's behavior predicts that of the other. Although the literature tends to use the term *influence*, we adopt the more neutral term *coordination*, which does not imply that one partner *does* something *to* the other.

The time-series model has been used extensively in infant research since the mid-1980s. Similar to adult findings, bidirectional coordination has been demonstrated in mother-infant interaction in many modalities (e.g., Beebe et al., 1985; Cohn, Campbell, Matias, & Hopkins, 1990; Cohn

& Tronick, 1988; Feldman & Greenbaum, 1997; Feldstein et al., 1993; Jasnow & Feldstein, 1986; Lester, Hoffman, & Brazelton, 1985; Martin, 1981; Martin, Maccoby, Baran, & Jacklin, 1981; Reiter, 1986).

Lester et al. (1985) used a form of time-series analysis, frequency domain analysis (spectrals), to examine the rhythmic structure of mother-infant facial-visual interaction in term and preterm infants, and found evidence of behavioral periodicities and mother-infant synchrony. They suggested that biologically based periodicities provide a temporal structure for the initial early organization of cognitive and affective experience. Feldman et al. (1996) also used spectrals to show a repetitive cyclic structure in mother-infant face-to-face play. They argued that this cyclic structure is a context for the integration of biological and social rhythms, which in turn mediate cognitive development.

In a classic paper, Cohn and Tronick (1988) detailed the bidirectional coordination process in mother-infant face-to-face affective communication. Over the group, mothers' behavior predicted that of infants, and vice-versa. Their work confirmed that "the conversation-like pattern of mother-infant face-to-face interactions at 3, 6, and 9 months is produced by bidirectional 'influence' or coordination. Bidirectional coordination is achieved through the stochastic organization of behaviors and not through mutual entrainment of periodic cycles" (p. 389). This differentiation between a stochastic organization (not perfectly predictable because it contains a random element), and entrainment, which implies coordination of perfectly regular periodic rhythms, is important, because as we noted in the Introduction, the rhythms addressed in this monograph are *nonperiodic.*

Time-series regression analysis has demonstrated bidirectional coordination in the timing of mother-infant vocal exchanges, across the group (Jasnow & Feldstein, 1986). This vocal dialogue model was translated into the mother-infant kinesic system, where time-series analysis demonstrated a similar bidirectional prediction of the durations of "movements" and "holds" in the changes of facial expression and direction of gaze (Beebe et al., 1985). Time-series analysis has also been used to investigate the affective exchange between depressed mothers and their infants (Cohn et al., 1990; Cohn & Tronick, 1989; Field, Goldstein, & Guthertz, 1990). Welkowitz, Bond, Feldman, and Tota (1990) also show bidirectional coordination in the conversational time patterns of parents and children using a time-series approach.

The Meaning of Degree of Coordination in Time-Series Analysis

The meaning of degree of coordination remains controversial. The literature on adults has debated the varying positions that high coordination is optimal (Chapple, 1970), high coordination indexes distress (Gottman, 1979), and midrange coordination is optimal (Warner et al., 1987). This debate has not been widely aired in the infant literature (see as an exception Cohn & Elmore, 1988; Dunham & Dunham, 1990). The current study addresses this debate.

Cohn and Elmore (1988) addressed degree of coordination in face-to-face interaction at age 3 months through an experiment. Using the "still-face" technique of Tronick, Als, Adamson, Wise, and Brazelton (1978), half of the mothers were instructed to become still-faced whenever the infant became positive; the other half were instructed to interact with the infant normally. The use of time-series techniques showed that the mother's degree of influence on the infant is higher in the experimental condition. Their conclusion is directly relevant to one of the goals of this monograph, which is a better understanding of the meaning of degree of coordination in infant social development: "Our findings suggest . . . that it may prove useful to begin concentrating on the size of influence-effects. . . . With respect to interpersonal influence, more may not be better. Increased interpersonal influence may indicate an interaction that is not going well. Too much influence may be as detrimental as too little (cf. Cohn, Matias, Tronick, Connell, & Lyons-Ruth, 1986). Further research is needed to determine whether there is an optimal range of interpersonal influence, as a function of the partner's developmental level, context, and type of interaction" (p. 501). In other research, also using time-series analysis, Cohn et al. (1986) studied 13 high-risk dyads with maternal depression and found lowered levels of coordination as a risk index. Only four mothers and two infants showed evidence of contingency. Thus, similar to Warner et al. (1987), Cohn and Elmore (1988) conceptualized a nonlinear model: "Difficult" interactions may show either high or low degrees of contingency.

Malatesta et al. (1989) examined degree of *maternal* facial coordination in mother-infant pairs where infants were subsequently classified at age 1 year as secure versus avoidant. Mothers of avoidant infants showed higher coordination. Tobias (1995) examined degree of coordination in mother-infant interaction at age 4 months as a function of the mother's own attachment rating, assessed during her pregnancy using the Adult Attachment Interview (Main & Goldwyn, 1988/1993). Using Tronick and Weinberg's method of coding (see Weinberg, Tronick, Cohn, & Olson, 1999), she found that infants and mothers had higher coordination when mothers were classified as "preoccupied" (which is conceptually similar to the infant classification of "anxious-resistant"), rather than secure. Weinberg et al. (1999) examined degree of coordination in male versus female infants, in the context of their finding that male infants have more difficulty in self-regulation than female. Dyads in which the infant is male show higher *synchrony* (a form of coordination) than those in which the infant is female. All of these studies are consistent with the hypothesis that higher coordination indexes more difficulty. However, because these studies compared only two conditions, it is possible that they consider only a portion of a larger nonlinear relationship.

Watson (1994) suggested that *degree* of contingency is a salient dimension of the infant's perception of the relationship between his or her own behavior and the response of the environment. He proposed that moderate levels of contingency are most interesting to infants, and that infants might prefer degrees of contingency that have become familiar (expected). Degree of coordination as measured by time-series analysis is conceptually similar to Watson's measure of contingency. His proposal that infants prefer familiar degrees of contingency received support from Bigelow (1998), in one of the few studies in the literature to examine coordination in both mother-infant and stranger-infant dyads in face-to-face play at age 4 months. When the stranger's degree of contingency approximated that of the mother, the infant's degree of contingency with stranger also matched the mother's. However, in interaction with strangers whose degree of contingency was greater or less than that of mother, infants showed greater degrees of contingency with their mothers than with strangers. Thus, Bigelow's study pointed to the importance of the infant's preference for the expected, when confronting a novel partner, rather than supporting a midrange hypothesis, or the hypothesis that high coordination indexes distress.

In conclusion, there is a varied and rich body of research on mother-infant vocal dialogues. Although the early work was more varied in approaches to measurement, current work is dominated by time-series analysis. The work using time-series analysis yields different possible interpretations of the meaning of degree of coordination. For the most part the studies reviewed here were not concerned with the prediction of outcomes, which we review next. Overall, the findings have become increasingly bidirectional, using a systems model of the regulation of the exchange, to which we now turn.

A DYADIC SYSTEMS VIEW OF COMMUNICATION

As in our work over the past four decades, we approach vocal dialogue as a dyadic system (see Beebe et al., 1985, 1992, 2000; Jaffe & Feldstein, 1970; Jaffe & Norman, 1964). In a dyadic systems view of communication, each person's behavior is created in the process of joint coordination. This systems assumption affects the way we record, the dyadic scoring of the vocal states, the selection of statistical methods to evaluate bidirectional coordination, and the choice of outcome measures, both of which are construed as fundamentally dialogic. This approach to vocal dialogue is specifically a systems view of *communication*, rather than a larger systems view of development.

Although communication can refer to linguistic content, a second meaning described by Bloom (1993) refers to the way communication has most often been studied in infant social interactions, ". . . a framing of the interaction—a 'getting into sync'—that involves a process in which persons act in ways that are responsive to the actions of those with whom they are in communication" (p. 84). This aspect of communication, often out of awareness, conveys "the affective quality of the relationship, . . . through observation of rhythm sharing, body movement, timing of speech, and silences" (p. 84). Altmann (1967) defined social communication more narrowly as ". . . a process by which the behavior of an individual affects the behavior of others" (p. 326). Communication occurs when each affects the probability distribution of the other's behavior. This definition converges on our definition of coordination. We use *coordination* of behaviors between partners as one empirical approach to the study of communication.

Our systems view of the coordination of dialogic rhythms was developed by Jaffe and Feldstein in the early 1960s at the William Alanson White Institute, a psychoanalytic institute dedicated to the understanding of *relationships*, thought to be underplayed in classical psychoanalysis. At that time, Jaffe and Feldstein were interested in the interpersonal, pragmatic features of dialogic timing that might be relevant to the communication of mood, the phenomenon of empathy, and the breakdown of effective dialogue. This interest led to the study of the on-off temporal patterns of vocal signals in face-to-face adult conversation. Sullivan's (1940) interpersonal theory heavily influenced this dyadic systems approach, particularly his view that "a personality can never be isolated from the complex of interpersonal relations in which the person lives and has his being" (p. 90). He suggested that personality is ". . . a temporal phenomenon, a patterning of experiences and interactions over time. . . . The only way . . . personality can be known is through the medium of interpersonal interactions" (Greenberg & Mitchell, 1983, p. 90). The Jaffe-Feldstein approach to coding vocal dialogue as dyadic states (defined in a later section) was a direct attempt to concretize Sullivan's ideas.

Sullivan was a psychiatrist and a contemporary of Winnicott, who was originally a pediatrician and later became a psychoanalyst. They shared the concept that a person can only be understood in the context of the relational field. Winnicott's (1965) famous remark that "There is no such thing as an infant" (p. 39) is analogous to Sullivan's similarly famous phrase, "the myth of personal identity." Winnicott and Sullivan, among many others (such as Bowlby, 1969; Fairbairn, 1941/1952; Lewin, 1935; and Spitz, 1963), participated in building a relational systems approach to the understanding of the person, in which individuals do not exist apart from the totality of their interpersonal relationships. This relational systems approach contrasts sharply with an alternative view, also very influential in the 20th century, that the individual is fundamentally alone, and is drawn into interactions and relationships, a position that Stolorow and Atwood (1992) termed the "myth of the isolated mind." Overton (1994) suggested that the latter view splits the relational matrix into separate independent individuals, and then searches for the glue that puts them together; the former begins with the relational matrix as a system, in which each component affects and is affected by the other. Through its own activity, the system further differentiates and reintegrates (Piaget, 1954; Werner, 1948). A relational systems approach informs the work presented here (see Overton, 1998).

Sullivan and Winnicott were also contemporaries of Werner and Piaget. Although Piaget (1965/1995) and Werner (1948) did not use the term *systems theory*, their emphasis on the continuous interaction of organism and environment set the stage for the development of systems views, particularly the interactionalist view of development, based on a constructivist or organismic model (see Lewis & Brooks, 1975; Reese & Overton, 1970), in which there is no pure sensory event independent of the perceiver. Piaget viewed development as occurring through interaction between an active, self-organizing organism and the external world, in a continuous dialectic between assimilation and accommodation. The sensory-motor schema is an organized internal model or structure formed by the organism's active process of ordering and reordering information.

Developments in many fields have moved from an individual-centered approach and linear views of causality toward systems and field approaches (Bowlby, 1969; Iberall & McCulloch, 1969; Kohlberg, 1969; Lewin, 1935; von Bertalanffy, 1968). Von Bertalanffy was a leading figure in theoretical biology who described the fundamental properties of a system as organization and primary activity: Each component of the system brings its own active self-regulation. In the course of development the system becomes more differentiated and complex. This point of view holds much in common with that of Piaget.

Sander, who began publishing in 1962, has been at the forefront of a relational systems approach to infant research. He was influenced by the work of von Bertalanffy (1968) and Weiss (1970) on biological systems views, by the work of Byers (1976) and Luce (1970) on biological rhythms, and by the work of Halburg (1960), Lashley (1954), and Pittendrigh (1961) on temporal ordering and coupling. He was also influenced by Piaget and psychoanalysis, particularly the views of Winnicott, who considered interactive process as central in personality organization. Sander (1977) suggested that ". . . organism, surround, and exchanges-between can be . . . discussed as a system. . . . Exchanges between interacting components in a system, through mutual modification, reach a harmonious coordination . . ." (p. 138). He emphasized that organization within the system exists from the outset. Both partners generate complexly organized behavior that must be interfaced or coordinated. Regulation in the system is based on the capacity for mutual modification of the partners, a bidirectional coordination. A further key aspect of Sander's systems approach is his emphasis on timing as central to coordination: ". . . the domain of time and the temporal organization of events . . . provide the framework for . . . unscrambling the difficulties in conceptualizing the interface between two ongoing organizations" (p. 137). Although Sander began writing around the same time as Jaffe and Feldstein in the early 1960s, and although there are remarkable similarities in their respective systems views and their emphasis on the importance of timing, neither was aware of the other's work until a decade later.

The concept that both partners in the dyadic system can mutually modify each other's behavior cannot be interpreted within any stimulus-response-like theory. However, it is easier to reject such a theory than the language it suggests. The language of direction of effects, as in "the infant influences the mother," lapses back into causal notions. Our way out of the inapplicability of linear cause-effect paradigms is to approach the timing of face-to-face communication as a dyadic system. Ruesch and Bateson (1951) were among the early voices articulating this systems approach to the bidirectional face-to-face exchange, describing the participants as simultaneous senders and receivers. This view was further developed in infant research by, among others, Stern (1971), Lewis and Rosenblum (1974), Fogel (1977, 1993a, 1993b), Trevarthen (1979, 1993), Cohn and Tronick (1988), Tronick (1989), and Beebe et al. (1985, 1992, 2000), all of whom provided further empirical explorations of this concept.

The notion of bidirectional exchange between partners resonates with current broad versions of systems theories of development. It is an aspect of the more general idea that components of a system are in a continuous process of bidirectional exchange. As Lewkowicz (2000) noted, many current versions of systems theory, such as those of Gottlieb (1992; Gottlieb et al., 1998) and Lerner (1998), view the method or means of development as a mutual interdependence between an actively perceiving infant and its structured environment. In Gottlieb's (1992; Gottlieb et al., 1998) "probabilistic epigenesis" view of development, new functions and structures result from horizontal (gene-gene, cell-cell, organism-organism) and vertical (such as gene-neuron, behavior-nervous system) reciprocal coactions

23

or coordinations. These bidirectional reciprocal coactions result in increased complexity of the system and the elaboration of emergent properties. The intrinsic action of the system results in rearrangement and reconnection of the components. Bidirectional reciprocal coactions (coordinations) operate as a central method of the system's development (Gottlieb, 1998; Lerner, 1998; Lewkowicz, 2000). Although bidirectional exchange has been a major theme of the past two decades of research on mother-infant face-to-face interaction, this construct has for the most part not yet been mined for its value in predicting the evolving trajectory of infant development. This study investigates bidirectional coordination both in the 4-month-olds' interaction, as well as in the prediction of developmental outcomes, as noted in the Introduction.

Current systems theorists also emphasize the central role of context in a systems view of development. Sameroff (1983) and Gottlieb et al. (1998) have proposed that one of the key dimensions of a system is its context sensitivity: The infant's capacities can be modified by specific features of the immediate surroundings. For example, the Rovee-Collier group (see Shields & Rovee-Collier, 1992) demonstrated striking context effects in infant memory studies. Using the paradigm of a mobile activated by the infant's foot-kick, even minor changes, such as in the color of the crib on re-testing, alter memory in the middle of the first year. Lerner (1998) proposed that context specificity must be integrated into the matrix of covariation that shapes developmental trajectories. Thelen and Smith (1994) proposed that context sensitivity permits the enormous flexibility of behavior to reorganize, and that context and function variability provide a critical source of transformations in development. They noted that observation under uniform conditions elicits a restricted set of behaviors, whereas novelty and variation elicit a broader range of organismic capacities. Bowlby (1969) also theorized that a wide range of abilities and flexibility is biologically adaptive for survival of the human species. In his view, the overriding importance of the parameter "familiar/strange" is a particularly critical variable in the appraisal of the environment (as well as a powerful activator of attachment behavior) (Hamilton, 1998). However, the role of various contexts, such as novelty, in the reciprocal bidirectional exchange, has received little attention in research on mother-infant face-to-face interaction. Nor has the role of context, such as novelty, been explored in conceptualizing Lerner's "matrix of covariation" that shapes developmental trajectories. Thus, in this study, as noted in the Introduction, novelty of partner (mother/stranger) and site (home/laboratory) are construed as social *contexts* within which to explore a range of variations of vocal rhythm coordination. We investigate the role of novelty in this coordination at age 4 months, as well as in the prediction of outcomes at age 12 months.

24

In so doing, we broaden the system under study, from mother-infant to stranger-infant, both at home and laboratory.

The Concept of Vocal "Rhythm" in Our Dyadic Systems View

Jaffe and Feldstein (1970) developed their dyadic systems model of communication through the empirical study of adult dyadic coordination of vocal rhythm. Although two partners coordinate many aspects of their communicative behavior, one of the most obvious is conversational rhythm, such as the turn taking that organizes their respective cycles of vocalization and pause. But immediately, we are confronted with the problem of "rhythm." As noted in the introduction, Lashley (1954) claimed that most of our motor behaviors are rhythmically organized. The best understood form of rhythm is one that is strictly regular, or periodic, such as the ticking of a clock. But a common misconception is that behavioral rhythms are *only* periodic (Lewkowicz, 2000; Martin, 1972). All definitions of rhythm share the notion of *recurrence*. We propose a general definition of rhythm as a recurrent temporal patterning of events, or nonrandom variation, which may or may not be strictly regular. Recently, Lewkowicz (2000), influenced by Martin (1972), suggested a definition of rhythm as a repeating sequence of *unequal* cycles. Although the rhythms that we study are by no means periodic, they nevertheless embody patterns with a definite mathematical structure. In our approach to conversational rhythm, the concept of recurrence can be translated into repeating on-off cycles of vocalization and pause within a speaker's turn, and the repeating turn-taking cycle as the two partners exchange turns.

Martin (1972) suggested that one implication of Lashley's work is the notion that rhythmic action might link speaking and listening, which Martin conceptualized as dynamically coupled rhythmic activities. When the listener hears the first few beats, he has a model with which to anticipate what will follow. Martin proposed that, in decoding the rhythm, the listener does not follow the speaker, but rather, ". . . the listener, given initial cues, actively enters into the speaker's tempo" (p. 503). These ideas provide one way of understanding how two speakers can coordinate their vocal timing; that is, anticipation of the rhythm may facilitate information processing as well as interpersonal coordination. This importance of the anticipation of rhythm can be linked to the infant's capacity to generate expectancies, discussed later.

A more specific definition of rhythmic patterns is offered by Martin (1972) as sequences of events in which some elements are marked or accented. The marked elements *recur* with some regularity, regardless of tempo or tempo changes. *Together*, the recurrence of a marked and unmarked element constitutes the simplest rhythmic pattern. In our research, the vocalization-pause cycle fits this description. The vocalization can be considered the marked element, and the pause the unmarked element.

In the 1950s a special rhythmic organization was discovered in the vocalization-pause cycles of ordinary adult *monologues*. Although these on-off vocal rhythms were irregular (nonperiodic), Mosteller (1949) and Verzeano (1950) discerned that they are nevertheless highly structured mathematically in a probabilistic (stochastic) fashion. Both vocalization and pause exhibit negative exponential distributions: The shortest durations are the most frequent, and each longer duration shows a constant proportional decrease in frequency. These are the necessary conditions for a Markovian rhythm. Jaffe, Cassotta, and Feldstein (1964) confirmed that Mosteller's model indeed fit the monologues of adult subjects telling stories. Moreover, the negative exponential distributions that Mosteller documented for vocalization and pause in monologue are found to be identical in dialogue (Jaffe & Feldstein, 1970). In addition, the durations of simultaneous speech states of dialogue show a negative exponential distribution. Thus, a Markovian process is present in dialogue that is remarkably similar to the rhythms that Mosteller documented in monologue. Furthermore, these Markovian dialogue rhythms conform to a nonperiodic model and constitute one possible approach to a theory of nonperiodic rhythms (Jaffe & Feldstein, 1970; for an alternative approach, see Warner, 1996). Although Markovian mathematics are not used in this monograph, they play a large role in Jaffe and Feldstein's research program. However, Jaffe and Norman's (1964) "bottom-up" attempts to generate dialogue rhythms from two monologues failed. Instead, they took an entirely different "top-down" tack, approaching dialogue as a dyadic system, to which we now turn.

The Jaffe-Feldstein Model of Vocal Rhythm as a Dyadic System

Although systems ideas are one of the most important intellectual currents of the 20th century (see Fogel 1993a, 1993b; Mason, 1953), our field is still searching for ways of translating systems approaches into data-analytic strategies. The basic systems notion that any action in a dyadic relationship is jointly defined by the behavior of both partners operationalizes the idea that, psychologically, individuals do not exist apart from the totality of their interpersonal relationships. Positing the interpersonal system as the unit of study led us to the concept of *dyadic states* (Jaffe, 1958; Jaffe & Feldstein, 1970; Jaffe et al., 1973b; Stern et al., 1975). The unique contribution of the Jaffe-Feldstein model of vocal dialogue as a systems view lies in its *dyadic coding of dialogic timing*. At any particular moment, any action of the individual is jointly defined by both the individual and the partner. The power of the dyad as the unit of analysis is particularly evident when social roles cannot be actualized in the absence of the other, such as speaker-listener, or mother-infant. Commonsense conversational phenomena, such as turns, interruptions, and switching pauses at the point of the turn exchange, cannot occur at the level of individual behavior—that is, in monologue. Similar to Sullivan's ideas, dyadic states do not fully exist at the level of the individual.

The concept of dyadic states was developed for face-to-face communication at a time when the reigning psychological model was stimulus-response (S-R) theory. Communication was studied primarily within information theory as a one-way process in which the passive receiver could not influence the sender during transmission (e.g., see Shannon, 1963). Although this model of communication was appropriate to the telephone (much of the research was done at Bell Telephone Laboratories), it was not adequate for face-to-face communication, a potentially simultaneous, bidirectional exchange. Ruesch and Bateson's (1951) concept that partners are simultaneously both senders and receivers influenced Jaffe's (1958, 1962) position that face-to-face communication requires an interpersonal feedback control model in which sending and receiving are concurrent and reciprocally evoked. More recently, Tronick (1989; Gianino & Tronick, 1988) described this process as the continual integration of self-regulation and mutual regulation processes. Fogel (1993a, 1993b) described the process as one in which all behavior is unfolding in the two individuals, who are simultaneously modifying and being modified by the changing behavior of the partner.

The Jaffe-Feldstein approach addressed both the dyad, and the individual in relation to the dyad. In a systems view, the individual always exists in a dyadic context; each person is "contextualized" by the partner (Sullivan, 1940; Winnicott, 1965). The series of sounds and silences of both partners is coded as a single sequence of dyadic states. However, although each dyadic state is jointly produced, each state can be unequivocally assigned to one of the partners, based on superordinate parsing of the interaction into *turns*. When either partner vocalizes while the other remains silent, it is clear who is speaker and who is listener. But in joint silence and joint vocalization, when both partners are doing the same thing, who is speaker and who is listener (who "has the floor")? A logical system of definitions must do justice to the dyad as well as to the individual. Our "turn rule" accomplishes this. Because it is physiologically difficult to simultaneously speak and comprehend another's speech (see Jaffe, 1978), turn taking developed as a biological solution to the limited cognitive capacity for verbal information processing. Our turn rule posits that the speaker who last vocalized alone retains the turn (even during subsequent joint silence and/or simultaneous speech) until the listener vocalizes alone, thereby becoming the turn holder. This turn rule parses

27

the behavioral sequence into mutually exclusive time domains that alternate between the speakers without overlap, even in the presence of co-action or joint silence. By uniquely specifying speaker and listener at each instant, the turn rule "recovers the individual" from the dyadic states, yielding symmetrical codes for the two people. This enables study of both the dyad and the individual in a dyadic context. The rhythms of dialogue are described as follows:

1. The *turn rhythm* is the slowest obvious cycle, with the turns of each partner defined via a sort of territorial parliamentary procedure based on the concept of speaking and listening (Jaffe, 1978). A sequence of two cycles, one by each partner, completes an *interpersonal turn rhythm.*

2. Within each partner's turn, the vocalization-pause cycle defines the turnholder's tempo. For example, the conductor of an orchestra beats the *tempo* of the music, which is given names such as largo, andante, and allegro.

3. The switching pause occurs at the moment of turn exchange and regulates turn taking; partners tend to match (positively correlate) durations of switching pauses so that each waits a similar amount of time before taking a turn. The switching pause is initiated by one partner, who falls silent, and is terminated by the other partner, who begins speaking.

4. As Sander (1977) noted, because rhythms exist in a spectrum of time levels from slower to faster cycles, they allow for events of the system to be interfaced at various temporal levels, permitting the coordination of both simultaneous and sequential events. Whereas the components of vocal rhythms above (turn, vocalization, pause, switching pause) are all sequential, two additional states define simultaneous or coactive events. Coaction, either interruptive or noninterruptive simultaneous speech, is a listener phenomenon in the Jaffe-Feldstein model. It refers to a vocalization by the partner who does not hold the turn. If the listener vocalizes simultaneously with the turn holder (speaker), but then backs off, the dyadic state becomes noninterruptive simultaneous speech, and the speaker does not relinquish the turn. But if the listener vocalizes simultaneously with the speaker, and then persists, taking the turn as the speaker yields, the dyadic state becomes interruptive simultaneous speech. Coaction tends to mark a high arousal moment, positive or negative affect (Stern et al., 1975).

5. Turns are exchanged through three patterns: (a) through a clean alternation (via a switching pause); (b) rarely, immediately without an

intervening switching pause, and (c) coactively (via interruptive simultaneous speech). Although all three patterns can appear in any interaction, the first characterizes more polite adult conversation, whereas the third predominates in mother-infant vocal exchanges (or adult argument, gossip, or lovemaking).

Procedural Representation of Dialogic Timing Pragmatics

The vocal timing model used in this study assesses more than on/off rhythm: it provides indices of different *moments* in the negotiation of a dialogic exchange, which we will call aspects of the "timing pragmatics" of social dialogue. In contrast to semantics and syntax, pragmatics refers to procedures that express intentions of the partners vis-à-vis each other (see Seboek, 1966). Examples of pragmatics in adult conversation are greetings and partings, asking questions, giving orders, apologizing, pleading, or soothing. At age 4 months, however, precursors of pragmatics are approach/avoidance, showing interest/pleasure/distress, or imitating. We construe the varying rhythmic patterns in infancy as procedures for regulating the timing pragmatics of social dialogue: when to vocalize, when to pause and for how long; as well as managing attention, activity level, turn taking, joining, interrupting, yielding, and tracking. However, at age 4 months, the pragmatic and expressive functions of these behaviors cannot be easily differentiated (see Overton, 1998).

We suggest that these various patterns of timing pragmatics come to be expected and procedurally represented by the infant. Here we briefly describe the presymbolic procedural representation of dialogic timing, for two purposes. The first is to set the stage for our proposal that the prediction of outcomes at age 12 months from vocal rhythm coordination at age 4 months can be viewed as based on common timing methods that may have similar functions at the two ages. The second is the articulation of presymbolic procedural representation as a critical form of organization in our systems view. In contrast to some current versions of systems theory, which privilege process over organization or structure (see Overton, 1998), in our view the infant's active construction of presymbolic representations provides a key organizational feature of the system, linking patterns of vocal rhythm coordination at age 4 months to outcomes at age 12 months.

Expectancies of interaction sequences are a critical organizational feature of the mother-infant communication system. The infant has intrinsic motivation to order information, detect regularity, generate expectancies, and act on these expectancies (Haith et al., 1988). Both partners generate patterns of expectation, constructed through the *sequence* of one's own actions in relation to those of the partner (patterns of coordination), and an associated self-regulatory range and style. This is one definition of *procedural knowledge* of the social environment. Whereas declarative memory refers to symbolically organized recall for information and events, procedural memory refers to skills or action sequences that are encoded nonsymbolically, become automatic with repeated practice, and influence the organizational processes that guide behavior (Emde, Biringen, Clyman, & Oppenheim, 1991; Grigsby & Hartlaub, 1994; Squire & Cohen, 1985). Although various controversies exist around the meaning of *procedural* (see Mandler, 1992; Mounoud, 1995; Muller & Overton, 1998), our use of the term includes both conscious and nonconscious processing, and a view of the infant as an active agent in the construction of procedural knowledge.

A considerable literature describes the infant's capacity to construct representations in a presymbolic, procedural format, based on expectations of action-sequences (Emde et al., 1991; Fagen, Morrongiello, Rovee-Collier, & Gekoski, 1984; Haith et al., 1988; Shields & Rovee-Collier, 1992; Stern, 1985, 1995). This view of representation uses a constructivist model (see Kuhn, 1962; Lewis & Brooks, 1975; Reese & Overton, 1970) in which the infant actively organizes information, based on an interaction between the external world and the infant's own perceptual preferences, previously established expectancies, and self-regulatory capacities. In previous work, we used the concept of patterns of expectation to define presymbolic representation in the first year (Beebe et al., 1997; Beebe & Lachmann, 1994; Beebe & Stern, 1977; see also Stern, 1977, 1985). In this monograph we view the coordination of timing patterns as operating through *expectancies*—the anticipation of the partner's pattern in relation to one's own. The rhythms themselves facilitate prediction, in the sense described by Martin (1972), that following the initial cues the listener actively enters into the speaker's tempo. Learning the regulation of dialogic timing patterns involves learning when to vocalize, when to pause and for how long, whose turn it is, when to join in simultaneously (coactive speech) and how to exchange turns. Furthermore, it involves coming to expect *how the dyad* coordinates these rhythmic patterns.

Prediction of outcomes at age 12 months would lend weight to the proposal that they depend on the very same interpersonal timing operations that we assess at age 4 months. As proposed in the Introduction, in both the cognitive (Bayley Scales) and attachment (Strange Situation) tests, the infant must also manage attention, take turns, regulate activity level, join, interrupt, and track. By analogy, the 4-month-old infant's management of vocal action, joint action, and turn taking may presage the way the 12-month-old infant attends, joins, ignores, or tracks the mother in the Strange Situation reunion, or the way the infant tracks the experimenter and takes his turn manipulating objects in the Bayley test. The common timing modes or methods may have similar functions at the two ages. We now turn to the literature on the prediction of 12-month-olds' attachment and Bayley Scales from mother-infant coordination.

PREDICTION OF AGE 1-YEAR OUTCOMES

Attachment

Definitions

Bowlby (1958, 1969) proposed that infant attachment behaviors are used to maintain proximity to and contact with the primary caretaker, contributing to a bond that ties infant and caregiver, continuing throughout life. Attachment is a construct that describes a *relationship* rather than an individual. Ainsworth and colleagues (Ainsworth, Blehar, Waters, & Wall, 1978) further developed Bowlby's theory, suggesting that the developing quality of attachment is highly dependent on maternal behaviors that are sensitive to the infant's signals and moods. Such sensitivity tends to promote a secure relationship in which the infant can use the mother as a base both for protection and nurturance as well as for exploration of the environment. The insecurely attached infant, on the other hand, spends either too much or too little time in proximity to the mother or exploring the environment, upsetting an attachment-exploration balance. The recurrent nature of the infant's experiences leads to the development of internal representations or "working models" of self and others that are proposed to influence the infant's emotional experiences and expectations throughout development (Arend, Gove, & Sroufe, 1979; Erickson, Sroufe, & Egeland, 1983; Lyons-Ruth, 1998; Main, Kaplan, & Cassidy, 1985).

The empirical test of attachment, the Strange Situation (Ainsworth et al., 1978), assesses the balance between attachment and exploration through a series of separations and reunions, yielding four categories of attachment: A, B, C, and D. In the *secure* pattern (B), the mother is sensitive to the infant's needs and the infant tends to use the mother as a secure base, to engage in active proximity seeking, contact maintenance, and positive social interaction following the reunion, and to recover easily from the separation. In the *anxious/ avoidant* pattern (A), mothers are predictably insensitive to their infants' needs and occasionally stressfully intrusive (Belsky, Rovine, & Taylor, 1984), and infants tend *not* to seek closeness and interaction with the mother, to greet her upon reunion, or to display separation distress. In the *anxious-resistant pattern* (C), mothers

31

are inconsistent in their response, generally nonnurturant, neglectful, and rejecting, but at times sensitive and caring. Their infants show strong proximity-seeking and contact-maintaining, limited exploration of the environment, inability to separate from mother and resume play after the separation, repeated expressions of anger, crying, and petulance, and seem inconsolable in spite of efforts by the mother to comfort them. A further pattern of infants who did not fit into the above patterns resulted in an additional classification, *disorganized/ disoriented* (D) infants (Main & Solomon, 1990), who show incomplete movements and expressions, simultaneous displays of contradictory approach/avoidance patterns, confusion and apprehension, and momentary behavioral stilling. These behaviors reflect a breakdown in behavioral organization under the stress of the heightened activation of the attachment system.

A critique by Lamb, Thompson, Gardner, Charnov, and Estes (1984) suggested that alternatives to the categorical classification procedure are needed, in the form of a continuous attachment metric. One such effort (Richters, Waters, & Vaughn, 1988) has transformed the scores of the interactive behavior scales of the Ainsworth coding into a single continuous scale that measures the *degree* of insecurity of attachment (see Method). The current monograph uses both the categorical and continuous measures so that they can be compared.

The Prediction of Attachment at Age 1 Year

Infant attachment security (Ainsworth et al., 1978) is an important predictor of developmental outcomes, such as school performance (Arend et al., 1979; Erickson et al., 1983; Lyons-Ruth et al., 1993), affect regulation (Kobak & Sceery, 1988), and psychopathology (Lewis, Feiring, McGuffog, & Jaskir, 1984; Lyons-Ruth et al., 1993; Sroufe, 1983, 1985). Maternal (parental) "sensitivity" (Ainsworth et al., 1978) has been considered the most important factor contributing to infant attachment security. Sensitivity involves alertness to infant signals, appropriateness and promptness of response, flexibility, and capacity to negotiate conflicting goals.

In studies predicting age 1-year Ainsworth Strange Situation outcomes from earlier interactions, we distinguish between macroanalytic and microanalytic coding of the latter. Microanalytic studies code videotaped or audiotaped interactions with explicit units of 1 s or less. Studies that use global judgments or clinical rating scales, or that code behavior (from videotape or on-line) using larger time segments, we term *macroanalytic.*

Macroanalytic studies. Numerous studies using more global assessments and clinical ratings to predict attachment at age 12 months have converged on a picture of the interactions in the early months of life that culminate in secure or insecure attachment outcomes A full review of this extensive literature is beyond the scope of this study. However, mothers of secure infants have been described as more contingently responsive and sensitive, more consistent and prompt in response to infant distress, more likely to hold their infants, less intrusive, and less tense and irritable. These studies described secure infants as more responsive than insecure infants in face-to-face play, as better able to elicit responsive caretaking, as more positive, as well as more able to express distress. Secure as compared to insecure infants cry less, have more varied means of communication, and quiet more readily when picked up (see, e.g., Ainsworth et al., 1978; Antonucci & Levitt, 1984; Bates, Maslin, & Frankel, 1985; Belsky et al., 1984; Blehar, Lieberman, & Ainsworth, 1977; Crockenberg, 1983; Egeland & Farber, 1984; Grossman, Grossman, Spangler, Seuss, & Unzer, 1985; Isabella & Belsky, 1991; Mikaye, Chen, & Campos, 1985; Stayton, Ainsworth, & Main, 1973; De Wolff & van Ijzendoorn, 1997).

Evidence for a midrange model predicting optimal attachment outcomes can be found in the studies of Belsky, Lewis, and colleagues. Coding on-line in 15-s units, Belsky et al. (1984) and Isabella and Belsky (1991) showed that higher degrees of maternal intrusion, intensity, and frequency of vocalization not contingent on infant vocalization predict avoidant (A) infant attachment. Conversely, maternal underinvolvement, failure to respond to infant vocalization, and bidding for attention when the infant is unavailable, predict anxious-resistant attachment (C). Midrange values predict secure (B). Coding online in 10-s units, Lewis and Feiring (1989) found that midrange scores of mother response and midrange scores of infant sociability and object play, predict secure infant attachment, whereas both higher and lower scores predict insecure.

In De Wolff and Ijzendoorn's (1997) recent metanalysis of 66 studies examining globally coded parental antecedents of infant attachment security, a range of definitions of parental sensitivity emerged, in the general domain of parental warmth and acceptance. De Wolff and Ijzendoorn emphasized that the modest size of the correlations leaves room for additional influences on attachment. They concluded that sensitivity cannot be considered to be the exclusive and most important factor in the development of attachment security, and instead a multidimensional approach to parenting antecedents is recommended. However, they focused on the parent's contribution without addressing the infant's role in the development of attachment.

Keller, Lohaus, Volker, Cappenberg, and Chasiotis (1999) also critiqued the concept of maternal sensitivity. They documented that their measure of interactive coordination is uncorrelated with Ainsworth et al.'s (1978) classic scales of maternal sensitivity, and they construed warmth (sensitivity) and contingency as two independent components of parenting. They

33

reiterated the argument of Tarabulsy, Tessier, and Kappas (1996) that the role of contingency in the development of different types of attachment is still unclear. The design of our current study responds to the preceding critiques by including the infant's as well as the mother's contributions, by using a broader concept than maternal sensitivity, that of dyadic vocal rhythm coordination, and by including challenging contexts, that of a novel partner and a novel site.

Microanalytic studies. In contrast to the macroanalytic studies, fewer than a dozen studies have predicted attachment from earlier inter-actions using second-by-second microanalytic approaches. Although the latter are more labor-intensive, they explicate finer details of behavioral organization.

Using regulation items on the Neonatal Behavioral Assessment Scale, Waters, Vaughn, and Egeland (1980) found that, when assessed at 7 (but not 10) days, infants classified as anxious-resistant score lower than in-fants classified as either secure or avoidant. Using vocal formant tension in the first month to predict 12-month-olds' attachment, Lester and Sei-fer (1990) found that B babies are midrange, A babies have high vocal tension ("holding distress in"), and C infants have low vocal tension ("let-ting out distress"). In an experimental paradigm, Izard, Haynes, Chisholm, and Beak (1991) found that more infant anger and sadness expressions during episodes of simulated maternal anger and sadness (from ages 2 to 9 months) predict B infants at age 13 months. Mikaye et al. (1985) found that infants who cry less tend to be classified as B attachment at age 12 months; infants classified as C show more fear in infancy than infants classified as A.

Two studies have predicted infant attachment from ongoing face-to-face interaction, similar to the design of the current monograph. Langhorst and Fogel (1982) documented greater infant avoidance in the attachment test when mothers are more likely to increase stimu-lation in response to negative infant cues at age 3 months, and less infant avoidance when mothers reserve stimulation for periods of infant gazing at mother. Malatesta et al. (1989) analyzed maternal facial changes contingent on infant facial changes (but not vice versa) from ages 2 to 7 months. Mothers of B infants show lower degrees of contin-gency than those of A infants. Low to moderate degrees of maternal contingency are more favorable for the child's expressive development at age 2 years.

Several studies have predicted attachment from mother and 6-month-old-infant behavior in the "still-face paradigm," developed by Tronick et al. (1978), which challenges the infant to "cope" with an unresponsive mother. Kiser, Bates, Maslin, and Bayles (1986) differentiated A, B, and C infants.

Tronick, Ricks, and Cohn (1982), as well as Cohn, Campbell, and Ross (1992), found that B, but not A, infants displayed positive eliciting behaviors when assessed during the still-face episode at age 6 months.

It is our contention that, although many studies have identified behavioral predictors of later attachment, nevertheless we still lack a full understanding of the methods or noncausal mechanisms of attachment formation and transmission. Various authors have concurred, such as Fox (1994), Hofer (1994), Seifer and Schiller (1995), and Tarabulsy et al. (1996). Tarabulsy et al. (1996) further argued that adequate documentation that interactive contingencies in infancy are in fact related to assessments of development is still lacking. Seifer and Schiller (1995) suggested that the best conceptualization currently available is that "if interactions are generally characterized as sensitive, infants will come to expect that their parent (or caregiver) will be available to help modulate states of negative arousal . . ." (pp. 154–155). They went on to argue that this statement remains too general, and "Despite the accumulating evidence for . . . cross-generational correspondence, there is little empirical work that has defined a mechanism by which this transmission occurs" (p. 155). Similarly, Pederson and Moran (1995) stated that ". . . our understanding of the role of maternal behavior in the emergence of distinctive attachment relationships has not been elaborated substantially beyond Ainsworth's pioneering work" (p. 114). In the current study variations in patterns of vocal rhythm coordination will be proposed as just such a (noncausal) mechanism or "style" of transmission.

We further argue that a systems model emphasizing bidirectional coordination and the coconstruction of experience has not yet been exploited in the investigation of the origins of attachment. Numerous authors have a similar view. Seifer and Schiller (1995) noted the dearth of research on the interactive origins of attachment in the 1st year, specifically emphasizing the need for a systems model. Fox (1994) noted that although notions of reciprocal regulatory control were central to Bowlby's (1969) thinking, they have not been similarly central in research on the origins of attachment. A number of critics observe that the infant is relatively neglected in research on the origins of attachment. Both the parent's and the child's contribution should be studied as a dyadic system, in the coconstruction of the relationship (Bowlby, 1969; Field, 1994; Fox, 1994; Hinde, 1982; Seifer & Schiller, 1995; Tarabulsy et al., 1996). Work using the face-to-face paradigm, particularly that of Tronick (1989) and Cohn and Tronick (1988), has been strongest in advocating a mutual regulation model. However, as Seifer and Schiller (1995) noted, "In general . . . the relations among assessments made in this [mutual regulation] paradigm with sensitivity and attachment assessments are as yet poorly understood" (p. 166).

Current critiques call for (a) evidence that interactive contingencies in early development indeed predict later outcomes; (b) framing research within a systems model, with greater attention to the role of the infant in this system; and (c) a specific investigation of the interactive origins of attachment within a mutual regulation model in which relationships are seen as coconstructed. These critiques provide the framework for the current study of the role of vocal rhythm coordination in the origins of attachment.

Cognition

Bayley Scales of Infant Development

The Bayley Scales of Infant Development (BSID) (Bayley, 1969, 1993) are designed to test mental and motor skills of infants aged 2–30 months, and to assess current functioning rather than to predict later IQ. The Bayley has two subscales, the Mental Development Index (MDI), which is used in the current investigation, and the Psychomotor Development Index (PDI). According to Buros (1978), the standardization of the BSID is excellent. Although the BSID was not designed to predict later IQ, it is correlated with numerous measures of childhood cognitive functioning. Flanagan and Alfonso (1995) documented correlations with the McCarthy Scales for Children's Abilities, the General Cognitive Index, and the Wechsler Preschool and Primary Scale of Intelligence. The BSID is also correlated with Apgar scores (Serunian & Broman, 1975), the Denver Developmental Screen test (Frankenberg, Goldstein, & Camp, 1971), and language and reading at ages 6 to 8 years (Siegel, 1989).

The Prediction of Bayley Performance From Mother-Infant Interaction

Numerous studies predict 12-month-olds' performance on the BISD, and other related cognitive assessments, from early mother-infant interaction. Lewis and Goldberg (1969) argued that infant experience with contingent maternal responsivity organizes a generalized expectation of responsiveness in the infant, which promotes both social and cognitive development. Various studies have demonstrated a positive relationship between maternal contingent responsivity and infant development (Beckwith, 1971a, 1971b; Beckwith, Cohen, Knopp, Parmalee, & Marcy, 1976; Finkelstein & Ramey, 1977; Ramey & Ourth, 1971). Lewis, Jaskir, and Enright (1986) suggested that the social ability of infants may be a more important factor in mental development than many other abilities: Mental development is a product of an interactive social system. It is in this sense that we construe the Bayley Scales as social as well as cognitive.

Infant response to novelty is a well-known predictor of performance on the BSID as well as other measures of cognitive development. For example, Fagan (1982) argued that novelty preferences are a convenient way to measure basic intellectual processes, and Berg and Sternberg (1985) concluded that novelty is central to the concept of intelligence at all ages. Novelty scores on visual attention tasks, construed as early indicators of intelligence by Fagan and Shepherd (1987), were found by Rose (1989) to predict Bayley MDI. Fagen and McGrath (1981) found that preferences for novelty at age 6 months predict intelligence in early childhood. Lewis and Brooks-Gunn (1981) concluded that the ability to process information, and particularly to recover from habituation in the face of a novel stimulus, is a key aspect of intellectual functioning in early infancy. In a similar approach, Ruddy and Bornstein (1982) showed that infants who demonstrate more and faster habituation at age 4 months have larger speaking vocabularies and higher Bayley scores at age 12 months. Bornstein and Sigman (1986) showed that rapidity of schema formation at age 4 months, assessed in a habituation task, predicts IQ at age 3 years. They argued that habituation and recovery of attention (novelty preference) are central to infant cognition and underlie the measures that predict later intelligence. A metanalytic review of the literature by McCall and Carriger (1993) suggests that habituation, recognition memory, and anticipation assessments in the 1st year of life predict later IQ assessed between 1 and 8 years of age. Habituation and recovery of attention (response to novelty), as well as recognition memory, tap the infant's capacity to shift attention from the familiar to the novel.

However, cognition is also predicted by infant sensitivity to temporal information in general. Lewkowicz (2000) has argued that temporally based perceptual and motor capacities in infancy are an important developmental foundation for the later emergence of cognitive abilities. Similarly, Dougherty and Haith (1997) used infants' visual reaction time and ability to visually anticipate events to predict later IQ assessed at age 4 years by the Wechsler Preschool and Primary Scale of Intelligence. The temporal processing of events is an important dimension of cognitive development, and the capacity to form expectancies of temporal information may be one of its underlying organizing processes.

Finally, several researchers have proposed that early mother-infant *vocal* interactions provide a specific framework for the child's later cognitive development (Beckwith, 1971a, 1971b; Beckwith et al., 1976; Bruner, 1983; Freedle & Lewis, 1977). Ruddy and Bornstein (1982) found that more infant vocalizing at age 4 months predicts higher Bayley scores at age 12 months. Roe et al. (1982) showed that 3-month-old infants who respond with more vocalizing to mother than stranger have higher verbal-cognitive scores at ages 3, 5, and 12 years. The Roe data examined vocal interactions in conjunction with response to novelty, yielding long-term predictions. Hardy-Brown, Plomin, and DeFries (1981) also documented that maternal contingent vocal responsivity and imitation at age 12 months are related to 12-month-old infants' communicative competence, based on measures that include language items from the BISD.

Thus, on the basis of studies of mother-infant interaction, as well as the study of temporal processing, we hypothesize that variations in the coordination of infant-adult vocal rhythms predict cognitive outcomes. Both the infant's expectation of maternal responsivity, as conceptualized by Lewis and others, as well as the infant's more general capacity to create expectancies of temporal information are relevant to this prediction. Furthermore, early vocal interactions themselves have been shown to predict cognitive development. Finally, because a large literature concurs that response to novelty is a central aspect of cognitive ability, we hypothesize that infant vocal coordination in the novel contexts of the laboratory with the stranger will be most informative about the infant's cognitive performance on the Bayley Scales.

III. METHOD

We examined 4-month-old-infants' vocal interactions with adults during face-to-face play, and assessed the significance of these interactions for attachment and cognition at age 12 months. Interactions were recorded for three partner configurations (mother-infant, stranger-infant, and mother-stranger), and at two sites (home and laboratory), yielding six partner/site conditions. Our main hypothesis is that degree of vocal rhythm coordination between the 4-month-old infant and the adult predicts outcomes at age 12 months. A secondary hypothesis is that bidirectional (reciprocal) coordination predicts outcomes at age 12 months. Analyses of partner and site novelty (stranger-infant as compared to mother-infant, lab as compared to home) are primarily exploratory, investigating the general proposal that vocal rhythm and timing coordination are differential relational features, providing one definition of the infant's first differentiation from mother, with a stranger, in a strange place. More specifically, guided by adult findings we hypothesize that coordination is greater between unacquainted partners. Also guided by infant cognition findings, we hypothesize that the highest novelty challenge (stranger in the lab) will be most informative about infant cognitive development.

PARTICIPANTS

Eighty-eight mother-infant pairs were assessed when the infants were 4 months old.

Recruitment. Within 24 hours of delivery, mothers who met eligibility criteria for the project were recruited from Babies Hospital, Columbia Presbyterian Medical Center, according to established procedures for obtaining informed consent. A female postdoctoral clinical psychologist explained to the mother that we were studying mother-infant communication and infant social development; that the project involved a home visit when the infant was 4 months old for audiotaping interaction with her infant and that she might also be invited to a lab visit at that time for audio-taping and videotaping; that she would be asked to complete some questionnaires; and that we would assess her infant's development at age 12 months in another home visit and a lab visit. Travel expenses would be reimbursed.

Inclusion criteria. Eligibility criteria included (a) primiparous birth; (b) mother at least 18 years old; (c) stable nuclear family situation; (d) mother's primary language was English for linguistic-phonetic reasons; (e) telephone in the home; (f) mother exhibited no gross psychopathology during initial contact; (g) absence of maternal positive prenatal urine drug screen; (h) no preclampsia or significant medical complications; (i) Caesarean section acceptable if no evidence of fetal distress; (j) singleton birth; (k) 1-minute Apgar less than 7 acceptable only if 5-minute Apgar greater than or equal to 7; (l) birth weight greater than 2,500 g; (m) infant not more than 3 weeks preterm or 2 weeks postterm; (n) no positive infant urine toxicology screen; (o) abnormal infant-blood gases acceptable if all other inclusion criteria met; (p) attending obstetrician confirmed suitability; and (q) baby discharged from hospital at same time as mother. Although mothers were recruited from both the "private" wards (mothers attended by private physicians) and the "public" wards, few of those from the latter were either willing to participate or met the eligibility criteria.

DESIGN

The study examined adult–4-month-old-infant face-to-face vocal interactions and 12-month-old-infant outcomes. The design at age 4 months involved three partner configurations, mother-infant, stranger-infant, and mother-stranger, at two sites, home and lab. The purpose of this design was to examine 4-month-old-infant–adult vocal interactions in relation to two kinds of novelty: partner and site. The mother-stranger interaction was included to compare adult-adult with adult-infant vocal interaction. In the face-to-face interactions, the order of mother-infant and stranger-infant interactions was counterbalanced; mother-stranger always occurred last.

Although 88 families began the study when infants were 4 months old, not all mother-infant pairs engaged in all project phases at 4 and 12 months of age. All 88 families were seen in the home; a randomly selected subset of 53 were seen in the lab as well. In the home visits, although all 88 mother-stranger interactions were recorded, only 84 mother-infant and 82 stranger-infant were recorded. In the lab, 53 mother-infant interactions were recorded, 52 stranger-infant, and 51 mother-stranger. Lost recordings were due to mechanical failures and occasionally a crying infant. A total of 410 interactions when infants were 4 months old was analyzed. When infants were 12 months old, 84 of the original 88 families were visited in the home to test infant cognition with the Bayley Scales; 82 of the original 88 families returned to the lab to test infant attachment with the Ainsworth Strange Situation. The Bayley testing was done in the home in order to procure greater cooperation from the families. The Ainsworth testing was done in the lab because this setting is an intrinsic aspect of the test. Of the 88 infants, 47 were male and 41 female. The average maternal age was 33 and mean social status (Hollingshead Four Factor Index, 1978) was 57. Most of the sample participants were white, middle- to upper-socioeconomic class; all lived in the greater New York metropolitan area; and 90% remained married throughout the study.

PROCEDURE

Scheduling took into account the infants' eating and sleeping patterns. Audiotaping both at home and in the lab used unidirectional air microphones embedded in a small circular container placed directly on the skin of each partner to serve as a contact microphone. The receiving face of the microphone was covered by a diaphragm, and the remaining part was shielded to some extent against extraneous noise. The microphone was attached to the skin by surgical tape in a place where clothes would not be likely to rub it.

Strangers. Infants as well as mothers interacted with a stranger. Strangers were 30 female graduate students recruited from local universities, selected for a warm interpersonal style, and paid a fee. Training sessions by a supervising investigator (BB) elaborated on methods of playing with infants face-to-face, and involved observation of a series of criterion interactions between mothers and infants, as well as several practice play sessions with an infant. Strangers were trained to avoid "chasing" an infant who was looking away, to be very responsive to a distressed infant, and to help such infants self-regulate. With 4-month-old infants, the 30 strangers engaged in 143 stranger-infant and 143 mother-stranger interactions. Apart from one of the strangers who interacted with 50 infants and their mothers, the average number of 4-month-old infants seen by each of the other 29 strangers was approximately 6 (SD = 4.1). Potential effects of the different strangers were covaried in every analysis involving a stranger, as detailed later. Strangers who participated in the Ainsworth or Bayley testing of the 12-month-olds were always new (unfamiliar to the infant).

41

Home. Two experimenters visited the home for audiotape (but not videotape) recording. Mothers chose a room, the infant was placed in an infant seat upon a table, and face-to-face interaction proceeded with the instruction that the mother play with her infant as she ordinarily would. The stranger also engaged the infant in face-to-face play, with order counterbalanced. Mother and stranger then conversed. For each interaction the recording lasted approximately 12 minutes. The average session durations and standard deviations across mother-infant and stranger-infant were 11.43 minutes and 2.19, respectively; those for mother-stranger were 13.96 and 1.27, respectively. To evaluate the possibility of sampling bias between the group seen at home only, as compared to the group seen both at home and in the lab, we assessed the attachment status of the two groups, using a continuous transformation of the attachment category (see the section on the degree of insecurity scale). ANOVA revealed a nonsignificant F ratio ($p = .77$).

Laboratory. The procedure at the lab was identical to that used at home, with the exception that sessions were video- as well as audiotaped. The average session durations and standard deviations across mother-infant and stranger-infant were 11.13 minutes and 2.40, respectively; those for mother-stranger were 10.87 and 3.98, respectively. If a baby became fussy to the point of crying for longer than 30 s, the interaction was interrupted. The period of crying was deleted from the tape, and taping was resumed after the infant was calm. Recordings took place in a sound proofed and partially sound-deadened booth.

AGE 4 MONTHS PREDICTOR VARIABLES

The primary set of predictor variables consisted of the coefficients of *coordinated interpersonal timing* (CIT) calculated by time-series analysis (described later). The second set included site (home or lab), partner configuration (mother-infant, stranger-infant, mother-stranger), and infant sex.

Vocal behavior. Vocal behavior (duration) of each interaction was recorded on two separate channels of a stereo tape recorder, which serve as inputs to a specialized computer system called the Automatic Vocal Transaction Analyzer (AVTA; Cassotta et al., 1967). The coding is accomplished by sending the two audio signals, one for each person, into AVTA, which performs an analogue-to-digital conversion. Both sequences of signals are sampled simultaneously every 250 ms to determine whether the signal in each channel is on or off, without regard to frequency or intonational characteristics of the sounds. Thus, the sole dimension examined in the on-off series was the *durations* of sounds and silences.

These time series are transformed and stored digitally in the computer as a sequence of four binary numbers: 0, 1, 2, and 3, which represent the four observable dyadic states of the dialogue: 0 = partners A and B are both silent; 1 = A is vocalizing while B remains silent; 2 = B is now vocalizing while A remains silent; and 3 = A and B vocalize simultaneously. The two-channel time series of the original recording can be perfectly translated from the dyadic code and vice versa, so the identities of the individuals are preserved. AVTA software converts the decimal numbers into a set of states (defined below) and averages their durations for a fixed time unit.

The dialogic approach of Jaffe and Feldstein (1970), augmented by Heller (1967), Feldstein (1972), and Feldstein and Welkowitz (1978), was used to code the vocal stream into the set of parameters defined below. *This approach is an exhaustive classification of everything that can possibly happen in a two-person, on-off vocal stream.* In the purely on-off system, during joint action or joint silence it is not possible to know whose pause it is, nor whose interruption it is. The turn rule resolves these problems, enabling automated determination of the turn holder at every sampling instant.

The turn rule. The basis for parsing the dialogue into vocal states for the two participants is the turn rule. A turn begins at the instant that either participant vocalizes alone, and it is held until the other vocalizes alone, at which point the turn is exchanged. Although the turn rule is the cornerstone of the definition of the vocal states, the analysis examines the coordination of the turns as well as durations of all sounds and silences of both partners within turns.

Vocal states. Five vocal state *durations* for each partner (Feldstein & Welkowitz, 1978) are computed by AVTA: vocalization, pause, switching pause, and interruptive and noninterruptive simultaneous speech (Fig. 1). All vocal states described for adult conversation occur for mother and infant.

1. A *vocalization* is a continuous utterance of one individual containing no silence greater than 250 ms (silences less than 250 ms are attributable to stop consonants in speech and are bridged by our A/D converter). Joint silence is classified in terms of its outcome.

2. A *pause* is a joint silence greater than or equal to 250 ms bounded by the vocalizations of the turnholder.

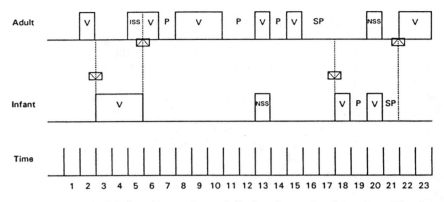

FIGURE 1.—A diagrammatic representation of an interactional sequence. The time axis represents successive 250-ms units. V = vocalization; P = pause; SP = switching pause; NSS = noninterruptive simultaneous speech; ISS = interruptive simultaneous speech. The arrows that point down denote the end of the adult's turns; those that point up denote the end of the infant's turns.

3. A *switching pause* is a joint silence greater than or equal to 250 ms initiated by the turn holder, but terminated by a unilateral vocalization of the partner, who thereby gains the turn. In unconstrained adult dialogue, the switching pause is assigned, for theoretical and empirical reasons, to the speaker whose turn it terminates (Jaffe & Feldstein, 1970).

Simultaneous speech is also classified in terms of its outcome—that is, whether or not it results in an exchange of turns. Simultaneous speech is a "listener phenomenon," initiated by the partner who does not hold the turn (the listener).

4. *Noninterruptive simultaneous speech* (NSS) is that which begins and ends while the partner who holds the turn vocalizes continuously.

5. *Interruptive simultaneous speech* (ISS) is part of a speech segment begun by the listener. It is initiated while the turn holder is vocalizing, but then continues after the turn holder stops. Only that part of the segment uttered coactively is considered interruptive simultaneous speech. The trailing portion, inasmuch as it is then a unilateral utterance, marks the beginning of the turn of the partner who initiated the interruption and is, therefore, considered his or her vocalization (see Fig. 1).

The *turn* itself is at a different conceptual level than the vocal states. Whereas the latter are uniquely defined, the turn can be a composite of all of them, including an unspecified number of repetitions of vocalizations, pauses, and noninterruptive simultaneous speech, as illustrated in Figure 1. It may not be obvious that these definitions plus our turn rule imply certain restrictions on the possible state sequences permitted by our model. For example, the pause of one partner cannot follow the switching pause of the other without violating the turn rule; that is, a switching pause terminates a turn, and the new turn of the other partner must begin with a vocalization. As another example, an ISS initiated by the listener *can* be followed by a pause of the interruptor, because the latter has gained the turn by the time the ISS ends. This logical rigor of definitions allowed a computer program to accomplish our coding.

Rhythmic Definitions of Vocal States

The vocal states can be construed as rhythms when individual on and off components are combined as on-plus-off cycles.

The *interpersonal turn rhythm* is a two-person cycle composed of a sequence of one partner's turn plus the other partner's turn.

Within the turn, the *vocalization-pause rhythm* defines the turn holder's tempo. For each partner, the *V + P cycle* (mean vocalization duration plus mean pause duration), in seconds per cycle, defines the "beat" (wavelength) of the rhythm. (Its reciprocal, $1/(V + P)$, is the tempo of the rhythm in cycles per second (familiar as Hertz). Matching the cycle of Vocalization + Pause (the beat, or the wavelength) is thought to be a major method of interpersonal coupling, often referred to as rhythmic entrainment (Winfree, 1975).

Within each partner's vocalization-pause rhythm, *the ratio V/P* indexes the relative activation (or inhibition) of the rhythmic sequence. This ratio is a traditional measure of fluency and speech rate in adult monologue (Feldstein, Crown, & Jaffe, 1991). Higher and lower ratios correlate with personality measures of extraversion/introversion, respectively (Feldstein, 1998). Speech is more flowing, or activated, with a high ratio (longer duration of sound relative to duration of silence), and more hesitant, or inhibited, with a low ratio (shorter duration of sound relative to that of silence).

Time-series regression analysis to assess CIT. Whereas the definitions above refer to the *durations* of vocal states and turns, we now move to the analysis of *interpersonal contingencies* of vocal durations (CIT), calculated by time-series regression (Gottman, 1981; Ostrom, 1978; Warner, 1996). Each interaction can be viewed as parallel streams of behavior in time—that is, a bivariate time series. A theory of interactive behavior (Gottman, 1981; Thomas & Malone, 1979) must take into account how the person is organized in relation to his or her own behavior (autocorrelation) as well as in relation to the partner's behavior (cross-correlation). But the results of using ordinary product-moment correlation to assess cross-correlation may be inflated because they include the effects of autocorrelation. The time-series model separately assesses and then removes (i.e., partials) the autocorrelation in each partner's contribution to the dyadic time series. Then, by means of lag correlations (controlled for autocorrelation), it assesses whether each partner's stream of behavior is predictable from that of the other, yielding an assessment of *direction of coordination.*

Other than turns, the time unit over which the vocal state durations were averaged was 5 s, yielding a vector of 144 units across a 12-minute interaction. Given the average vocal state durations of approximately 1 s (Feldstein & Welkowitz, 1978; Jaffe & Feldstein, 1970), the 5-s unit is long enough to include at least one and, more often, several occurrences of a particular state. The time unit for *turns*, however, was 30 s, because they constitute a sequence of states.

Each of the two series for each adult-infant pair was subjected to an SPSSX ARIMA (Auto Regressive Integrated Moving Average) modeling procedure in order to remove autocorrelation effects from the data, and the ACF subprogram of SPSSX was used to allow for visual and statistical checks of which model provided the best fit to the data. After inspecting the error distributions of approximately 35 interactions, an "AR2" model was selected as most appropriate on the basis of a diagnosis of the residuals. An AR2 model is an ARIMA model that uses two lags to remove autocorrelational effects from a time series. Dr. Rebecca Warner consulted on the adequacy of our visual diagnostics. It should be noted that neither ISS nor NSS could be as consistently fitted by an AR2 model, perhaps because the frequency of their occurrence is usually less and their average duration usually shorter than the other vocal states. Turns, on the other hand, were generally too long to fit an AR2 model. Therefore, none of these three (ISS, NSS, turns) was used in the analyses predicting outcomes. However, in the remaining analyses, the CIT of all six vocal parameters was considered. In this study, autocorrelational effects were removed from both the criterion (dependent) and predictor (independent) variables. The AR2 model used specified no differencing and a zero-order moving average. After selecting the model, the AREG subprogram of SPSSX Trends was used to compute the time-series analyses.

The degree to which a partner coordinated his or her current behavior with the other's behavior of the previous minute was examined. A minute had been used in our past research (e.g., Crown, 1991; Jasnow et al., 1988; Jasnow & Feldstein, 1986) and in that of others (e.g., Cappella, 1996). Thus, for each parameter, a set of 12 successive 5-s "lags" was used to examine the prediction of each participant's autocorrelation-corrected behavior from that of the partner. Lag-0 was omitted. The statistic used to index degree of coordinated timing was the proportion of the variance (R^2) of one partner's behavior that accounted for the 12 lags of the other partner's behavior. In addition, an *optimal lag* was defined as the lag that accounted for the most variance. Only pairwise comparisons were performed: Adult and infant behavior were compared only within the same vocal state (e.g., average pause of infant with average pause of adult), which was the same strategy used in all our related studies (e.g., Beebe et al., 1988; Crown, 1991; Jasnow & Feldstein, 1986; Jasnow et al., 1988).

Definitions of bidirectional coordination at age 4-months: Across-group and per dyad. Based on the time-series analyses, two definitions of age 4-months bidirectional coordination were used. (1) The across-group definition uses Cohn and Tronick (1988): For example, for mothers and infants, across the group, the proportion of mothers for whom the CIT indices were statistically significant (I → M) and the proportion of infants for whom the CIT indices were significant (M → I) yield a description of bidirectional across-group coordination. (2) Per dyad coordination requires that, *within each dyad,* I → M and M → I are both significant.

AGE 12 MONTHS OUTCOME VARIABLES

The two outcome variables were the Ainsworth Strange Situation, assessed for 82 infants, and the Bayley Scales of Infant Development, assessed for 84 infants.

Ainsworth Strange Situation. This test (Ainsworth et al., 1978) is a lab procedure involving infant, mother, and a stranger, with eight brief episodes of separation and reunion, designed to examine the balance between an infant's exploratory and attachment behavioral systems with a primary caregiver. The two brief separations of the infant from the mother (episodes 5 and 8) are key for determining the attachment classification. The infant's ability to use mother as a secure base is appraised through seven scales of proximity-seeking, contact-seeking, contact maintaining, resistant, avoidant, distance interaction, and search behavior during separation and reunions. Interobserver reliabilities (Ainsworth et al., 1978) ranged from .93 to .97 for all scales except distance interaction and search. In our study, Dr. Mary Jo Ward supervised the training and coding reliability and also coded 20 of the 82 infants for reliability. Intraclass correlation yielded an $R = .73$ ($F(19, 20) = 6.407$), $p < .05$. A (nonchance) kappa coefficient yielded a $k = .59$. The coding yielded 16 *avoidant* (A), 55 *secure* (B), 4 *anxious-resistant* (C), and 7 *disorganized* (D) infants (classifications are described in the literature review, "Prediction of Age 1-Year Outcomes"). The distribution is relatively similar to that of a normal American sample (Sagi, van Ijzendoorn, & Koren-Karie, 1991). Although the number of infants classified as C and D is small, given that this is the first large study of its kind, the advantage of analyzing these classifications was considered to outweigh the danger of the nonreplicability of the findings. Particularly the analysis of the D classification is exploratory, because very little research has explored its interactive antecedents.

Degree of insecurity scale (DIS). In addition to the traditional four attachment categories, a continuous transformation of attachment (Richters et al., 1988) was used to examine nonlinear relationships between CIT and attachment. The Richters et al. transformation used discriminant function analysis with four scales of proximity-seeking, contact-maintaining, proximity- and interaction-avoidance, and contact-resistance, as well as crying/noncrying. The DIS was obtained by multiplying the scale scores by the weights supplied by Richters et al. Higher scores indicate greater insecurity.

The *Bayley Scales of Infant Development* (1969) is the only instrument that measures standardized "mental development" as early as age 1 year. The child participates in a series of tasks and games that are rated by the experimenter. Of the three parts of the Bayley Scales, the Mental Development Index (MDI), the Psychomotor Development Index (PDI), and the Infant Behavior Rating Scale (IBR), only the MDI was used. The MDI split-half reliability from the original standardization sample ranged from .81 to .93 (median = .88). The MDI is a standard score (multiplied by 100), with a mean of 100, standard deviation of 16. Two graduate students, A. Rotter and R. Schwartz, were trained by Dr. I. Wallace, at that time at Yeshiva University. The MDI was administered in the subjects' homes after training consisting of a dozen periods of one-way vision screen observation, videotaping of testers, and testing of 15 subjects. Calculated for 20 infants, interrater reliability was 83% agreement, maintained throughout testing.

DATA-ANALYTIC PROCEDURES

Data analyses addressed both 4-month-olds' vocal state *durations* as well as the *coordination* (the CIT) of these durations. Thus the vocal states have two forms: durations and CIT. The data-analytic strategies were (a) bivariate time-series regression analysis, described previously, to assess 4-month-olds' CIT for each vocal state for each partner of each interaction; (b) multivariate analyses of variance to explore differences among vocal state durations, as well as CIT, as a function of novelty of site (home/ lab) and partner (mother/stranger), at age 4 months; (c) McNemar's test of symmetry to evaluate differences in percentages of dyads showing *per dyad* bidirectional coordination (see the definition previously given) as a function of novelty of partner or site; (d) multiple regression analyses to predict the 12-month-olds' outcome measures from 4-month-olds' CIT; (e) a series of chi-square tests to examine the relationship between per dyad bidirectional coordination and attachment, and a series of ANOVA, to examine the relationship between per dyad bidirectional coordination and cognition. We thus explored two approaches to the question of whether 12-month-olds' outcomes are bidirectionally predicted: across-group and per dyad. The multiple regression analyses in (d) above address whether, across the group, the equations using the infants' indices of CIT (A → I), as well as the equations using the adults' indices (I → A), predict outcomes. The chi-square tests and ANOVA described in (e) above address whether the outcomes can be predicted from the distinction between dyads who do, and do not, show per dyad bidirectional CIT.

Although these analyses involved many inferential tests, the analyses in each Results chapter (chapters IV, V, and VI) are independent of those in the other Results chapters. In the multiple regression analyses we entered the variables in only one order. Although we performed analyses to test the main hypothesis of a relationship between 4-month-olds' vocal rhythm coordination and subsequent outcomes, we also did exploratory analyses of modes of rhythmic coordination and the role of novelty. In the tests of the main hypothesis, we used the conventional alpha level of .05. In exploratory analyses, however, we were as interested in *patterns* of the data, and effect size, as in statistical significance. We discuss exploratory results (in the analyses of novelty) that do not meet conventional levels of significance, if the effect size is substantial and if they fit a pattern of results that are formally significant. Abelson (1995) and Rosenthal and Rosnow (1991), among others, have argued that significance tests contribute additional evidence in support of a particular explanation but cannot provide the sole or even the most critical evidence. An explanation needs to be tempered by coherence within the context of a viable theory. It is true that 5% of the tests that are ostensibly significant could be so by chance. We decided not to adjust the significance levels because this study was one of the first large studies of its kind, and we decided to accept the risk of a Type II over a Type I error.

Multivariate analysis of variance. To evaluate the role of partner and site novelty in mother-infant (MI) and stranger-infant (SI) interactions when infants were 4 months old, MANOVA were performed to explore differences among vocal state durations, as well as CIT, as the dependent variables. (Because of the differing number of participants involved, separate MANOVA were performed.) Infant sex was used as the between-subjects variable, and partner configuration (MI versus SI), site (home versus lab), and direction of lag (or direction of coordination) from the time-series analysis were used as the within-subject variables in a split-plot MANOVA. Preliminary analyses showed that, although the set of strangers accounted for a significant proportion of variance in some instances, there was no interaction with any of the vocal measures.

Multiple regression analysis. Univariate multiple regression analyses examined the relationship of 4-month-olds' CIT to the two outcome measures for 12-month-olds. The multiple regression equations described below were the only ones performed; a variety of models was not explored. Any potential shared variance among the CIT indices was removed. We also partialled out of each of the outcomes (attachment, Bayley Scales) any variance that was contributed by the other outcome. The effect of the sex of the infant and the different strangers was also covaried.

Attachment. A set of multiple regression equations examined the relation of the coefficients of CIT to the attachment categories (A, B, C, and D). A measure of CIT (e.g., switching pause coefficients) served as the criterion variable. The primary predictor variables were infant sex and the set of attachment categories, dummy-coded with category B as the reference category. They were entered as a set, which allowed the computer to choose, on the basis of its variance contribution, which of the categories entered the equation first. Infant sex and the MDI of the Bayley Scales were used as a set of covariates in the model to partial out their variance contributions, thus examining the unique relation between attachment and the CIT variables. Attachment was not used as the criterion variable because we wanted to know the relation of each of the categories to CIT.

Whereas each mother interacted only with her own infant, each stranger interacted with different numbers of mothers and 4-month-old infants. To control for this source of variance, the set of strangers was used as a covariate, dummy-coded such that each variable in the set represented the number of interactions in which a particular stranger engaged. This covariate was entered prior to the Bayley scores.

To explore curvilinear relations between the CIT and the continuous DIS, the regression analysis used a hierarchical model—that is, the order of the equations was determined by the investigators. Thus, the predictor variables were sex, the coefficients of switching pauses, pauses, and vocalizations, each followed by its respective squared coefficients. These were followed by the product variables of sex by each of the vocal measure coefficients, entered as a set so that the product that contributed the most variance to prediction of the criterion variable entered the equation first. Whereas the coefficients themselves represented the linear aspects of the vocal measures in their relationship to the DIS, the squared coefficients (power polynomials) represented their quadratic aspects. The product variables yielded information about the interactions of sex with each of the vocal measures. This model was used to separately analyze the CIT coefficients of (a) mothers (with infants); (b) infants (with mothers); (c) strangers (with infants); (d) infants (with strangers); (e) mothers (with strangers); and (f) strangers (with mothers), each at home and at the lab.

Bayley MDI. The multiple regression model used to predict the Bayley used the MDI scores as the criterion variable in each of a set of equations. The primary independent variables were the coefficients of CIT of vocal states. However, infant sex, the dummy-coded set of strangers, and attachment (DIS) were included as covariates, thus examining the unique relation between the Bayley and the CIT variables. Again, the model was hierarchical so that we could investigate the curvilinear relations between coordination and Bayley scores. Thus, each vector of the power polynomials of a measure of vocal coordination followed the measure itself for each of the vocal measures, as in the attachment model. These variables were followed by a set of the product variables of sex by vocal states in order to assess possible interaction effects.

Sequence of the analyses. The Results are organized in chapters IV, V, and VI. Chapter IV evaluates *durations* of vocal states from the points of view of stability and variability, as a function of partner and site novelty, and then explores a rhythmic construction of these same durations (see definitions given previously). Chapter V subjects these same vocal state durations to time-series regression analyses, yielding coefficients of coordination (CIT), and again examines them as a function of novelty of partner and site. In chapter VI, the 4-month-olds' CIT indices were used to predict the 12-month-olds' outcomes. We could have used the raw durations of the vocal states to predict outcomes, but we chose the CIT indices because more information about the nature of the interaction was inherent in CIT. Furthermore, by using time-series regression analysis, each dyad could be separately evaluated for direction of coordination.

IV. RESULTS: THE TIMING OF SOUND AND SILENCE

In this chapter we address two of the study goals: an examination of how novelty of partner and site may relate to vocal rhythms using a strictly durational approach, and a description of how vocal rhythms may be interpersonally coupled. For clarity of terminology, when referring to the *durations* of vocal data, as we do in this chapter, we use the term *couple* when any of the vocal timing patterns show ordinary correlation. In contrast, when we address the interpersonal *contingencies* of these vocal durations by time-series analysis, a lagged form of correlation, as we do in the next two chapters, we use the term *coordination*.

The first section in this chapter, "The Timescale of Sound and Silence Durations at Age 4 Months," presents data on the frequency and durations of the vocal states, and their intercorrelations within individuals. This section describes the vocal rhythms in terms of their separate components, the vocal states—vocalization, pause, switching pause, and simultaneous speech—as well as turns, a composite of all the states. In the second section, "Comparisons of Vocal State Durations Across Novelty of Partner and Site," the durations of the vocal states are compared in the various novelty conditions of mother-infant and stranger-infant, in home and lab, to see whether partner and site novelty organize vocal durations. In the third section, "Rhythmic Interpretation of Sound and Silence Durations," we turn to an interpretation of the vocal data that integrates the separate components into various rhythms. Forms of interpersonal coupling may become evident in a rhythmic analysis that may not be apparent from the isolated components of the rhythms. Examining rhythmic cycles and their interpersonal correlations is one way of addressing the question of *how* vocal rhythms couple.

THE TIMESCALE OF SOUND AND SILENCE DURATIONS AT AGE 4 MONTHS: DESCRIPTIVE DATA ON ADULT-INFANT DIALOGUES

Table 1 presents the percentage of session time spent vocalizing. Adding together all types of vocalization, infants at home vocalized 17.2%

TABLE 1

PERCENT OF SESSION TIMES SPENT IN SPEAKING TURNS AND THE FIVE VOCAL STATES FOR THE ADULTS AND INFANTS

Vocal Measures		Home						Laboratory					
		MI:M	MI:I	SI:S	SI:I	MS:M	MS:S	MI:M	MI:I	SI:S	SI:I	MS:M	MS:S
	N	84	84[a]	82	82	88	88	53	53	52[b]	52	51	51
T	X	75.3	25.3	80.1	19.7	43.7	56.1	81.3	18.5	87.7	12.2	39.8	60.2
	SD	15.4	15.4	18.3	18.2	16.7	16.8	14.1	14.1	11.0	10.9	15.0	15.0
V	X	46.6	17.2	48.5	14.8	37.3	48.8	53.1	13.6	56.5	9.6	34.2	52.7
	SD	13.6	13.1	15.5	16.2	14.4	16.0	15.1	11.8	13.3	8.9	12.8	14.9
P	X	22.8	3.9	28.3	2.1	4.6	5.4	24.7	2.2	28.7	1.0	3.7	5.5
	SD	10.8	3.5	14.0	2.5	7.6	5.0	10.4	3.1	11.2	1.5	3.5	4.1
SP	X	5.0	4.1	3.2	2.8	1.8	1.9	3.5	2.7	2.5	1.6	1.9	2.0
	SD	2.8	2.2	2.4	2.3	1.5	2.9	2.9	2.3	2.2	1.6	1.8	1.9
ISS	X	2.0	1.8	1.5	1.4	2.2	2.4	1.9	1.5	1.7	1.7	2.3	2.7
	SD	2.0	1.8	1.6	1.5	1.3	1.4	2.1	1.7	2.0	3.2	1.0	1.3
NSS	X	1.5	2.9	1.5	2.3	2.9	2.0	1.9	1.5	1.7	1.7	2.3	2.7
	SD	2.3	3.2	3.8	3.7	2.4	1.7	2.0	2.3	1.7	4.5	2.2	1.8

Note.—MI = Mother-Infant; SI = Stranger-Infant; MS = Mother-Stranger. Following the colon, M = Mother; S = Stranger; I = Infant. To retrieve 100% of session time, the turn is omitted. T, V, P, SP, ISS, and NSS = turns, vocalizations, pauses, switching pauses, interruptive simultaneous speech, and noninterruptive simultaneous speech, respectively.

[a]The N for this cell for turns is 82.

[b]The N for this cell for turns is 48 and is 52 for the other vocal states.

and 14.8% of the time, with mother and stranger respectively, and somewhat less in the lab setting. Tables 2 and 3 present duration and frequency data for interactions of mother-infant and stranger-infant, with mother-stranger for comparison. Because of variations in session length, all frequency data are reported as average frequencies per minute. Intraindividual consistency of the durations of the vocal states was addressed by estimating split-half reliabilities. The split-half estimates for mother-infant and stranger-infant interactions are shown in Table 4. Averaged across vocal states and over partners, infants' coefficients averaged .50 (SD = .23), mothers'coefficients (with infants) averaged .52 (SD = .29), and strangers' (with infants) .57 (SD = .23). Thus, infants interacting with adults had essentially the same stability as adults interacting with infants.

The durations of these states show a largely "split-second vocal world" when adults interact in face-to-face play with 4-month-old infants (Stern 1971, 1977). The timescale of mean durations of vocal states at age 4 months is shown in Table 2 and illustrated in Figure 2. All *infant* state durations are under 1 s; *adults* (with infants) also generally operate in this range, with the one exception of adult vocalization, where the means range from 1.27 to 1.58 s. Adult-adult state durations are also split-second, with the exception of vocalizations (where the mean is approximately 2 s).

Table 5 shows *intraindividual* correlations among vocal state durations. In this analysis we asked whether the durations of the different vocal states tend to be intercorrelated within individuals, a measure of individual "consistency." In Table 5, among mothers, and among infants, significant correlations are found between the two silence states, *pauses* and *switching pauses*, and the two types of *simultaneous speech*, and also among mothers (but not infants) between *vocalizations and pauses*. However, the silence states and the coaction states are not themselves intercorrelated. The same finding is evident in the stranger-infant interactions and in the mother-stranger interactions, with the exception that vocalization and pause are correlated for both partners, and mothers (with strangers) do not show the correlation of the two types of simultaneous speech. Thus, there is a remarkable similarity in the consistency of intraindividual correlations of state durations across mother-stranger, mother-infant, and stranger-infant; overall the same states tend to be correlated with the same sign within each partner.

These findings are consistent with the study of adult dialogue rhythms (Feldstein & Welkowitz, 1978; Jaffe & Feldstein, 1970), where durations of pause and switching pause were positively correlated, vocalization and pause were negatively correlated, and neither type of pause was related to vocalizations or simultaneous speech. Matarazzo, Sazlow, and Hare (1958) and Warner (1992) factor-analyzed this type of conversational on-off activity

TABLE 2

Average Durations in Seconds of Speaking Turns and the Five Vocal States for the Adults and Infants

Vocal Measures		Home						Laboratory					
		MI:M	MI:I	SI:S	SI:I	MS:M	MS:S	MI:M	MI:I	SI:S	SI:I	MS:M	MS:S
	N	84	84[a]	82	82	88	88	53	53	52[b]	52	51	51
T	$\bar{X}$	7.57	2.21	10.84	1.74	5.15	4.58	10.93	1.85	21.12	1.19	3.01	5.00
	SD	6.69	1.64	10.69	1.37	12.01	3.48	9.77	1.58	29.46	.52	1.27	2.50
V	$\bar{X}$	1.29	.85	1.18	.90	1.88	2.15	1.45	.91	1.58	.79	1.65	2.24
	SD	.37	.43	.56	.67	1.03	.83	.62	.42	1.42	.25	.51	.75
P	$\bar{X}$	.95	.66	.90	.52	.49	.48	.90	.54	.83	.42	.45	.49
	SD	.36	.32	.36	.25	.18	.19	.38	.36	.24	.23	.12	.20
SP	$\bar{X}$	.91	.84	.73	.66	.50	.49	.85	.78	.73	.54	.49	.47
	SD	.50	.47	.34	.32	.20	.22	.47	.50	.31	.24	.23	.22
ISS	$\bar{X}$	.41	.39	.37	.36	.39	.40	.39	.37	.41	.44	.44	.44
	SD	.18	.16	.16	.16	.12	.13	.16	.13	.22	.20	.12	.12
NSS	$\bar{X}$	.50	.42	.47	.39	.56	.51	.47	.41	.57	.46	.52	.56
	SD	.33	.18	.26	.15	.53	.15	.33	.14	.42	.21	.44	.16

Note.—MI = Mother-Infant; SI = Stranger-Infant; MS = Mother-Stranger. Following the colon, M = Mother; S = Stranger; I = Infant. T, V, P, SP, ISS, and NSS = turns, vocalizations, pauses, switching pauses, interruptive simultaneous speech, and noninterruptive simultaneous speech, respectively. The average session durations and standard deviations across MI and SI are 11.43 and 2.19, respectively, for the home, and 11.13 and 2.40, respectively, for the lab; those for MS are 13.96 and 1.27, respectively, for the home, and 10.87 and 3.98, respectively, for the lab. [a]The N for this cell for turns is 48 and is 52 for the other vocal states. [b]The N for this cell for turns is 82.

TABLE 3

AVERAGE FREQUENCIES PER MINUTE OF SPEAKING TURNS AND THE FIVE VOCAL STATES FOR THE ADULTS AND INFANTS

Vocal Measures		Home						Laboratory					
		MI:M	MI:I	SI:S	SI:I	MS:M	MS:S	MI:M	MI:I	SI:S	SI:I	MS:M	MS:S
	N	84	84[a]	82	82	88	88	53	53	52[b]	52	51	51
T	X	7.75	7.69	6.46	6.40	8.14	8.12	6.18	6.13	5.09	4.95	8.27	8.27
	SD	3.24	3.25	3.31	3.33	2.65	2.67	2.91	2.93	3.68	3.69	2.84	2.73
V	X	22.09	11.43	25.05	8.67	12.77	14.41	22.84	7.61	25.33	6.28	16.25	19.49
	SD	5.58	5.25	8.00	5.29	3.68	4.61	6.65	4.23	7.65	5.19	5.84	5.13
P	X	14.34	3.72	18.59	2.26	4.64	6.27	16.67	1.84	19.80	1.23	5.64	8.90
	SD	5.72	3.35	8.69	2.63	3.64	3.89	7.74	2.01	7.55	1.80	4.38	4.28
SP	X	3.33	3.02	2.66	2.49	1.99	2.19	2.28	1.92	1.95	1.58	2.72	3.02
	SD	1.47	1.23	1.55	1.94	1.15	1.24	1.12	1.07	1.60	1.42	1.80	1.70
ISS	X	2.43	2.38	2.20	2.06	3.26	3.69	2.41	2.12	2.01	2.10	4.21	4.87
	SD	1.71	1.71	1.53	1.53	1.79	1.79	1.45	1.48	1.52	2.11	1.74	1.93
NSS	X	1.35	3.45	1.29	2.93	3.26	2.25	.95	2.67	.65	2.63	4.74	2.73
	SD	1.76	3.26	2.53	3.64	2.35	1.57	1.39	2.32	.77	3.36	2.53	1.66

Note.—MI = Mother-Infant; SI = Stranger-Infant; MS = Mother-Stranger. Following the colon, M = Mother; S = Stranger; I = Infant. T, V, P, SP, ISS, and NSS stand for turns, vocalizations, pauses, switching pauses, interruptive simultaneous speech, and noninterruptive simultaneous speech, respectively.
[a]The N for this cell for turns is 82. [b]The N for this cell for turns is 48 and is 52 for the other vocal states.

TABLE 4

Split-Half Estimates (r) of the Internal Consistency of Mother-Infant and Stranger-Infant Dialogues When Infants are 4-Months Old

		Dyad Types			
		Home		Laboratory	
	States	Mother-Infant	Stranger-Infant	Mother-Infant	Stranger-Infant
Adults	V	.78** (76)	.80** (81)	.48** (47)	.94** (48)
	P	.79** (76)	.85** (81)	.63** (47)	.68** (48)
	SP	.59** (76)	.58** (78)	.12 (47)	.46** (46)
	NSS	.26 (51)	.32 (47)	.42* (28)	.57** (25)
	ISS	.48** (70)	.52** (72)	.73** (44)	.38** (42)
Infants	V	.76** (76)	.83** (81)	.54** (48)	.29* (48)
	P	.24* (76)	.08 (81)	.20 (43)	.10 (48)
	SP	.51** (76)	.44** (78)	.39** (46)	.25 (46)
	NSS	.54** (70)	.64** (47)	.52** (43)	.53** (25)
	ISS	.62** (69)	.74** (72)	.24 (44)	.85** (42)

Note.—V, P, and SP, NSS, and ISS = average durations of vocalizations, pauses, switching pauses, noninterruptive and interruptive simultaneous speech, respectively. Numbers in parentheses are the degrees of freedom in terms of the number of interactions. The average duration of the interactions was 10–14 min. *$p \leq$ .05, **$p \leq$ .01.

data and concluded that the two main factors represented sound and silence, respectively. But even the highest of these within-person correlation coefficients leaves a large proportion of variance to be explained, leaving open the question of interpersonal correlations, addressed below.

One implication of these correlations is that the vocal state durations are not independent of each other, in the ways described above. Thus, in the analyses to follow, examining vocal durations in relation to novelty of site and partner, the results for one vocal state will not be completely independent of another vocal state, although it is difficult to specify the degree of dependence. It might be expected therefore that the analyses to follow would yield relatively similar results, but note that this is not the case.

COMPARISONS OF VOCAL STATE DURATIONS ACROSS NOVELTY OF PARTNER AND SITE

In these analyses, we addressed whether significant differences in the durations of the vocal states could be detected as a function of novelty of partner and site. To reduce the number of analyses, we limited our focus to adult-infant interaction, and particularly the infant. Two approaches

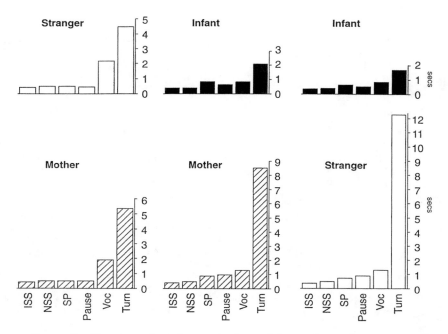

FIGURE 2.—Durations of vocal states (and turns) for mother and stranger, mother and infant, and stranger and infant. Interactions occurred in the home; infants were 4 months old.

were used: (1) Correlational analyses addressed whether, across the group, *individuals* showed similarities in the pattern of vocal durations used across these contexts; (2) multivariate analyses then addressed differences in *group* vocal durations as a function of these contexts.

Correlational Analyses: Are Individuals Stable Across Site and Partner?

These analyses compared (a) mothers and infants across sites of home and lab, and (b) infants across partners of mother versus stranger, in home and lab. Pearson product moment correlation coefficients were calculated.

Mother and infant stability across sites. The first comparison correlated the average durations of the mothers interacting with their infants, at home and in the lab; the second comparison correlated the average durations of the infants interacting with their mothers, at home and in the lab. Table 6 shows that the magnitude of the correlation coefficients is

TABLE 5

INTRAINDIVIDUAL CORRELATIONS AMONG VOCAL-STATE DURATIONS
OF THE MOTHERS, INFANTS, AND STRANGERS

		Mothers				
		P	SP	V	ISS	NSS
	P		0.81*	−0.46*	−0.15	−0.19
	SP	0.71*		−0.31*	−0.16	−0.24*
Infants	V	−0.11	−0.08		0.20	0.22*
	ISS	−0.14	−0.15	0.36*		0.75*
	NSS	−0.22*	−0.19	0.35*	0.70*	
		Strangers				
	P		0.79*	−0.47*	−0.26*	−0.70*
	SP	0.63*		−0.37*	−0.08	−0.04
Infants	V	−0.07	−0.17		0.21	−0.03
	ISS	−0.13	−0.14	0.40*		0.69*
	NSS	−0.28*	−0.26*	0.27*	0.70*	
		Mothers				
	P		0.79*	−0.25*	−0.23*	0.053*
	SP	0.76*		−0.12	−0.18	0.20
Strangers	V	−0.33*	−0.41*		0.33*	0.03
	ISS	−0.12	−0.08	0.22*		0.04
	NSS	−0.17	−0.25*	0.38*	0.63*	

Note.—The vocal states are pauses (P), switching pauses (SP), vocalizations (V), interruptive simultaneous speech (ISS), and noninterruptive simultaneous speech (NSS). The coefficients above the diagonals are from the persons named above the coefficient; those below the diagonals are from the persons named at the side of the coefficients. The N for each of the Mothers' and Infants' coefficients is 84; that for each of the Strangers' and Infants' coefficients and each of the Mothers' and Strangers' coefficients is 83. *$p < .05$.

low to moderate for both mothers and infants, indicating that both vary somewhat in temporal pattern from home to lab. Infant pause, mother and infant switching pause, and mother simultaneous speech (ISS) show a significant but moderate stability from home to lab.

Infant stability across mother and stranger. The average infant durations with their mothers as contrasted with strangers were correlated, separately for home and lab, as presented in Table 7. The low correlations indicate that infants employ different temporal patterns when interacting with mothers versus strangers, at home and in the lab.

It appears that the low to moderate correlations indicate, in general, that the pattern of vocal state durations of mothers and infants as individuals differs somewhat from home to lab. We now turn to an analysis of these questions in terms of differences across groups.

TABLE 6

Estimates (r) of Mother with Infant and Infant with Mother Cross-Site Stability of Vocal State Durations from Home to Laboratory

States	Mother	Infant
V	.19	.04
P	.26	.35*
SP	.42*	.34*
NSS	.20	.19
ISS	.34*	.21

Note.—V, P, SP, NSS, and ISS refer to the average durations of vocalizations, pauses, switching pauses, and noninterruptive and interruptive simultaneous speech, respectively, during mother-infant face-to-face interactions when infants are 4 months old. Because the coefficients compare home and laboratory, only those dyads that interacted in both sites were used. $N = 49$. $*p \leq .05$, $**p \leq .01$.

Multivariate Analyses of the Effects of Site, Partner, and Infant Sex

Do adults (with infants) differ by site, partner, and infant sex? Split-plot multivariate analyses of variance for mother and stranger (interacting with infants in home and lab) included site as an independent within-subject factor, representing repeated measures, because mothers and strangers interacted with the same infants at both sites. Partner is treated as a within-subject variable and infant sex as a between-subject variable. The dependent variables were the durations of the five vocal states. The degrees of freedom for the multivariate effects are 5 and 40; for the univariate effects, they are 1 and 44.

There was a significant main effect of site for adult durations ($F = 5.18$, $p = .001$, $\eta^2 = .39$), with univariate effects for vocalization (longer in the lab) ($F = 6.32$, $p = .016$, $\eta^2 = .13$), switching pause (longer at home)

TABLE 7

Estimates (r) of the Cross-Partner Stability of Infants' Vocal State Durations from Mothers to Strangers in Home and Laboratory

States	Home	Laboratory
V	.03	.07
P	.10	.00
SP	.19	.05
NSS	.04	−.05
ISS	.17	.04

Note.—V, P, SP, NSS, and ISS refer to the average durations of vocalizations, pauses, switching pauses, and noninterruptive and interruptive simultaneous speech, respectively, during mother-infant face-to-face interactions when infants are 4 months old. The N for the home coefficients is 82; that for the laboratory coefficients is 51.

($F = 4.20$, $p = .046$, $\eta^2 = .09$), and simultaneous speech (ISS: $F = 14.02$, $p = .001$, $\eta^2 = .24$), clarified below. Univariate effects for pause did not reach significance ($p = .065$), although they showed the same pattern of longer duration at home. There was also a main effect of partner ($F = 3.41$, $p = .012$, $\eta^2 = .299$) with significant univariate effects for simultaneous speech (ISS: $F = 8.87$, $p = .005$, $\eta^2 = .17$). Univariate effects for switching pause did not reach significance ($p < .065$). A significant interaction of site by partner ($F = 3.40$, $p = .012$, $\eta^2 = .30$) clarified the role of simultaneous speech (ISS) in both main effects above. In the home, the durations of ISS were longer for mothers than strangers (each with infants), but in the lab this pattern was reversed. Thus, at home, mothers tended to chime in longer (and take the turn); in the lab the strangers chimed in for a longer duration.

A three-way interaction effect of site by partner by infant sex ($F = 2.41$, $p = .053$, $\eta^2 = .23$) was found, with no univariate effects. For example, vocalization durations, which were shorter in the home for stranger than for mother with male infants, showed the reverse pattern with female infants; in the lab all these relationships were reversed. No other main or interaction effects were significant. Thus, three adult vocal states varied by site (vocalization, switching pause, and ISS); in addition, ISS varied by partner as well as site; and vocalization varied by site, partner, and infant sex. For both mother and stranger, switching pauses were shorter in the lab than at home and vocalizations were longer in the lab; for mothers ISS was longer at home, but for strangers, ISS was longer in the lab.

In summary, this analysis shows consistent effects of novelty of site and partner for adult vocal durations. These effects can be interpreted as greater vocal activity with novelty. For both mothers and strangers, both vocalization and switching pause showed a consistent pattern of greater activity in the lab. Longer vocalizations indicate greater activity; shorter switching pauses indicate that the turn is exchanged more rapidly, hence greater activity. For simultaneous speech (ISS), the picture of greater activity in the lab was only true for the stranger. Although the pause did not reach significance ($p < .065$) in the main effect for site, nevertheless it showed the same pattern of shorter duration, thus more activity, in the lab. The effect of novelty of partner in this analysis is a joint effect of an interaction of both partner and site, as noted above for ISS. Mother had longer, thus more active, ISS in the home; the stranger had longer, more active ISS in the lab. Longer ISS can be interpreted as more pressure to take the turn, because the listener joins in and persists to the point of taking the turn.

Do infants (with adults) differ by site, partner, and infant sex? Split-plot MANOVA for infants (interacting with mother and stranger, in home and

61

lab) included site and partner as independent within-subject factors, representing repeated measures, because the same infants participated in both sites and with both partners. Infant sex was treated as a between-subject variable. The dependent variables were the durations of all five vocal states. The degrees of freedom for the multivariate effects are 5 and 40; for the univariate effects, they are 1 and 44.

The analysis showed a main effect of partner ($F = 2.55$, $p = .043$, $\eta^2 = .24$), with univariate effects for infant switching pause ($F = 6.08$, $p = .018$, $\eta^2 = .12$) and pause ($F = 7.71$, $p = .008$, $\eta^2 = .15$), both longer with mother than stranger. The univariate effect for vocalization did not reach significance ($p < .085$). A main effect for site was not formally significant ($F = 2.32$, $p = .061$, $\eta^2 = .23$), but the univariate effects for switching pause ($p = .005$) and pause ($p = .005$) were significant, although not formally interpretable. An interaction of site by sex was also not formally significant ($F = 2.17$, $p = .076$, $\eta^2 = .21$). No other main or interaction effects were significant. Interpreting the significant main effect of partner, infant durations of pauses and switching pauses were longer with mother than stranger. With the stranger, infants shortened their durations of pause and switching pause, consistent with a pattern of greater activity: The infant paused a shorter time before resuming a vocalization, and paused a shorter time before taking a turn, as seen in the shorter switching pause.

A further examination of the univariate effects for pause and switching pause in the infant MANOVA, inspecting cell means, grand mean, and row and column effects, evaluated a linear novelty hypothesis. Expected and observed infant values were compared for the four conditions of home/mother (double-familiarity), lab/mother, home/stranger, and lab/stranger (double-novelty). The within-cell standard deviations varied from .231 to .496. With $N = 45$, the sample mean standard errors varied from .0044 to .0739, and the largest departure of expected cell means from observed was .02, which suggests that a simple linear model adequately describes the data pattern. Thus infant pause and switching pause become shorter as a function of novelty of both partner and site. Because the values for double-familiarity are at one end and for double-novelty are at the other, this picture yields a linear novelty gradient for infant pause durations, which are most active in the lab with the stranger, as illustrated in Figure 3 for pause and switching pause. The adult data in Figure 3 are included for illustration only.

Because the turn is a composite of the other vocal states, it was tested separately, for infants only. Split-plot MANOVA for infants (interacting with mother and stranger, in the home and in the lab) included site and partner as independent within-subject factors, representing repeated measures, because the same infants participated in both sites and with both partners. The degrees of freedom are 1 and 45. There were main effects

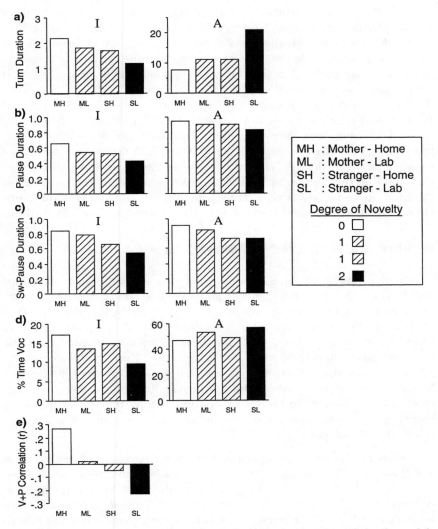

FIGURE 3.—Vocal parameters and vocal rhythms as a function of the four adult-infant conditions: mother-home, mother-lab, stranger-home, stranger-lab. I = infant; A = adult. Durations are in seconds.

for site ($F = 5.29$, $p < .02$) and partner ($F = 10.07$, $p < .003$), with no interaction effects. This result indicates that with novelty, from home to lab, and from mother to stranger, the infant turn shortens, with the longest turn in the double familiarity condition of mother at home (mean = 2.36 s), and the shortest turn in the double novelty condition of stranger in the lab (mean = 1.23 s). The mean durations of infant turn across the four partner/site conditions are illustrated in Figure 3. Although not formally tested, the percentage of time vocalizing seems to share the same pattern as turn (greatest with mother at home and least with stranger in the lab), also illustrated in Figure 3.

In sum, across the groups, the site of the interaction, the particular partner, and to a lesser extent the sex of the infant organize these adult-infant vocal durations. For the infant, there is a novelty gradient from the double familiarity of mother-infant at home to the double novelty of stranger-infant in the lab. However, in pause and switching pause infant durations become more active with novelty, whereas in the turn infant durations become less active. Thus with novelty infant vocal durations show both increasing and decreasing activity levels, in different rhythms.

RHYTHMIC INTERPRETATION OF SOUND AND SILENCE DURATIONS

To this point, we have demonstrated that the vocal state durations are, in general, sensitive to partner and site. The component vocal states are now recast in terms of *rhythmic cycles* (see Method), which provide additional information not evident in their isolated components. As we noted in the Introduction, there is currently no unifying theory of the interpersonal coupling of nonperiodic rhythms. Thus, examining rhythmic cycles and their interpersonal correlations is one way of addressing how rhythms couple. That is, what particular dimensions of the patterns of sound and silence are correlated between two partners? Two modes of coupling the vocalization-pause rhythm are examined, in relation to the effect of site and partner novelty.

Modes of rhythmic coupling of vocal durations: Interpersonal correlations of V + P and of V/P. Matching the cycle of V + P (Vocalization plus Pause), which is the beat or the wavelength, is considered to be a major method of interpersonal coupling, often referred to as *rhythmic entrainment.* Here we evaluate whether interpersonal coupling is best characterized as matching the beat (V + P), matching level of activity (V/P), or both. Table 8 shows that V + P durations are uncorrelated in five of our six partner-site configurations. However, V/P is correlated in all six. The single exception showing a V + P correlation, mother with infant at home, is the only condition that uses *both* interpersonal coupling methods, matching V + P and V/P. Although matching of cycle durations (interpersonal correlation of V + P durations) is considered to be the mode of periodic rhythmic coupling (e.g., Warner, 1988), this particular mode is largely absent in our data once novelty is introduced (see Fig. 3).

TABLE 8

Interpersonal Correlation Coefficients of V + P (Cycle Duration)
and V/P (Vocalization to Pause Ratio)

Context	V + P		V/P	
	r	p	r	p
HMI	.270	.017	.514	.001
LMI	.023	.876	.285	.049
HSI	−.049	.680	.320	.006
LSI	−.226	.118	.375	.013
HMS	−.183	.107	.554	.001
LMS	.037	.802	.388	.006

Note.—V = vocalization; P = pause; H = home; L = laboratory; M, S, and I = mother, stranger, and infant, respectively. Correlations were computed on the subset of the 90% who returned for the attachment evaluation ($N = 82$).

In summary, in this chapter we have shown that vocal state durations vary in temporal pattern when compared across sites and partners. For both infants and adults, with increasing novelty from mother and infant at home to stranger and infant in the lab, there is a pattern of greater activity of vocal rhythms: pause and switching pause for infants, vocalization and switching pause for adults, simultaneous speech (ISS) for strangers only. Infants show a pattern of decreasing activity as well, in turn durations. These results can be described as a *novelty gradient* that shows an orderly progression of greater (and lesser) activity of vocal states, as the dyad moves from double familiarity of mother and infant at home to double novelty of stranger and infant in the lab. The fact that vocal durations and vocal rhythms systematically show greater degrees of activity across this novelty gradient suggests that both infants and adults flexibly adjust to these differing partners and sites. We also noted that, although matching of tempo or beat (vocalization on-off cycle length) is usually considered a central means by which rhythms are coupled (Winfree, 1975), in fact tempo matching occurred only for mother and infant at home. In contrast, matching the balance of vocal activity to inactivity (ratio of durations of vocalizations to pauses) within a cycle occurred in every partner-site configuration. It appears that matching of behavioral level of activity is a far more pervasive form of interpersonal coupling than matching of tempo in these nonperiodic rhythms. This finding elucidates how rhythmic coupling of vocal durations occurs. Furthermore, only mother and infant at home showed both patterns.

V. RESULTS: COORDINATED INTERPERSONAL TIMING (CIT) AT AGE 4 MONTHS

To this point we have addressed the durations of vocal rhythms and their component vocal states. We now move beyond vocal duration to the complex issue of investigating by time-series analysis whether these durations show evidence of interpersonal *contingencies*, for which we reserve the term *coordination*. In this chapter we describe the coordination of vocal rhythms, explore the roles of partner and site novelty, and investigate possible methods of coordination, or organizing patterns, which elucidate *how* this coordination occurs.

The analysis of contingencies by time-series regression analysis addresses several issues that the analysis of sheer durations cannot. First, whereas the analysis of duration was based on a correlational approach over the group, the analysis of contingency by time-series regression is a more complex correlational approach, which can address coordination within the individual dyad. Second, whereas simple correlations cannot establish who is adapting to whom, time-series analysis can answer the question of who is coordinating with whom, which addresses the issue of bidirectional coordination. As noted earlier, no causality is implied in this analysis, because it addresses coordination by asking whether each partner's behavior can be predicted from that of the other. Third, a specific advantage of time-series regression analysis over simple correlational techniques is that a form of self-regulation, self-predictability (autocorrelation), can be assessed and statistically removed from the estimate of interpersonal coordination.

The first section of this chapter describes CIT. The same vocal variables evaluated in the previous chapter as durations are now evaluated for evidence of coordination. First we address the strength (degree) of the coefficients of coordination, to see whether our data are similar to previous reports using similar methods. We then turn to the intraindividual intercorrelation of these coefficients, asking whether the different CIT coefficients are independent of each other. Next, we evaluate the signs of the coefficients because these carry clues as to the underlying method, or particular patterns, of the coordination. We then turn to the question of whether coordination is bidirectional (where each partner is predicted from the other), and whether our data replicate previous reports. However, we also investigate bidirectional coordination *at the level of the dyad*, as well as across groups. The latter was the method of previous studies. These two approaches address current debates over the definition and importance of bidirectional coordination, as noted in the Introduction. We then address the possible impact of novelty on the prevalence of bidirectional coordination, asking whether bidirectional coordination (assessed per dyad) differs in mother-infant versus stranger-infant dyads, at home and in the lab. We also investigate whether adult-infant dyads differ in prevalence of bidirectional coordination, compared to adult-adult dyads. Finally, we describe a 20–30 s rhythm in the CIT data.

The second section of this chapter again returns to the exploration of the role of partner and site novelty in the coordination of vocal rhythms, but using multivariate techniques to examine the variation of CIT as a function of bidirectional coordination across groups. This multivariate analysis for CIT parallels that of the previous chapter for durations.

DESCRIPTIVE ANALYSES OF CIT

The "Strength" of the Coefficients of CIT

Table 9 presents the means of the coefficients of CIT for adults coordinating with infants and infants coordinating with adults, as well as for adults coordinating with adults, included for purposes of comparison. The means index the average degree to which one set of partners coordinated with the other set, in terms of the average proportions of variance accounted for. These means range from 10–33% of the variance and are within the same range as reported by other infant researchers using time-series regression such as Cohn and Tronick (1988), Beebe et al. (1985), and Warner (1996). They can be considered low to moderate.

Intraindividual Intercorrelations of the Coefficients of CIT

Tables 10, 11, and 12 show the intraindividual intercorrelations of CIT for infants and mothers, infants and strangers, and mothers and strangers, respectively, at home and lab sites, for all five vocal states. Tables 10 and 11 show similar pictures of a great deal of significant intercorrelation both at home and in the lab. In Table 10, for mothers, and for infants, at home, all of the coefficients of coordination are significantly intercorrelated;

TABLE 9

COEFFICIENTS (R^2) OF COORDINATED INTERPERSONAL TIMING OF TURNS AND THE FIVE VOCAL STATES FOR THE ADULTS AND INFANTS

Vocal Measures		Home						Laboratory					
		MI:M	MI:I	SI:S	SI:I	MS:M	MS:S	MI:M	MI:I	SI:S	SI:I	MS:M	MS:S
T	N	86	86	80	80	62	62	51	51	45	45	61	61
	X	.161	.202	.145	.176	.100	.093	.240	.200	.214	.196	.282	.271
	SD	.244	.247	.180	.200	.099	.101	.238	.234	.203	.196	.366	.373
V	N	82	82	87	87	62	62	51	51	45	45	51	51
	X	.139	.126	.127	.126	.098	.094	.115	.124	.143	.148	.104	.119
	SD	.089	.077	.084	.107	.044	.034	.075	.070	.097	.131	.073	.125
P	N	82	82	82	81	61	61	49	49	41	40	51	51
	X	.134	.133	.100	.132	.091	.084	.128	.135	.096	.158	.083	.099
	SD	.089	.080	.063	.092	.067	.037	.090	.082	.055	.226	.057	.089
SP	N	82	82	82	84	62	62	51	51	41	43	51	51
	X	.134	.145	.139	.176	.100	.101	.118	.156	.143	.190	.087	.095
	SD	.109	.098	.113	.176	.070	.061	.073	.133	.146	.176	.066	.011
ISS	N	86	86	80	80	62	62	51	51	45	45	61	61
	X	.234	.206	.228	.194	.094	.091	.226	.219	.230	.272	.240	.249
	SD	.261	.223	.213	.203	.101	.099	.222	.205	.174	.253	.345	.346
NSS	N	86	86	80	80	62	62	51	51	45	45	60	61
	X	.290	.224	.245	.305	.109	.098	.277	.280	.326	.236	.248	.245
	SD	.333	.243	.316	.313	.110	.072	.270	.298	.301	.289	.361	.351

Note.—MI = Mother-Infant; SI = Stranger-Infant; MS = Mother-Stranger. Following the colon, M = Mother; S = Stranger; I = Infant. T, V, P, SP, ISS, and NSS = turns, vocalizations, pauses, switching pauses, interruptive simultaneous speech, and noninterruptive simultaneous speech, respectively.

TABLE 10

INTRAINDIVIDUAL CORRELATIONS (r) AMONG THE VOCAL-STATE CIT FOR INFANTS
(WITH MOTHERS) AND FOR MOTHERS (WITH INFANTS) IN THE HOME AND LABORATORY

		Infants (with Mothers)				
		V	P	SP	ISS	NSS
	V		.438	.371	.388	.611
Infants	P	−.152		.440	.275	.552
	SP	.077	.223		.311	.463
	ISS	.265	−.156	.391		.512
	NSS	.059	−.073	.225	.273	
		Mothers (with Infants)				
		V	P	SP	ISS	NSS
	V		.556	.559	.569	.453
Mothers	P	.377		.544	.311	.217
	SP	.173	.213		.371	.245
	ISS	.152	.242	.153		.496
	NSS	.252	.413	.120	.250	

Note.—V = vocalizations; P = pauses; SP = switching pauses; ISS = interruptive simultaneous speech; NSS = noninterruptive simultaneous speech. The coefficients above the diagonal are for the home ($N = 84$), and those below the diagonal are for the laboratory ($N = 53$). The critical value ($p < .05$) for the home is .183, and that for the laboratory is .231.

in the lab, three are significant for the infant and five for the mother. In Table 11, for both strangers and infants at home, all but one CIT index are significantly intercorrelated. However, in Table 12, for both mothers and strangers at home, only one CIT index is intercorrelated. The picture is very different in the lab, where every correlation is significant for both mother and stranger. Thus, with the increased novelty of the lab, mother and stranger each show more coherence in CIT.

Sign of CIT

To examine the signs of the coordination, we used a nonparametric Sign Test to evaluate how many dyads showed a negative versus positive coordination, for each vocal state. The test yields a z score, significant if it is above $\pm .96$, as shown in Tables 13 and 14. The directional t tests evaluate whether the general trend of the dyads is significantly positive or negative in sign. Tables 13 and 14 show the directional t for the *pattern* of signs of CIT, for home and lab, respectively. The home data, with the larger N, show a robust pattern of sign tests, such that vocalization, pause, and turn are negative, whereas switching pause and simultaneous speech

TABLE 11

INTRAINDIVIDUAL CORRELATIONS (r) AMONG THE VOCAL-STATE CIT FOR INFANTS
(WITH STRANGERS) AND FOR STRANGERS (WITH INFANTS) IN THE HOME AND LABORATORY

		Infants (with Strangers)				
		V	P	SP	ISS	NSS
	V		.768	.509	.230	.588
	P	.094		.578	.253	.663
Infants	SP	.285	.317		.232	.411
	ISS	.436	.172	.095		.168
	NSS	.205	.383	.179	.254	
		Strangers (with Infants)				
		V	P	SP	ISS	NSS
	V		.620	.657	.531	.682
	P	.228		−.156	.443	.586
Strangers	SP	.562	.015		.499	.645
	ISS	.501	.162	.303		.567
	NSS	.472	−.124	.372	.363	

Note.—V = vocalizations; P = pauses; SP = switching pauses; ISS = interruptive simultaneous speech; NSS = noninterruptive simultaneous speech. The coefficients above the diagonal are for the home ($N = 82$), and those below the diagonal are for the laboratory ($N = 52$). The critical value ($p < .05$) for the home is .183, and that for the laboratory is .231.

(ISS, NSS) are positive. The same patterns appear in the lab, with smaller N, although not as robustly. Thus, coordination of sound and silence encompasses both systematic "matching" (positive sign), as well as an inverse "compensatory" pattern (negative sign).

The negative sign for vocalization, pause, and turn CIT indicate that, as one partner coordinates to a greater degree, the other partner coordinates to a lesser degree. The positive sign for switching pause CIT indicates that, at the moment of the turn switch, each person "matches" by increasing or decreasing degree of coordination in the same direction as the partner. The positive sign for simultaneous speech (ISS and NSS) is also a matching phenomenon: As either person increases or decreases coordination, the partner does likewise.

Uni- and Bidirectional Significance of CIT per Dyad

The analyses of durations of vocal variables in chapter IV were all across-group, whereas the time-series analyses reported here are conducted for each dyad. A coordination coefficient is assigned to each person in each dyad, the significance of which can then be tested for a

TABLE 12

Intraindividual Correlations (r) Among the Vocal-State CIT for Mothers
(with Strangers) and for Strangers (with Mothers)
in the Home and Laboratory

		Mothers (with Strangers)				
		V	P	SP	ISS	NSS
Mothers	V		.007	.116	.061	.241
	P	.805		−.107	.003	.081
	SP	.289	.867		.087	.114
	ISS	.560	.508	.356		−.058
	NSS	.857	.821	.316	.676	
		Strangers (with Mothers)				
		V	P	SP	ISS	NSS
Strangers	V		.185	−.002	.222	.058
	P	.897		−.067	.049	−.013
	SP	.914	.902		−.032	.008
	ISS	.707	.669	.689		.066
	NSS	.902	.839	.897	.763	

Note.—V = vocalizations; P = pauses; SP = switching pauses; ISS = interruptive simultaneous speech; NSS = noninterruptive simultaneous speech. The coefficients above the diagonal are for the home ($N = 88$), and those below the diagonal are for the laboratory ($N = 52$). The critical value ($p < .05$) for the home is .183, and that for the laboratory is .231.

single case. CIT estimates the degree of contingency between the partners' vocal time series, predicting the adult's behavior from that of the infant (I → A), and vice versa (A → I). Coordination can be bidirectional, unidirectional, or absent, as shown in Table 15. The analysis is presented with three approaches: (a) for all six vocal variables combined; (b) for vocalization, pause, and switching pause combined; and (c) for simultaneous speech (ISS, NSS) and turn combined.

Each dyad was classified in terms of both partners' coefficients of CIT, using the three approaches. Using all six variables, CIT was termed bidirectional if at least one coefficient of any of the six vocal variables was significant for both partners, unidirectional when only one of the partners had at least one significant coefficient, and absent when no coefficient of either partner was significant. Using identical logic, in any of the three variable approaches (e.g., vocalizations, pauses, and switching pauses; or ISS, NSS, and turns), coordination was termed bidirectional if the coefficients of any of the three were significant for both partners.

The rationale for these three approaches is as follows. The definition of bidirectional coordination using all six variables operationalizes the idea that all aspects of vocal rhythms are in play at once, as a system.

71

TABLE 13

SIGNS OF CIT FOR TURNS AND THE VOCAL STATES OBTAINED
IN INTERACTIONS IN THE HOME

Vocal Measures	Minus	Plus	Z Score	t Test	Vocal Measures	Minus	Plus	Z Score	t Test
MI:TURNS	49	34	1.6465	−4.872	MI:SPAUSE	26	58	3.4915*	98.266
SI:TURNS	50	29	2.3627	−6.595	SI:SPAUSE	26	53	3.0377*	147.026
MS:TURNS	54	30	2.6186*	−13.055	MS:SPAUSE	32	54	2.3723*	112.927
IM:TURNS	48	35	1.4269	−1.252	IM:SPAUSE	28	56	3.0551*	93.301*
IS:TURNS	39	40	0.1125	6.342	IS:SPAUSE	26	53	3.0377*	88.836
SM:TURNS	55	29	2.8368*	17.117	SM:SPAUSE	36	50	1.5097	121.562
MI:VOCS	38	46	0.8729	69.213	MI:ISS	17	64	5.2222*	257.959
SI:VOCS	50	30	2.2361*	−14.906	SI:ISS	15	62	5.3561*	49.954
MS:VOCS	72	14	6.2543*	−292.293	MS:ISS	29	56	2.9286*	141.398
IM:VOCS	34	50	1.7457	31.942	IM:ISS	18	62	4.9193*	230.222
IS:VOCS	46	35	1.1180	−31.663	IS:ISS	11	66	6.2676*	301.723
SM:VOCS	71	15	6.0386*	−294.374	SM:ISS	35	50	1.6270	109.832
MI:PAUSE	45	39	0.6547	0.500	MI:NSS	18	55	4.3305*	150.742
SI:PAUSE	46	33	1.4626	−22.981	SI:NSS	24	46	2.6295*	119.247
MS:PAUSE	61	24	4.0132*	−141.758	MS:NSS	45	40	0.5423	8.510
IM:PAUSE	51	28	2.5877*	−46.844	IM:NSS	22	51	3.3942*	140.707
IS:PAUSE	51	28	1.9640*	−41.281	IS:NSS	27	43	1.9124	74.061
SM:PAUSE	56	29	2.9286*	−150.979	SM:NSS	49	36	1.4100	−19.287

Note.—Of the two letters that precede the names of the vocal states (MI, IM, SI, IS, MS, SM), the coordinating partners are symbolized by the first letter and the partners with whom they coordinated are symbolized by the second letter. M = mother; I = infant; S = stranger. Minus and Plus are the numbers of dyads with negative and positive coordination for the vocal states. The z scores are the results of a Sign Test for each state and the directional ts tested the significance of the direction of coordination. *$p < .05$.

Theoretically, we prefer this approach because it addresses the entire system. The rationale for examining vocalization, pause, and switching pause as a group separately from ISS, NSS, and turn is based on our decision to use only vocalization, pause, and switching pause to predict the age 12-months' outcomes, as seen in the next chapter, as well as the fact that the latter three variables fit the AR2 model of the time series more consistently (see Method).

Bidirectional coordination *per dyad* provides an additional purely dyadic measure. Table 15 shows that 47–72% of adult-infant dyads are bidirectional using all six variables; 16–31% using vocalization, pause, and switching pause; and 24–46% using simultaneous speech (ISS, NSS) and turns. Using the six-variable approach, bidirectionality of CIT in the adult-infant interactions at age 4 months is *robust but certainly not ubiquitous*. Only approximately half of the mother-infant dyads at home show bidirectionality. With the maximum novelty of stranger-infant in the lab, the percentage of bidirectional dyads goes up to 72%.

TABLE 14

SIGNS OF CIT FOR TURNS AND THE VOCAL STATE OBTAINED
IN INTERACTIONS IN THE LABORATORY

Vocal Measures	Minus	Plus	Z Score	t Test	Vocal Measures	Minus	Plus	Z Score	t Test
MI:TURNS	30	18	1.7321	8.668	MI:SPAUSE	9	41	4.5255*	160.712
SI:TURNS	25	17	1.2344	−3.558	SI:SPAUSE	14	29	2.2875*	110.676
MS:TURNS	27	14	2.0303*	−18.913	MS:SPAUSE	16	26	1.5430	26.402
IM:TURNS	22	26	0.5774	7.786	IM:SPAUSE	15	35	2.8284*	61.935
IS:TURNS	16	26	1.5430	6.902	IS:SPAUSE	19	22	0.4685	61.935
SM:TURNS	22	19	0.4685	−0.985	SM:SPAUSE	19	23	0.6172	12.173
MI:VOCS	27	23	0.5657		MI:ISS	10	38	4.0415*	198.860
SI:VOCS	25	20	0.7454	8.249	SI:ISS	9	34	3.8125*	38.126
MS:VOCS	31	11	3.0861*	−72.030	MS:ISS	18	24	0.9258	27.154
IM:VOCS	32	18	1.9799	−19.582	IM:ISS	4	43	5.6887*	244.861
IS:VOCS	22	23	0.1491	−7.887	IS:ISS	6	38	4.8242*	151.366
SM:VOCS	31	11	3.0861*	102.403	SM:ISS	24	18	0.9258	−102.403
MI:PAUSE	9	41	4.5244*	160.712	MI:NSS	14	29	2.2875*	81.533
SI:PAUSE	14	29	2.8275*	110.676	SI:NSS	15	26	1.7179	13.866
MS:PAUSE	16	26	1.5430	26.402	MS:NSS	29	13	2.4689*	−21.561
IM:PAUSE	15	35	2.8284*	61.935	IM:NSS	6	37	4.7275*	212.487
IS:PAUSE	19	22	0.4685	20.809	IS:NSS	7	34	4.2167*	145.461
SM:PAUSE	19	23	0.6172	12.173	SM:NSS	24	18	0.9258	−37.663

Note. Of the two letters that precede the names of the vocal states (MI, IM, SI, IS, MS, SM), the coordinating partners are symbolized by the first letter and the partners with whom they coordinated are symbolized by the second letter. The Minus and Plus are the numbers of dyads with negative and positive coordination for the vocal states. The z scores are the results of a Sign Test for each state and the directional *t*s tested the significance of the *direction* of coordination. *$p < .05$.

Table 15 can also be used to calculate the proportion of mothers and of infants for whom the CIT indices were statistically significant, *across the group*. Using the six-variable approach, 64% of mothers in the home had significant CIT indices (adding the 47% bidirectional dyads plus the 17% unidirectional mothers). Similarly, 67% of infants in the home had significant CIT indices (adding 47% bidirectional dyads plus 20% unidirectional infants). The comparable numbers for the lab are 76% of mothers and 75% of infants. The comparable numbers for the stranger-infant dyads in the home are 77% of strangers and 73% of infants. In the lab, 84% of strangers and 80% of infants show significant CIT indices.

Partner and Site Novelty in Relation to per Dyad Bidirectional Coordination: Adult-Infant Dyads

To evaluate Table 15 for differences in percentages of bidirectional dyads (assessed *per dyad*) as a function of novelty of partner or site,

73

TABLE 15

DIRECTIONALITY OF CIT: PERCENTAGE OF INTERACTIONS AT INFANT AGED 4 MONTHS IN WHICH EITHER, NEITHER, OR BOTH PARTNERS COORDINATE

Site	Partners	Direction of Coordination			
		Bi	A→I	I→A	Neither
A. All Six Vocal States					
Home	Mother-Infant	47	20	17	16
	Stranger-Infant	61	12	16	11
	Mother-Stranger	35	24	30	11
Laboratory	Mother-Infant	62	15	14	9
	Stranger-Infant	72	8	12	8
	Mother-Stranger	34	24	18	24
B. Vocalizations, Pauses, Switching Pauses					
Home	Mother-Infant	16	26	18	40
	Stranger-Infant	20	24	22	34
	Mother-Stranger	15	28	31	26
Laboratory	Mother-Infant	31	24	10	22
	Stranger-Infant	22	40	16	22
	Mother-Stranger	16	28	16	40
C. ISS, NSS, Speaking Turns					
Home	Mother-Infant	24	25	20	31
	Stranger-Infant	37	16	24	23
	Mother-Stranger	12	13	23	52
Laboratory	Mother-Infant	35	14	29	22
	Stranger-Infant	46	10	22	22
	Mother-Stranger	10	18	20	52

Note.—Entries are the percents of dyads showing significant coordination ($p \le .05$). Bi = bidirectional coordination within each dyad; A → I = infant behavior predicted from the lagged adult behavior; I → A = adult behavior predicted from the lagged infant behavior. In the Mother-Stranger analysis, A → I translates into M → S and I → A into S → M. In part A of the table, the home analysis is based on Ns of 76, 75, 78, respectively, for Mother-Infant, Stranger-Infant, and Mother-Stranger; in the laboratory, the Ns are 52, 50, 50. In part B of the table, the comparable Ns, are 76, 74, 78, and 51, 50, 50. In part C, they are the same as in part A.

McNemar's test of symmetry was used (two-tailed). The N's in these analyses are slightly lower than those indicated on Table 15 because of the necessity for complete data sets. We first evaluated the two extremes of novelty: the double-familiarity of mother-infant at home versus the double-novelty of stranger-infant in the lab. Across the variables of simultaneous speech (ISS, NSS) and turn (Table 15C), stranger-infant dyads in the lab showed a significantly greater percentage of bidirectional dyads than mother-infant dyads at home ($\chi^2 = 5.04$, $p < .05$). The other two sets of variables, across all six, and across vocalization, pause, and switching pause, were not significant.

We then examined the relation of home versus lab novelty to mothers and infants alone, in terms of per dyad bidirectionality. We dub these "mother and infant at home-base" versus "mother and infant going visiting." None of the comparisons was significant. However, strangers and infants showed more bidirectional dyads in the lab than the home ($\chi^2 = 5.04$, $p < .025$), in ISS, NSS, and turn (Table 15C). We conclude that the relationship of novelty to per dyad bidirectional CIT is carried primarily through the coactive states of simultaneous speech (the turn was rarely significant). The stranger-infant interaction is more sensitive to home/lab novelty than the mother-infant.

Per Dyad Bidirectional Coordination in Adult-Infant Versus Adult-Adult Dyads

McNemar's test (two-tailed) of symmetry was used to test for differences in per dyad bidirectional coordination in adult-adult (mother-stranger) versus adult-infant dyads in Table 15. Four comparisons of prevalence of bidirectional dyads were made:

1. The home mother-stranger versus home mother-infant comparison yielded nonsignificant but marginal differences for the two sets of vocalization, pause and switching pause, and the two simultaneous speech states and turn (both $p < .06$).

2. In comparing home mother-stranger versus home stranger-infant, the set of all six variables ($\chi^2 = 10.62$, $p < .001$) and the set of two simultaneous speech states and turn ($\chi^2 = 11.17$, $p < .001$) were significant, yielding more bidirectional stranger-infant dyads.

3. In comparing lab mother-stranger versus lab mother-infant, the set of all six variables ($\chi^2 = 4.03$, $p < .04$) and the set of two simultaneous speech states and turn ($\chi^2 = 4.76$, $p < .03$) were significant, yielding more bidirectional mother-infant dyads.

4. In the comparison of lab mother-stranger versus lab stranger-infant, the set of all six variables ($\chi^2 = 14.45$, $p < .0001$) and the set of the two simultaneous speech states and turn ($\chi^2 = 14.45$, $p < .0001$) were significant, yielding more bidirectional stranger-infant dyads.

We conclude that, in general, these infant-adult interactions are more bidirectionally coordinated than these adult-adult interactions. Evidently infants and adults rely more on a reciprocal, two-way coordination of vocal rhythms than do conversing adults who can rely on language as well as vocal rhythms to coordinate. As the one exception, mother and infant at home versus mother and stranger at home do not show this

75

clear difference. Similar to the role of novelty described above, the coaction states (simultaneous speech) carry this adult-adult versus adult-infant difference. But unlike the novelty findings for bidirectional coordination, the set of all six variables also indicates this difference.

A 20–30-s interaction rhythm in CIT. The faster vocalization-pause rhythm and slower turn rhythm, described in chapter IV, are obvious to the naive ear, but an even slower rhythm of 20–30 s, not behaviorally detectable, becomes obvious only with time-series analysis. The time-series results presented thus far were based on each partner's coordination with the other's behavior over the course of the previous minute (twelve 5-s lags: see Method). However, for most dyads, some degree of coordination was detected at many possible lags within this previous minute. Adult partner and infant are potentially contingent upon what the other did 5 s before, 10 s before, and so forth, up to 60 s before. Thus, we determined *which* of the 12 lags accounted for the greatest percent of variance (not necessarily significant) in predicting the partner's behavior, and termed it the *optimal lag*. The average of the optimal lags that best predicted the partner was 20–30 s and was similar for infants and adults, for all the vocal states. A previous study by Feldstein et al. (1993) conducted a series of ANOVA that compared the optimal lags of a subset of the current data ($N = 15$) to a comparable data set ($N = 13$) at a second lab. The ANOVA yielded nonsignificant F ratios for each of the vocal parameters. Thus, there is a remarkable similarity in the mean optimal lag durations for mother-infant and stranger-infant interactions. This finding was construed as an interaction "rhythm" for the following reasons: At the average optimum lag of 20–30 s, each partner was most coordinated with the other, meaning that this optimum coordination *recurred* every 20–30 s, over the approximately 12-minute sample. Thus each partner displayed a recurrent pattern, which is construed as a rhythm. Both partners followed the same rhythm.

CIT AT AGE 4 MONTHS IN RELATION TO SITE, PARTNER, DIRECTION OF COORDINATION, AND INFANT SEX

We now return to an exploration of the role of partner and site novelty in the coefficients of coordination (CIT). As we noted in the Introduction, the finding that in adult conversations unfamiliar partners tend to coordinate their behaviors to a greater degree than familiar partners has not been investigated for infant-adult interactions. Here we present a series of analyses of variance examining whether, across the group, the magnitude of the coefficients of coordination varied as a function of novelty of partner and site, as well as direction of coordination, and infant sex. This parallels, for CIT data, the analysis for duration data presented in the previous chapter.

Analyses of Variance

Because of considerations of degrees of freedom, two analyses of variance for the adult-infant interactions were performed, one each for home and lab. Because we consider these analyses exploratory, results are evaluated using the joint considerations of significance level, pattern of significant results, and effect size (percent of variance accounted for: η^2). An alternative structure to the analysis of variance was explored, which combined both home and lab adult-infant data ($N = 36$), but so little was found that we do not report it.

Home adult-infant CIT. Split-plot multivariate analyses of variance for adults and infants in the home included partner configuration (mother-infant versus stranger-infant) and direction of lag (adult coordinated with infant or vice versa) as independent within-subject factors, and infant sex as a between-subject variable. The dependent variables were the CIT coefficients of the vocal states (without turns). The final N for the analysis was 59. The degrees of freedom for the multivariate effects are 5 and 53; for the univariate effects, they are 1 and 57.

An interaction effect of sex by direction of coordination did not reach formal significance ($F = 2.26$, $p = .062$, $\eta^2 = .176$). A significant univariate effect for simultaneous speech (ISS: $F = 4.75$, $p = .033$, $\eta^2 = .077$) indicates that within infants, female infant CIT (with adults) (A → I) is higher (.173) than that of male infants (.142); within adults, adult CIT with male infants (I → A) is higher (.199) than that with female infants (.163). Because the interaction effect did not reach formal significance, these univariate effects are not formally interpretable. No other main or interaction effects were significant.

Laboratory adult-infant CIT. Split-plot multivariate analyses of variance for the lab were identical to those for the home, $N = 26$. The degrees of freedom for the multivariate effects are 5 and 20; for the univariate effects, they are 1 and 24. Despite the fact that the lab analysis had half the degrees of freedom of the home analysis, it is more powerful in articulating effects. There was a main effect for infant sex ($F = 3.89$, $p = .013$, $\eta^2 = .493$) with a significant univariate effect for pause ($F = 5.02$, $p = .035$, $\eta^2 = .173$). Averaging across infant and adult pause coordination, CIT is higher in dyads with a female infant (.133) than in dyads with a male infant (.096). Thus, infant sex is related to the magnitude of coordination differently in home and in the lab, but emerges as a main effect only in the lab.

There was also a main effect for partner configuration ($F = 3.85$, $p = .013$, $\eta^2 = .490$), with significant univariate effects for switching pause ($F = 5.49$, $p = .03$, $\eta^2 = .185$) and simultaneous speech (NSS: $F = 4.485$, $p = .045$, $\eta^2 = .157$). Mother and infant have higher switching pause co-ordination than do stranger and infant. Because switching pause is one major way of exchanging the turn, this finding indicates that mother-infant turn taking is more tightly coordinated than that of stranger and infant. In contrast, stranger and infant coordinate the coactive moment of NSS more than do mother and infant. In addition, two interactions, one of partner configuration by direction of coordination and one of sex by partner configuration by direction of coordination, are not formally significant, although they account for substantial proportions of variance (32.4% and 20.4%, respectively). No other main or interaction effects were significant. Considered together, the analyses performed separately for home and lab adult-infant CIT indicate that the lab was associated with a larger number of significant effects than the home, perhaps because of the novelty of the lab or the more highly controlled conditions.

In summary, in this chapter we noted that the analyses of vocal durations by time-series analysis revealed estimates of coordination between partners that are similar in strength to other studies. Although previous analyses of adult-infant coordination using time-series analysis have not usually evaluated the sign, we found that vocal rhythm coordination encompasses both systematic matching as well as inverse "compensatory" (negative sign) patterns. We will use these signs in the Discussion chapter to clarify further just how coordination works. Unlike previous studies, we evaluated whether coordination was bidirectional on a per dyad basis, as well as across group. Per dyad bidirectional CIT in interactions of adults with 4-month-old infants was robust but certainly not ubiquitous. Novelty was an important dimension: Stranger-infant dyads in the lab showed a greater preponderance of per dyad bidirectional coordination than mother-infant dyads at home. Strangers and infants also showed more per dyad bidirectionality in the lab than in the home. In contrast to adults interacting with each other, adult-infant dyads show more per dyad bidirectionality, suggesting a specific adaptation that adults make to infants. The 20–30 s rhythm found in the "optimal lags" of CIT suggested yet another rhythmic pattern. As a further approach to examining novelty, using multivariate techniques we found that, across the group, novelty of partner and novelty of site were also associated with magnitude of CIT, similar to the previous analysis of vocal durations. But only in the lab did significant differences emerge: Mother and infant coordinated turn taking (through the switching pause) to a greater degree; stranger and infant coordinated the simultaneous moment to a greater degree. Sex differences also emerged in the lab data: Female infant coordination was higher.

VI. RESULTS: CIT RHYTHMS AT AGE 4 MONTHS PREDICT OUTCOMES AT AGE 12 MONTHS

To this point we have documented various temporal patterns of mutual adjustment in the vocal interactions of adults and 4-month-old infants, both in the duration data of chapter IV and the coordination of durations in chapter V. In both, we explored how communication might work in terms of various rhythmic modes or methods of coordination. We also showed that novelty of partner and site elucidated the organization of adult-infant vocal interaction in both types of data. We now turn to an evaluation of the hypothesis that coordination of vocal rhythms at age 4 months (CIT of vocalization, pause, and switching pause) predicts age 12-months infant attachment (Strange Situation) and cognition (Bayley Scales).

In the first section of this chapter we present the descriptive statistics for the Ainsworth Strange Situation and the Bayley Scales. The second section presents the results of the multiple regression equations predicting attachment, using both the standard scoring of four categories (secure, avoidant, anxious-resistant, and disorganized) as well as a continuous approach developed by Richters et al. (1988; see Method). The continuous approach was used to examine possible nonlinear relationships between CIT and attachment. Following the presentation of the results of the predictions, we evaluate the role of partner and site novelty in these predictions. We then return to the measure of per dyad bidirectionality of CIT (presented in the previous chapter) to investigate a possible relationship to attachment. Whereas the multiple regression approach can identify bidirectional predictions across the group, the per dyad analysis can identify bidirectional predictions that are based on a pattern of bidirectional coordination within each individual dyad. Both approaches explore a central tenet of current systems theories of development, that bidirectional coordinations between components of a system (such as infant and partner) provide one critical engine of development, as noted in the Introduction. The third section presents the results of the predictions of the Bayley Scales and again evaluates how variations of CIT according to partner and site novelty affected these predictions. We then return to the measure of per dyad bidirectionality of CIT and its relationship to the Bayley Scales.

DESCRIPTIVE STATISTICS OF AGE 12-MONTHS OUTCOME MEASURES

Attachment. The Ainsworth Strange Situation (conducted in the lab) yielded 16 avoidant (A), 55 secure (B), 4 anxious-resistant (C), and 7 disorganized (D) infants (19.5%, 67%, 4.5%, and 8.5%, respectively), a total of 82. The transformation of the 82 attachment classifications into a continuous degree of attachment insecurity scale (DIS; see Method) yielded a mean of .503 ($SD = 1.826$). In this scale, higher scores indicate greater insecurity.

Bayley I. Conducted on a separate home visit, the mean MDI of the Bayley Scales for 84 infants was 111.68 ($SD = 12.62$). Note that in this test, higher scores indicate better functioning.

A significant negative correlation (−.51) was found between the DIS and the Bayley MDI. Because the two outcomes were correlated, and we wanted to examine the *unique* relation between the vocal CIT variables and each of the outcomes, we partialed out of each of the outcomes any variance that was contributed by the other. The effect of the sex of the infant and the different strangers was also covaried when relevant. We report significant findings from these partialed equations. However, in comparing the partialed and unpartialed equations, differences between results were minor.

PREDICTING ATTACHMENT FROM CIT AT AGE 4 MONTHS

Although infants are labeled by the attachment classification at age 12 months, it should be understood that we are referring to the 4-month-old's CIT pattern of the *future* secure or insecure infant. Table 16 summarizes the significant multiple regression equations predicting attachment from CIT across the group, presenting both the standard categorical approach (A, B, C, D) as well as the continuous "degree of insecurity" scale.

Categorical approach. In the categorical equations of Table 16, each analysis used the secure B pattern as the reference variable and compared it to an insecure category, one by one, to see which of the insecure categories could be discriminated from the secure, across the group. Thus, each equation yielded two values: one for B, and one for an insecure

TABLE 16

SIGNIFICANT PREDICTIONS OF ATTACHMENT CATEGORIES AND DEGREE OF INSECURITY
(CONTINUOUS ATTACHMENT TRANSFORM) BY CIT

Vocal Measures	Home		Laboratory	
Mother-Infant	$M \rightarrow I$	$I \rightarrow M$	$M \rightarrow I$	$I \rightarrow M$
D vs. B	P (.053)	P (.049)	SP (.208)	SP (.132)
DIS				SP (.058)
Stranger-Infant	$S \rightarrow I$	$I \rightarrow S$	$S \rightarrow I$	$I \rightarrow S$
A vs. B	SP (.075)		SP (.038)	
C vs. B				V (.025)
DIS		V (.104)	V^2 (.142)	
Mother-Stranger	$M \rightarrow S$	$S \rightarrow M$	$M \rightarrow S$	$S \rightarrow M$
A vs. B		SP (.054)		
D vs. B		P (.059)		
DIS				

Note.—The prediction of the attachment categories and Degree of Insecurity (DIS) have partialed from them the other outcome, the Bayley MDI. Attachment categories D vs. B, means that category D was significantly differentiated by the CIT coefficients of the predicting vocal state from category B, and similarly for A vs. B and C vs. B. The same logic applies to the remaining rows in the table. P = pauses; SP = switching pauses; V = vocalizations. The r^2s associated with the prediction (MR) equations are in parentheses. The entries in the table are those predictors whose variance contributions yielded a $p \leq 05$; significant results that account for less than 1% of the variance were omitted. The power of 2 means that the relationship is quadratic. The N for the analyses of the attachment categories was 82, and the Degree of Insecurity, 82.

classification (A, C, or D). CIT discriminated all four attachment classifications, although different classifications were predicted from different partner configurations.

To further understand these categorical predictions, we examined the plots of the equations reported in Table 16, to examine the magnitudes of the CIT values that yielded findings. We then rank ordered the magnitudes of CIT, illustrated by Figures 4 and 5. Figure 4 shows that the

LOW CIT	MIDRANGE CIT	HIGH CIT
I I	I	I II I II
	SS S SS S S	S S

FIGURE 4.—Rank ordering of low, midrange, and high CIT ranges yielding significant age 12 months' attachment predictions of secure (S) and insecure (I = A, C, D).

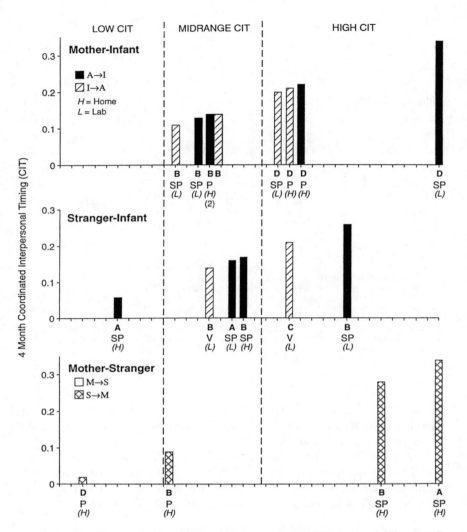

FIGURE 5.—Rank ordering of low, midrange, and high CIT ranges yielding significant age 12 months' attachment predictions by partner configuration. A, B, C, and D refer to categories of attachment. V = vocalization; P = pause; SP = switching pause. Each equation evaluated a contrast between the secure and a particular insecure category, yielding two CIT values, one each for secure and insecure. Values vary by partner configuration, direction of influence, site, and vocal state, as well as by specific attachment classification.

degree of coordination of secure infants clustered in the midrange of CIT, whereas that of insecure infants tended to cluster at the extremes (tightly or loosely coordinated).

Figure 5 shows a detailed breakdown of Figure 4, rank ordering (on the x axis) the magnitudes of CIT (on the y axis). Organized according to mother-infant, stranger-infant, and mother-stranger findings, and indicating home/lab, direction of coordination, and vocal variable, Figure 5 illustrates the findings of Table 16. The eight bars of B and D in the mother-infant section of Figure 5 represent the four equations in the first line of Table 16, each of which differentiated D versus B by the degree of age-4-months' CIT. In these mother-infant interactions, CIT in the midrange of the distribution predicted secure (B) attachment, whereas high CIT predicted disorganized (D). It is noteworthy that the D versus B distinction is predicted both from infants' coordination with mothers ($M \rightarrow I$) and mothers' coordination with infants ($I \rightarrow M$), with exactly symmetrical vocal states involved, hence "coconstructed" across the group.

The stranger-infant interaction further differentiates the A and C (but not the D) classifications from the B. The six bars of the stranger-infant interactions in Figure 5 represent the three equations in the stranger-infant section of Table 16: Infants' coordination with strangers ($S \rightarrow I$) in the home differentiated A versus B, infants' coordination with strangers ($S \rightarrow I$) in the lab differentiated A versus B, and strangers' coordination with infants ($I \rightarrow S$) in the lab differentiated C versus B. Two of the three equations place secure attachment (B) in the midrange, and insecure in the high or low ranges. Avoidant attachment was associated either with low *or* midrange infant CIT, depending on home/lab context. The avoidant infant relates to the stranger with low CIT at home, but with midrange CIT in the lab. The one finding where high CIT predicts secure (B) is the infant's coordination with the stranger in the lab. The D attachment was not differentiated in the stranger-infant data: The D here is mother-specific.

Table 16 also shows that the mothers' ($S \rightarrow M$) degree of coordination with strangers in the home when the infant is age 4 months discriminates the A and D from B. These predictions are unidirectional, based on the mothers' CIT with strangers. With the stranger, the mother of the avoidant infant shows very high CIT, whereas the mother of the disorganized infant shows very low CIT. The mother of the B (secure) infant coordinates with the stranger in midrange in one case, and in the high range in the other.

Summarizing the categorical attachment predictions, combining equations for all three partner configurations, eight out of the nine yielded the picture of secure (B) in the midrange and insecure in the higher or lower ranges of CIT. Bidirectional or coconstructed predictions (across the group) were not ubiquitous. The B showed robust bilateral predictions from mother-infant and stranger-infant interactions, and the D showed a robust bilateral prediction from the mother-infant interaction. However, from the stranger-infant interaction, the A was predicted from infants' coordination with strangers (S → I), and the C from strangers' coordination with infants (I → S), both unilateral. Furthermore, the predictions of B, D, and A from the mother-stranger interaction were all unilateral, based on the mothers' coordination with strangers (S → M).

Continuous approach. Using the continuous DIS approach, Table 16 also shows that attachment is predicted mainly by the interactions of the strangers with the 4-month-old infants. These stranger-infant predictions were coconstructed across the group, based on infants' coordination with strangers, and vice versa. The mother-infant interaction yielded one significant finding, the stranger-infant yielded four, and the mother-stranger none. Most of the findings were linear, such that higher degrees of CIT predicted higher degrees of insecurity.

Attachment predictions and site. In order to roughly compare the power of the prediction from different conditions, we added the percentages of variance accounted for in a particular condition in Table 16. In the mother-infant interaction, the prediction of disorganized versus secure attachment from the lab accounts for 3.3 times the variance of the prediction from home. In the stranger-infant interaction, the lab findings account for 1.6 times the variance of the home findings. The predictive advantage of the lab may lie in its greater control of the environment, in its novelty, and/or in its developmental challenge ("mother and infant going visiting"). However, only when the stranger comes into the mother's home does the mother's coordination with the stranger predict infant attachment.

Attachment predictions and partner configurations. Again adding the percentages of variance from Table 16, the stranger-infant interaction is as strongly associated with the attachment outcomes as is the mother-infant interaction, although in different ways. The mother-stranger interaction is about one-quarter as strong in its association to attachment as the other two dyad configurations. *Thus patterns of stranger-infant as well as mother-infant CIT during face-to-face interactions at age 4 months provide indices of the developing attachment system at age 12 months.* Across all three partner configurations, and across categorical and continuous approaches, the predominant vocal state predicting attachment is switching pause, appearing in one-half of the significant equations.

Per dyad bidirectional coordination in secure versus insecure dyads. Whereas the preceding analyses showed that *degree* of coordination *across the group* predicts attachment, and that some of these findings are based on bidirectional coordinations across the group, we now reconsider our measure of per dyad bidirectionality and its relation to attachment. A series of chi-square tests examined the relationship between per dyad bidirectionality

84

(presence/absence) and attachment (secure versus insecure of A, C, and D) in each condition: mother-infant, stranger-infant, and mother-stranger, each at home and lab. The analyses used the three sets of vocal variables described in the previous chapter (Table 15): the set across all six; the set of vocalization, pause, and switching pause; and the set of the two simultaneous speech states and turn. Only one chi-square value was significant ($\chi^2 = 3.99$, $p < .046$), which we infer to be a chance finding. The remaining range of chi-square values was .000 ($p = 1.0$) to 2.89 ($p = .084$). Thus there seems to be no relationship between secure/insecure attachment and this measure of per dyad bidirectional CIT. Note that this finding is very different from that above documenting that attachment is predicted by the CIT indices of both partners, across the group.

PREDICTING 12-MONTH-OLDS' BAYLEY (MDI) FROM CIT AT AGE 4 MONTHS

Table 17 presents predictions of infant Bayley (MDI) from CIT at age 4 months, and Figure 6 is a schematic of these findings. Figure 6 shows the dramatic finding that the highest novelty condition, stranger-infant in the lab, yields entirely symmetrical findings (in vocal state and direction of coordination) for infant and stranger. Thus, these predictions of Bayley scores are coconstructed across the group, by strangers' coordination with infants, and infants' coordination with strangers. Both linear

TABLE 17

SIGNIFICANT PREDICTIONS OF THE BAYLEY MENTAL DEVELOPMENT INDEX BY CIT

Interacting Pair	Home		Laboratory	
Mother-Infant	M → I	I → M	M → I	I → M
	V^2 (.044)			SP (.055)
Stranger-Infant	S → I	I → S	S → I	I → S
			SP (.123)	SP (.281)
			SP^2 (.328)	SP^2 (.149)
			V (.126)	V (.089)
			V^2 (.093)	V^2 (.171)
Mother-Stranger	M → S	S → M	M → S	S → M
			P^2 (.063)	

Note.—These predictions have partialed from them the other outcome, Attachment. The r^2s associated with the prediction (MR) equations are in parentheses. P = pauses; SP = switching pauses; V = vocalizations. The entries in the table are those predictors whose variance contributions yielded a $p \le 05$; significant results that account for less than 1% of the variance were omitted. The power of 2 associated with a vocal state means that the relationship is quadratic. The N for the analyses is 84.

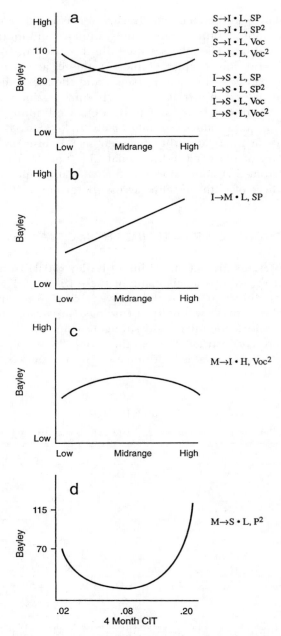

FIGURE 6.—Predictions of Bayley scores at age 12 months from CIT at age 4 months. S → I = infant predicted by stranger; L = lab; H = home; SP = switching pause; Voc = vocalization; P = pause. SP², Voc², and P² stand for the quadratic version of the equation.

and quadratic best-fit curves converge at the high end of CIT, so that higher CIT predicts higher Bayley scores. The plots of these equations show that the low end of CIT is less interpretable because the linear and nonlinear predictions are more discrepant, yielding greater scatter.

Comparing partner configurations. To compare the prediction of the Bayley Scales from the different partner configurations, we added the percentages of variance accounted for in particular conditions, as shown in Table 17. The stranger-infant interaction accounts for approximately 8 times the variance of the mother-infant interaction. The mother-stranger interaction is roughly comparable to that of the mother-infant. Across all three partner configurations, the predominant vocal states predicting Bayley are switching pause and vocalization, each appearing in 7 of the 17 significant equations.

Per Dyad Bidirectional Coordination and Bayley Scales

Parallel to the analyses relating per dyad bidirectional coordination to attachment, a series of ANOVA examined per dyad bidirectionality (presence/absence) in relation to Bayley scores for each condition: mother-infant, stranger-infant, and mother-stranger, each at home and lab. The analyses used the three sets of vocal variables: all six; vocalization, pause, and switching pause; and the two simultaneous speech states and turn. There were no significant findings. The F values ranged from $F = .01$ ($p = .90$) to $F = 2.62$ ($p = .113$). Thus we conclude that there is no relationship between the Bayley scores and this measure of per dyad bidirectional CIT. *This finding is very different from that discussed previously documenting prediction of the Bayley from CIT indices of both partners, across group.*

In this chapter we have shown that attachment and Bayley scores at age 1 year are not related to per dyad bidirectional CIT, but they *are* predicted from CIT indices across the group: in all three partner configurations, from both the home and the lab sites, and from both directions of coordination (A → I and I → A). *Thus across-group variations in adult-infant vocal rhythm coordination at age 4 months are indeed systematically related to attachment and cognition outcomes at age 12 months.* In summary:

1. In both mother-infant and stranger-infant interactions, the I → A and the A → I indices of CIT across the group were predictive of the outcomes at age 12 months (although not necessarily symmetrically). Thus, outcomes are predictable across the group from both infant and adult.

2. Across all partner configurations at age 4 months, midrange CIT values differentially predicted *secure* attachment, whereas low and

high extremes differentially predicted insecure. A high degree of coordination indicates a highly predictable interaction, a more tightly organized system.

3. The D findings were the most robust of the insecure categories, predicted from both mothers' CIT with infants and vice versa, based on the highest ranges of CIT, and *completely symmetrical* for mothers and infants (regarding direction of coordination, vocal state, and site).

4. In contrast to attachment, higher CIT predicts higher Bayley scores, particularly in the stranger-infant interaction in the lab.

5. The lab as compared to the home, and stranger as compared to mother, amplified the predictive power of vocal rhythms for attachment and even more markedly for the Bayley Scales. The condition of stranger and 4-month-old infant provided a unique source of information about developmental outcomes: (a) It had 8 times more power, in percentage of variance accounted for, to predict 12-month-olds' Bayley scores than did the mother-infant interactions; (b) the capacity to predict attachment was as great from the stranger-infant as from the mother-infant interaction (although different types of information were operative); (c) whereas the mother-infant interaction discriminated the future D from the B, the stranger-infant interaction was necessary to further differentiate the A and C categories from the B.

6. Predictions of attachment and Bayley Scales share the switching pause as a predominant vocal state accounting for findings. The switching pause regulates the turn exchange. For the Bayley, vocalization was also a predominant state.

7. Thus *degrees* of CIT at age 4 months mean different things in different developmental subsystems (attachment, cognition), in different sites (home, lab), and with different partners (mother, stranger). High CIT can index more *or* less optimal outcomes, depending on the particular outcome measure.

8. The percentage of variance accounted for in the prediction of attachment can be considered low to modest, ranging from 4% to 21%. In predicting the Bayley Scales, the percentage of the variance accounted for is low to strong, ranging from 4% to 33%.

VII. DISCUSSION

In the 1970s, rhythmic coordination between adult partners was known to convey important emotional information regarding the perceived warmth, similarity, and empathy of the speakers (e.g., Feldstein & Welkowitz, 1978), and a decade later it became clear that unfamiliar adult partners coordinate vocal rhythms to a greater degree than familiar ones. We applied this adult work to the study of infant-adult face-to-face vocal rhythms, as a system that widens from mother-infant at home to stranger-infant in the laboratory at age 4 months, and in relation to 12-month-olds' attachment and cognition. After noting the timescale of vocal rhythms, we address the question of *how* the coordination of vocal rhythms might work, reframing the results of both vocal durations, as well as the CIT of these durations, as modes of rhythmic coordination. The inclusion of a wider ecology revealed the context-sensitivity of vocal rhythms and their coordination at age 4 months, as a function of partner/site novelty, defining mother-specific and stranger-specific organizations, addressed next. CIT predicted infant social and cognitive development at age 12 months, confirming our central hypothesis. These predictions are discussed, and a refinement of the concept of the coconstruction of developmental outcomes offered. We then turn to the question of *why* vocal rhythm coordination would predict infant development, arguing that vocal rhythms are procedures for regulating the timing pragmatics of adult-infant dialogue, with implications for infant presymbolic representation. After noting limitations of the research, we provide a summary of the study and its implications.

THE TIMESCALE OF SOUND AND SILENCE

There is a dramatic match between the temporal ranges of infant auditory discrimination and the sound-silence durations of adult-infant interaction. Lewkowicz (1986) showed that 0.4–1.6 s is the ballpark of infant discrimination of vocal duration, and we find the timescale of vocal events to be largely less than 1 s. This time frame, shared by 4-month-old infants and adults, provides the perceptual underpinning for the coordination of behavioral timing patterns. The largely split-second time frame replicates the work of Keller et al. (1999), Papousek et al. (1985), Stern (1977), as well as our own (Beebe et al., 1988). This match between timing perception and duration of behavior can be seen from a systems point of view as reflecting a coherent perceptual-motor system. Our finding that infants and adults display a degree of across-session stability (split-half reliability) of vocal durations comparable to that of adults suggests a certain degree of intrapersonal stability, which nevertheless coexists with a sensitive adjustment to partner and site contexts. The similarities of timescale and across-session stability indicate strong commonalities in the timing system of adult-infant and adult-adult "conversations."

MODES OF RHYTHMIC COORDINATION

The timing of adult-infant dialogue can be conceptualized as a dyadic coordination of rhythms that are modified in changing environments, and that underlie social relatedness, mother-infant bonding, and cognitive processes. But how does coordination work? As we noted in the Introduction, there is currently no unifying theory of the interpersonal coordination of nonperiodic (irregular) rhythms, the subject of this study. Originally the study of coordination occurred in the context of periodic (regular) rhythms. For some regularities, such as walking, breathing, or heartbeat, the presence of biological clocks (oscillators) was suggested as an underlying regulatory process (e.g., Lenneberg, 1967). The theory of coupled oscillators remains the standard explanation for the coordination of periodic rhythms, and entrainment of regular cycles is the central metaphor of this coordination (Chapple, 1971; Iberall & McCulloch, 1969; Lester et al., 1985; Pavlidis, 1969; Trevarthen, 1993; Winfree, 1975).

In this study we identified a family of modes of interpersonal temporal coupling in rhythmic durations, and their coordination, which are potential contributors to an eventual theory of the coordination of nonperiodic rhythms: (1) interpersonal correlations of tempo, based upon the mean vocalization-plus-pause *cycle* duration; (2) the level of activity (the ratio of vocalization to pause durations) within these cycles; (3) the examination of whether CIT is bidirectional, across the group and within each dyad; (4) two modes of turn regulation (matching and compensatory) based on the CIT findings; (5) the midrange optimum coordination of CIT identified in the prediction of attachment; and (6) group matching of the optimum lag in the CIT analyses, construed as a much slower

interaction rhythm. These rhythmic modes appear at many different organizational levels, and some, inferred from the matching of group means, may represent ways in which dyadic partners arrive at the same range prior to fine-tuning coordination within each individual dyad.

Interpersonal Correlations of the Durations of Vocalization-Plus-Pause Cycle

In this study, conversational coupling was not generally based on a correlation of mean cycle durations (of vocalization-plus-pause). So metaphors of entrainment, attunement, or "we're on the same wavelength" (in the sense of tuning a radio receiver to a broadcast wavelength) are not generally applicable across the data set. The one exception, a positive correlation of vocalization-plus-pause cycle between mother and infant at home, suggests that this mode of coupling may be employed only in maximally familiar contexts. That a subset (63%) of these infants and mothers showed almost zero correlation of vocalization-plus-pause cycles when they came to the lab is a demonstration that a change of context alters the forms of vocal rhythmic coupling.

Interpersonal Correlations of Activity Level Within the Vocalization-Plus-Pause Cycle

A second mode of temporal coupling is matching of the average activity level of two partners (ratio of mean durations of vocalization to pause). The greater the numerator relative to the denominator, the more fluent or active the speech is judged, by clinicians and psycholinguists (Jaffe, Anderson, & Rieber, 1973). Positive correlation of this activity level was a significant mode of coupling in all six conditions (three partner configurations at two sites), and thus very general. Lester et al. (1985) and Feldman (Feldman & Greenbaum, 1997; Feldman et al., 1996) have also argued that interaction rhythms are mediated by homeostatic control mechanisms that affect the balance between behavioral excitation and inhibition, facilitating infant regulation of environmental input. *Homeostatic* refers to noncausal mechanisms or methods that maintain a relatively stable state of equilibrium around a goal or set point. In coding cross-modal attunements for global matches in intensity, time, or shape, Stern, Hofer, Haft, and Dore (1985) found that the dimension of change in intensity over time (activation contour) was the most frequent dimension of matching, occurring in 97% of attunements. Our pervasive matching of activity level may be analogous.

Matching of activity level within cycles is thus a more general mode of coupling in our data than matching cycle of durations (entrainment).

Why might this be so? Cycles can vary considerably in length and yet still have the same ratio of sound to silence. For example, compare a 3-s cycle, composed of a 1-s vocalization and a 2-s pause, to a 6-s cycle, composed of a 2-s vocalization and a 4-s pause. Both the first faster tempo and the second slower tempo have the same vocalization to pause ratio, 1:2. The scale of the timing has changed, and yet the ratio remains constant. This change of scale is similar to the phenomenon of scalar timing, originally suggested by Stern and Gibbon (1979) as a method that the mother uses to keep the infant from habituating. Zlochower and Cohn (1996) showed that whereas control mothers indeed used this method, depressed mothers did not, implying that this scalar method has adaptive value in development.

Bidirectional Coordination (CIT) at Age 4 Months: Across-Group and per Dyad

We turn now from the findings based on vocal duration to those based on the coordination of durations (CIT). The *degree* (magnitude) of CIT, regardless of statistical significance, was a powerful predictor of outcomes. However, CIT of each dyad can also be assessed for statistical significance, which is necessary for evaluating whether coordination is bidirectional. Whereas our basic measure is one of coordination, an assessment of the *pattern* of directionality can be construed as a particular form or mode of coordination.

Most descriptions of a bidirectional pattern of coordination have been based on across-group rather than per dyad evaluations. For example, Cohn and Tronick's (1988) conclusion that mother-infant coordination is bidirectional was based on an across-group analysis, *that is*, mothers as a group coordinated with infants, and vice versa. Whereas we addressed vocal timing, and Cohn and Tronick used degree of facial-visual engagement (monadic phases), similar calculations are possible to compare our across-group results to theirs. Both examined mother-infant dyads in the lab, and our vocal data across all six variables are most comparable to their monadic phase scoring, which considers several kinesic variables at once (gaze, face, vocalization). Our proportion of dyads where mother was contingent upon infant in the lab was .76, somewhat higher than the range observed by Cohn and Tronick (.55–67); our proportion of dyads where infant was contingent upon mother in the lab was .75, twice their range (.33–.39). The comparable proportions in our data for mother and infant at home was .64 for mothers, and .67 for infants; for stranger and infant at the lab, .84 for strangers, and .80 for infants; and for stranger and infant at home, .77 for strangers, and .73 for infants. Thus, our across-group findings for mothers (with infants) in the lab are similar to those of Cohn and Tronick, but infants (with mothers) in the lab suggest greater coordination. A further difference is that the current study defined coordination purely by lagged predictions, whereas Cohn and Tronick summed across both lagged and unlagged effects. Unlagged effects cannot evaluate direction of effects.

However, in order to utilize the full power of the time-series method, each dyad can be *separately* evaluated for direction of effects. Although this feature of time-series analyses offers a powerful methodological advance in infancy research, few researchers have pursued a *per dyad* examination of bidirectional coordination (as an exception, see Gottman, 1981). But the very idea of bidirectional coordination is fundamentally a within-dyad rather than an across-group concept: Is each partner adjusting to the other? Evaluating each dyad as bidirectional (coordination significant for both partners), unidirectional (coordination significant for only one partner of the dyad), or absent, we found that bidirectional coordination was present in 47% to 72% of adult-infant recordings (using all six vocal parameters), depending on partner/site condition. Both methods, across-group and per dyad, show that bidirectional coordination is robust but by no means ubiquitous. The across-group method yields somewhat higher estimates of bidirectionality than the per dyad method.

The meaning of per dyad bidirectional coordination between adults and 4-month-old infants was clarified by its relation to partner and site novelty. The double-novelty condition (stranger-infant in the lab) showed a greater proportion of bidirectional dyads than the doubly familiar condition (mother and infant at home). And the stranger-infant interaction itself showed a greater per dyad bidirectionality in the lab than the home. These differences were primarily carried through the coactive moment of simultaneous speech and turn. Because per dyad bidirectional coordination was such a systematic function of novelty, it seems to be more an index of *degree of mutual interactive vigilance* than of intuitive concepts of attunement, reciprocity, or relatedness. From this point of view, increased per dyad bidirectionality is a mutual social adaptation that copes with uncertainty, reduces the complexity of the system, and can be seen as efforts by both partners to make the interaction more predictable under conditions of novelty or challenge. This interpretation was proposed by Crown (1991) who found that unfamiliar (novel) adult dyads had higher coordination than acquainted dyads. Our data thus suggest that, similar to adult-adult dyads, adult-infant dyads also respond to novelty with increased coordination. These results also fit Gottman's (1979) finding of higher degree of heart rate coordination in distressed marital pairs. To our knowledge only Gottman (1981) has published case-by-case comparisons of direction of effects, for three mother-infant dyads. Anecdotally, in one of the three cases that he analyzed, the dyad with a fussy baby was the only one demonstrating bidirectional effects.

Per dyad bidirectional coordination was also clarified by our finding that adult-infant dyads show more bidirectionality than adult-adult dyads. At the project's outset, a model of polite adult conversation was conceived as the final form toward which infant vocal development is tending (Werner, 1948), and we anticipated that dialogues between two adults would be more coordinated than those between adults and infants. The reverse turned out to be the case: Adult–4-month-old-infant dyads showed more per dyad bidirectional coordination than adult-adult dyads. This difference was identified through analyses using the coactive simultaneous speech states, as well as all six vocal variables. We believe that preverbal adult-infant dialogues favor bidirectional coordination (more dyadic predictability) precisely because they are developmentally more restricted to this interpersonal mode than are two adults who can rely on symbolic forms of communication as well. The fact that the coactive states were associated with both the adult-infant and the adult-adult per dyad bidirectionality findings adds weight to the interpretation of coaction as a heightened moment (see Flaster, 1995; Stern et al., 1975).

Two Modes of Turn Regulation in CIT: Matching Versus Compensatory

Another facet of coordination is found in the *sign* of the findings. The coefficient of coordination for each vocal variable can be positive or negative, indicating two modes of turn regulation: (a) dyadic regulation of turn exchange (positive sign of switching pause CIT); and (b) dyadic regulation of activity level within the turn (negative sign of vocalization and pause CIT). The data suggest that both types of feedback facilitate turn taking, but in different ways.

In our model, the switching pause marks a moment that is destined to become a highly complex interaction in the life of every infant— namely, a graceful, synchronized exchange of speaker-listener roles. The positive signs of switching pause CIT indicate that, at the moment of turn exchange, tightness of coordination for adult and infant varies in parallel, thus making the exchange more predictable. A similar finding is well-known in adult conversations. Jaffe and Feldstein (1970) and Crown (1991) have shown that adults match switching pause durations. Jasnow and Feldstein (1986) also showed a positive sign for switching pause coordination at age 9 months. The positive correlation of switching pause CIT supports our previous findings that aspects of adult dialogic structure are already in place at age 4 months (Beebe et al., 1985, 1988).

But the CIT findings for vocalization and pause carried negative signs: Here the partners coordinated with each other's durations in compensatory fashion such that as one tightened coordination, the other loosened, and vice versa. Vocalization and pause coordinations occur alternately, during each partner's speaking turn. This compensatory mode of coordination constitutes a *dyadic regulation of relative tightness of coordination within the turn.* Here, rather than keeping the behavior similar, as in the switching pause match, the task seems to be keeping a relatively constant *dyadic* degree of activation across both partners' turns, a homeostatic or cybernetic mode of regulation. Whereas *homeostatic* generally refers to maintaining the internal environment constant, *cybernetic* refers to how the organization of a system is maintained. One implication of this negative feedback pattern is a reduction in variance, with a bias toward the midrange of the CIT distribution, which bears a striking resemblance to the fifth mode of coordination described below. In kinesic interactions, the durations of mother and infant movements (of face, head, gaze) and holds (sustained postures) also showed compensatory adjustment of activity levels, when analyzed by time-series analysis (Beebe et al., 1985).

Optimal Midrange Coordination

A further rhythmic mode is the concept of optimal midrange coordination, identified by across-group bidirectional predictions of secure attachment from midrange coordination. One common explanation of midrange phenomena comes from the field of cybernetics. A thermostat is a well-known example, in which a set point defines a new range around which the temperature may vary. The set point defines the midrange. Our finding suggests that attachment involves a dyadic control system in which extremes of coordination are optimally counteracted, biasing the system toward the set point. In a simulation experiment, Tononi, Sporns, and Edelman (1994) found that maximal information transmission occurred in the midrange of coordination.

The Optimum Lag as a Slow Interaction Rhythm

A final mode of rhythm coordination can be found in the optimum lag findings. The magnitude of the lagged cross-correlations was studied over a moving window of 1 minute of history. For most dyads, contingencies occurred at many possible lags, so that either partner was potentially contingent upon what the other did 5 s before, 10 s before, and so on, up to 60 s before. The percentage of variance accounted for peaked at a mean value of about 20–30 s for both adults and infants (Feldstein et al., 1993). We refer to this peak as the optimum lag. Thus, at any particular moment in the play session, on average, each partner was most contingent on what the other did 20–30 s before, defining another potential interaction rhythm. (But whether or not partners matched optimal lags

95

on a per dyad basis would require further analysis.) The 20–30 s rhythm is not obvious to the naked ear and its detection required extensive data processing. In contrast, the vocalization-pause and turn rhythm cycles in dialogue are audible to the untrained observer, with durations closer to conscious experience.

Similar slow rhythms have been reported by Brazelton et al. (1974), who found a 20–30-s cycle in infant attention, by Lester et al. (1985) who found a 10–45-s cycle in the coordination of facial engagement, and by Cohn and Tronick (1988) who found a 20-s lag in facial engagement correlation. Slower rhythms have been found to be more soothing, to facilitate memory, to account for the classic superiority of distributed over massed practice, and to facilitate synchronization (Fields, Eshete, Stevens, & Itoh, 1997; Kogan, 1996; Yin, 1995). The remarkable similarity in the mean optimum lag durations for mother-infant and stranger-infant interactions is reminiscent of D. Newtson's (personal communication, April 26, 1993) metaphor that behavior is a wave flowing through both people. In the optimum lag measure, all the vocal states were doing the same thing—that is, they were all riding the same wave, or interaction rhythm.

In summary, we have documented a number of modes of coordination that illustrate the complexity of the processes through which two partners may coordinate their vocal rhythms. The dyad's actions of sound and silence fit together at many temporal levels, in many different patterns. Interpersonal bonding may in part be constructed from all the particular rhythmic patterns that are shared between two individuals at any point in time. In contrast to most approaches to rhythmic coordination, all of the modes illustrated in our data are nonperiodic. These modes provide a range of alternatives to the usual periodic concept of how rhythms coordinate, namely, entrainment of regular cycles. Our description of these modes may spur further conceptualization of a theory of the coordination of nonperiodic rhythms.

VOCAL RHYTHM COORDINATION AND "CONTEXT" AT AGE 4 MONTHS: PARTNER/SITE NOVELTY AND INFANT SEX

In this section we turn to the importance of the infant's experiences of a stranger, as compared to his or her mother, and of a new place, the laboratory, as compared to the home. Novelty of partner and site were fertile variables with which to explore the novelty sensitivity of the adult-infant system for the 4-month-old infant, varying in systematic ways with vocal durations, rhythmic cycles, degree of coordination, and per dyad bidirectional coordination.

Interaction between the stranger and the 4-month-old infant showed a surprising degree of articulation, with various differentiations from the mother-infant interaction in every kind of vocal rhythm data examined. Construing mother and infant at home as the core dyadic matrix (doubly familiar), the organization of stranger and infant in the lab (doubly novel) can describe the infant's early experience with an unfamiliar other in an unfamiliar place. The way stranger and infant coordinated vocal rhythm in the lab provides a window on an early moment of the infant's differentiation from mother. In general the vocal rhythms of infant and stranger were more active than those of infant and mother, but there was also a pattern of constriction: Infant turn durations were shorter with stranger in the lab, as compared to mother at home. Nested within the shorter infant turn duration with stranger, durations of pauses and switching pauses were shorter, indicating a faster resumption of vocalization, or a faster turn exchange, hence more active. This phenomenon of simultaneous behavioral activation and inhibition at different levels of organization is well-known in other data such as that of Field (1981), in which infant heart rate activation is associated with gaze aversion.

A further central difference was that stranger and infant in the lab showed more bidirectional coordination of simultaneous speech (per dyad and across-group measures) than mother and infant at home, suggesting that the dyad adjusts to novelty and challenge by augmenting interpersonal predictability. The coactive moment of simultaneous speech was found by Stern et al. (1975) to be one of heightened arousal. Flaster (1995) also identified the coactive moment of simultaneous speech as the most powerful of the vocal states in showing that the infant's degree of coordination with the stranger can be predicted from that with the mother.

The analysis of per dyad bidirectional coordination clarified that novelty of site carries a different meaning for mother-infant versus stranger-infant dyads: Mother and infant maintained their preponderance of bidirectionality from home to lab, whereas stranger and infant increased it. Furthermore, these findings clarify the meaning of mother versus stranger for the infant. That the mother-infant system does not change in per dyad bidirectionality from home to lab suggests that, in this dimension, the core mother-infant dyadic matrix remains stabilized when a novel site is introduced. In this sense, mother remains home base for the infant even at the lab.

Reciprocally, mother and infant at home base were more flexible than stranger and infant, with richer relational resources, in the sense that they used the additional rhythmic mode of coupling of cycles, as well as the coupling of activity level of cycles found in all partner-site conditions. They were also least bidirectionally coordinated, and one-way coordination was more common for both. This finding suggests that bidirectional coordination was not as necessary to maintain interpersonal predictability, hence a more flexible system. A further dimension of flexibility of the mother and infant at home was revealed by the comparison of adult-adult versus adult-infant per dyad bidirectional coordination. In all comparisons, adult-infant dyads showed more bidirectional coordination than adult-adult, with the exception of home mother-stranger compared to home mother-infant. This finding suggests that mother at home is not working as hard to adapt her adult vocal rhythm style to the infant. This more relaxed or "less infantized" maternal management of bidirectionality constitutes one meaning of the core home mother-infant matrix.

These differences between mother-infant and stranger-infant vocal rhythm organizations can be further illuminated by considering them within the Piagetian framework of the balance between assimilation/accommodation. The system is tilted toward assimilation when there is a match between the infant's action schemas and the provisions of the environment. Elements of the environment can be assimilated into the infant's preexisting schemas, thus conferring meaning on these elements. With novelty, and perceptions that are discrepant from those expected, the system tilts toward accommodation, such that the infant's action schemas differentiate and elaborate. Accommodation opens new possibilities in response to novelty. As schemas differentiate through action, they become detached from their original objects, becoming more flexible and useable for different purposes (see Bloom, 1994; Muller & Overton, 1998; Overton, 1994).

For 4-month-old infants, the organization of mother and infant at home can be construed as tilted toward assimilation, whereas stranger and infant in the lab can be construed as tilted toward accommodation. Evidence of the infant's accommodation is seen in the differences between the two conditions of doubly familiar and doubly novel. Increasing vocal activity and per dyad bidirectionality shown in the stranger-infant dyads, as well as the turn constriction, may index the system's shift from assimilation to accommodation. This accommodation or differentiation process provides a way of conceptualizing how the infant differentiates from mother. These more active (and constricted) forms of vocal rhythm coordination then confer a new meaning on the stranger. Variations of vocal rhythm coordination become detached from mother and available for creating other forms of relatedness with the stranger. In this process infant and mother become more differentiated. Simultaneously, however, Flaster's (1995) finding from these data that the infant's degree of CIT with stranger (in the lab) could be predicted from that with mother indicates that the infant's differentiation with the stranger is systematically related to the interaction with the mother. In sum, the different rhythmic patterns with the stranger provide a way of conceptualizing the infant's initial experience of the unfamiliar other. Thus, as we proposed in the Introduction, vocal rhythm and timing coordination are differential relational features at this age, providing one way of defining the infant's first differentiation from the original mother-infant matrix.

Bigelow (1998) also examined mother-infant and stranger-infant face-to-face interactive contingencies (face and vocalization) at age 4 to 5 months. Although mothers' and strangers' degree of contingency with infants was similar, infants' degree of contingency was greater with mothers. Her finding that it is the familiar partner, mother, to whom the infant is more responsive is very different from our finding that infant and stranger have a greater bidirectional coordination. However, our findings are per dyad analyses based on time-series analysis; hers are across-dyad analyses using a different method of assessing interpersonal contingency. Nevertheless, the two sets of findings do share the idea that degree of coordination is sensitive to the familiarity/novelty of the partner.

Our findings are consistent with adult work on coordination and novelty of partner, as we proposed in the Introduction. Cappella (1996) reported that interpersonal attraction was associated with higher coordination when adult partners were unacquainted strangers than when they were intimate. This finding is similar to that of Crown (1991), who found higher coordination in unacquainted partners. Hedge et al. (1978) also demonstrated that a partner's temporal patterns of gaze and vocalization become more similar in conversations between strangers as opposed to those between friends, indicating a more tightly organized system with fewer dimensions. Our findings taken together with the adult findings suggest that interactions between unacquainted strangers are more coordinated or tightly organized than are those between acquainted partners. However, Bigelow's (1998) findings provide an important exception to this general view. Thus, there are contradictory views of the role of novelty in interpersonal coordination: Interpersonal predictability is enhanced versus constricted with a familiar, as compared to a novel, partner. This issue needs further research.

A further dimension of vocal coordination at age 4 months was the finding that both infant and adult partner in dyads with a female infant showed higher pause CIT than dyads with a male infant. This bidirectional finding indicated that dyads with a female infant were more sensitive to the coordination of the pause, which is highly correlated with the rate of the vocalization-pause cycle. Although significant, the difference was small: CIT was approximately .10 for male and .13 for female. These are both midrange values for this data set. Weinberg et al. (1999) find that female infants are better regulated than males at this age. Analogous to the Weinberg et al. findings, perhaps this greater coordination of the pause in both partners facilitates the female infant's social capacity at this age. However, unlike Weinberg et al., we showed female coordination to be higher, whereas they showed male coordination to be higher.

VOCAL RHYTHM COORDINATION AND OUTCOME PREDICTIONS

In this section we turn to our question of the functional significance of vocal rhythm coordination for two important aspects of infant development at age 12 months, attachment and cognition. Although the meaning of vocal timing coordination was partially clarified by its relation to partner and site novelty, as discussed above, it was further clarified by its relation to the outcome measures. Vocal rhythm coordination at age 4 months did indeed predict both cognition and attachment at age 12 months. However, it was not presence or absence of coordination, but rather its *degree*, that was critical, and the meaning of degree of coordination was highly dependent on context: outcome measure, partner, and site. Organism and environment are always coordinated in time, and the degree of coordination is flexible and changes according to context (see Fogel, 1993a, 1993b; Thelen, 1998; Warner, 1988). Coordination is highest in environmental contexts of danger *or* intense concentration. Coordination is looser in safe situations. Adaptation is enhanced by the capacity to rapidly change the strength of coordination—what is adaptive in one second may not be in the next. In the present study, midrange degree of coordination was optimal for attachment, but higher degrees of coordination (between stranger and infant in the lab) were optimal for Bayley scores.

COGNITIVE PREDICTION

Our highest novelty condition for infants at age 4 months, stranger-infant in the laboratory, was the primary predictor of the infant's Bayley performance at age 12 months. Highest CIT scores were optimal for Bayley scores, consistent with the position that coordination is higher in conditions of high attention, concentration, and novelty (Crown, 1991; Thelen, 1998). Note that the Bayley Scales are a test of the infant's response to a stranger; when the infant was 12 months old, the examiner was a new stranger. The Bayley prediction was dramatically coconstructed, across the group. Both infant and stranger showed symmetrical patterns of prediction (based on vocal variables, site, and linear/nonlinear form). That vocalization (part of the voc-pause rhythm) and switching pause (part of the turn rhythm) were the best predictors of the Bayley Scales fits the conversational demands of this test. The Bayley test requires careful infant

100

attention to the words of the stranger (vocalizations), as well as careful turn taking (regulated by switching pauses), as the stranger demonstrates the tasks and the infant takes his turn performing them. We believe that a high degree of the 4-month-old-infant's coordination, through vocalization and switching pause, is analogous to, and in fact a precursor of, the 12-month-old infant carefully following the stranger's demonstrations of tasks in the Bayley Scales.

As expected, as noted in the Introduction, our doubly novel context (stranger-infant in the lab) was most powerful in predicting the Bayley Scales. Recall that strangers and infants in the lab showed the highest per dyad bidirectional coordination at age 4 months, paralleled by the bidirectional predictions of the Bayley. This finding is consistent with a large body of research on infant attention and information processing that has converged on the robust finding that individual differences in infant response to novelty predict later IQ (see, e.g., Bornstein, 1985; Bornstein & Sigman, 1986; Colombo, Mitchell, Dodd, Coldren, & Horowitz, 1989; Fagan & McGrath, 1981; Lewis & Brooks-Gunn, 1981; O'Connor, Cohen, & Parmalee, 1984; R. A. Weinberg, 1989). Berg and Sternberg (1985) argue that novelty is central to the concept of intelligence at all ages. Bornstein and Sigman (1986) note that habituation and recovery of attention (novelty preference) are central to infant cognition and underlie measures that predict later intelligence. Fagan (1982) suggests that novelty preferences are a convenient way to measure basic infant intellectual processes, such as encoding, abstraction, detection of invariant features, and categorization.

Our findings are also consistent with research showing that infant response to novelty specifically predicts the Bayley Scales (see, e.g., Fagan & Shepherd, 1987; Rose, 1989). Fagen and McGrath (1981) find that preferences for novelty at age 6 months predict intelligence in early childhood. Lewis and Brooks-Gunn (1981) argue that the ability to process information, and particularly to recover from habituation in the face of a novel stimulus, may be a key aspect of the infant's early cognitive development. Faster habituation suggests faster schema formation. Infants who demonstrated more, and faster, habituation at age 4 months, and thus *who were more responsive to novelty,* had larger vocabularies and higher Bayley scores at age 12 months, and higher intelligence scores as toddlers (Bornstein & Sigman, 1986; Ruddy & Bornstein, 1982). These studies suggest a potential explanation of our finding that infants who showed most highly coordinated CIT in the maximum novelty condition had higher Bayley scores. Both measures tap novelty responsivity and efficient information processing. The fact that higher Bayley scores were predicted by the stranger (as well as the infant) coordinating in the high range suggests the hypothesis that a highly responsive partner facilitates the infant's cognitive development.

The findings of Feldman et al. (1996) most parallel our result that rhythmic interpersonal coordination predicted cognitive outcomes. In that study, infants who showed a cyclic pattern during face-to-face interaction at age 3 months (coded by the method of Cohn and Tronick (1988), and analyzed with a measure derived from time-series analysis) had higher Stanford-Binet scores at age 2 years. The measure of mother cyclicity did not predict. Feldman et al. emphasized the importance of the repetitive cyclic structure of mother-infant face-to-face play as a context for the integration of biological and social rhythms, "which in turn mediate the development of cognitive skills" (p. 350). Repetition, rhythm, and the interpersonal co-ordination of rhythms are central means by which the infant acquires cognitive expectancies and creates order and predictability in the world (Lewis & Goldberg, 1969; Stern et al., 1977; Stern & Gibbon, 1979).

Finally, the infants' Bayley scores were moderately negatively correlated with degree of attachment insecurity: Greater insecurity was associated with lower Bayley scores. It is not surprising that these two processes share some variance: An insecure attachment climate may compromise developing cognitive capacities, or vice versa. This finding is a partial replication of others already in the literature (see, e.g., Lyons-Ruth, Repacholi, McCleod, & Silva, 1991; Morisset, Barnard, Greenberg, Booth, & Spieker, 1990).

PREDICTION OF ATTACHMENT

A powerful way of understanding the attachment findings is to conceptualize interactive regulation on a continuum, with an optimum midrange and two poles defined by excessive or inhibited monitoring of the partner. Across all partner configurations at age 4 months, midrange CIT values differentially predicted secure attachment, whereas low and high extremes differentially predicted insecure. We designate 4-month-old infants as secure or insecure with the understanding that they *will* be so classified at age 12 months.

Secure (B) 4-month-old infants operated in the midrange of CIT with both mother and stranger. The midrange may give secure infants more flexibility than the insecures, who tended toward extremes of the range. Assuming that the B infant expects mother to be consistent and adequately responsive, neither vigilant nor inhibited coordination would be required. We suggest that, for secure 4-month-old infants and their mothers, the coordination of interpersonal rhythms remains in the background, whereas in C and D infants with high CIT, monitoring and coordination has become salient, presumably with high arousal and vigilance.

Avoidant (A) 4-month-old infants were low coordinators with the stranger, analogous to their pattern in the attachment test of showing little distress during separation from mother and avoiding her upon reunion. These infants are described as minimizing response to fear by an organized shift of attention away from mother toward the inanimate environment (Cassidy, 1994; Main & Hesse, 1990), which allows self-regulation and proximity, but at a price. We interpret our A infant's low CIT with stranger at age 4 months as a correlate of the 12-month-old's attention shift away from the interpersonal involvement in the Ainsworth Strange Situation, in the service of self-regulation. Avoidant infants have an elevated cortisol level (Spangler & Grossman, 1993) suggesting a greater self-regulatory burden. A videotape microanalysis comparing a subset of A versus B infants of the current study showed that A infants used more self-touch than the B, suggesting difficulty in self-regulation (Koulomzin, 1993; Koulomzin, Beebe, Jaffe, & Feldstein, 1993).

Anxious-resistant (C) 4-month-old infants respond to separation from mother with great distress, but are unable to be comforted by her return, simultaneously approaching her while angry, and reluctant to return to play. Our strangers were highly coordinated with these 4-month-old infants. We suspect that these infants may signal distress and overarousal, which elicited high stranger CIT. The strangers were trained to be very responsive to a distressed infant, and to help them self-regulate. We interpret high stranger CIT with future C infants as working harder to connect, to get the engagement going. Further kinesic microanalysis may clarify how the C infant may trigger the stranger's high coordination. Cassidy (1994) noted that, unlike the minimization strategy of the A, the C heightens, and becomes overinvolved. Whereas minimization of the A is reflected in the *infant's* use of the low CIT range with the stranger, heightening of the C is reflected in the *stranger's* use of the high range.

When the attachment figure herself becomes frightening, none of the B, A, or C patterns of organization are consistently sustained. Whereas the B infant tracks shifts in mother's location, the A infant shifts attention away from the mother, the C infant shifts attention toward the mother, and the D infant fails to exhibit a consistent pattern and instead shows moments of "disorganization" (Main & Hesse, 1990). The disorganized D infant is "in conflict" in the ethological sense of simultaneous activation of incompatible behavioral systems, both approaching and avoiding the mother, such as opening the door for the mother at the reunion, and then sharply ignoring her. Many of these infants compromise by "freezing," "stilling," or falling prone to the floor. Some exhibit apprehensive behaviors such as fearful facial expressions, oblique approaches, or vigilant postures (Lyons-Ruth, 1998; Main & Hesse, 1990). The highest cortisol levels among insecure infants have been documented in the D infant (Spangler & Grossman, 1993).

Although there were only seven such infants, the D findings were the most robust of the insecure categories. The mother-infant interaction (but not the stranger-infant) identified the future D attachment classification, based on the highest ranges of CIT at age 4 months. We interpret high CIT as vigilance, arousal, or hyperreactivity. The discrimination of the D was based on a bidirectional prediction across the group, and was the only *completely symmetrical* attachment prediction (based on direction of coordination, particular vocal state, and site): a coconstructed organization of social timing, unique to the D mother and infant. Because D infants and mothers showed the highest CIT, and thus the highest degree of interpersonal predictability, they were in this sense the *most* interpersonally organized dyads of the entire database.

Pursuing the concept of D attachment as the simultaneous activation of infant approach and avoidance, CIT in the high range (vigilant hypertrackers) can be seen as a form of *vocal approach.* Videotape observation of these same dyads revealed that infant vocalization was predominantly distressed (i.e., fussing, whimpering) so that the high coordination occurred during periods of infant vocal distress. Regarding avoidance, videotape observation revealed that these infants were *visually* disengaged for long periods, arching away or losing postural tonus, thus combining high levels of distressed vocal approach with high levels of avoidance in the gaze-orientation modality, a form of intermodal conflict. To our knowledge, this is the first synthesis of the concept of approach-avoidance and degree of rhythmic coordination.

The Role of Partner Configuration in Predicting Attachment

Mother-infant, stranger-infant, and mother-stranger coordination revealed very different patterns of prediction to attachment. Only the B infants looked similar with mother and stranger. The A, C, and D infants showed distinct prediction patterns (D vs. B predicted from mother-infant; A vs. B and C vs. B from stranger-infant). Whereas the B and D were bidirectional predictions, the A and the C were *unilateral* predictions. The mother's coordination with the stranger also differentiated the D and A from the B. These different prediction patterns allow us to further define differences between the mother-infant and the stranger-infant interactions. We infer that infants in different attachment classifications experience mother versus stranger differently. For example, the D infant seemed to "relax" the high coordination in the presence of the stranger, as if retaining the capacity to identify a safe adult (M.S. Moore, personal communication, April 17, 1994).

104

In addition, the coordination pattern may change with a partner change. For example, the D mother coordinated in the highest ranges of the entire sample with her infant, and in the lowest ranges with the stranger. The A infant and mother showed opposite ranges of CIT when interacting with the same stranger: infant in the low CIT range and mother high. In this sense, the developing coordination patterns associated with attachment outcomes are better characterized as sensitive to who the partner is, rather than as stable individual differences generalized to any interaction.

Furthermore, prediction of all four attachment classifications involved the stranger. Stranger-infant and mother-stranger interactions identified more varied contingency structures and a wider range of attachment outcomes than did the mother-infant condition, which differentiated only B from D. Imagine the stranger as a nonspecific catalyst for the coconstruction, with mother and infant separately, of a dance that mother and infant will later perform in the Strange Situation. For example, the A infant at age 4 months displayed inhibited coordination with the stranger, an analogue of the avoidant coordination with mother in the attachment reunion. Bowlby (1969) believed that attachment is dyadically organized and unique to a particular figure. The fact that the infant and stranger showed more variation in their predictions to attachment suggests that at age 4 months the infant has the flexibility to respond very differently to the stranger as compared to the mother.

Perhaps our most unique finding was that mother-stranger coordination (in the absence of the 4-month-old infant) discriminated infant attachment, and in one instance, the Bayley score. As they talked, mother and stranger evidently generated with each other an aspect of their relatedness to the infant, with whom both had just played. The way mother at home coordinated with the stranger embodied some significant aspect of the developing attachment climate. And note that both mother and stranger were integral parts of the Ainsworth and Bayley tests.

In sum, our findings that varying degrees of vocal rhythm coordination in mother-infant, stranger-infant, and mother-stranger interactions predicted all four attachment classifications lead us to propose vocal rhythm coordination as one important means of attachment formation and transmission. The fact that low, moderate, and high degrees of coordination had such different implications for attachment security clarifies the meaning of coordination for attachment, one of the central goals of this study, as noted in the Introduction. Although only the mother-infant vocal timing data are directly relevant to attachment formation and transmission per se, the stranger-infant and mother-stranger data amplify aspects of the system's organization, as we suggested in the Introduction. Our proposal that vocal rhythm coordination is an important means of attachment formation and transmission directly addresses a current "transmission gap" in the understanding of the origins of attachment (see, e.g., Seifer & Schiller, 1995; van Ijzendoorn, Juffer, & Duyvesteyn, 1995).

Convergent Evidence for an Optimum Midrange Degree of Coordination for Attachment

Current research bolsters a model in which midrange interactive contingencies are optimal for infant attachment, and high or low degrees may identify different routes to disordered interactions. In our review of studies predicting attachment, we noted that a number of studies fit the optimal midrange model: Lester and Seifer (1990), Belsky et al. (1984), Isabella and Belsky (1991), and Lewis and Feiring (1989). In addition, predicting cognition rather than attachment, Roe, Roe, Driva, and Bronstein (1990) found a curvilinear relationship such that only midrange-talkative mothers both initiated vocalizations and allowed the infant to do the same, and these infants showed higher cognitive scores at ages 3 and 5 years. At either pole of most and least talkative mothers, infants had lower cognitive scores. Leyendecker, Lamb, Fracasso, Scholmerich, and Larson (1997) have findings most similar to the current study. They also confirm an optimal midrange model of coordination: Secure infants and their mothers were midrange, whereas insecure infants and their mothers received higher or lower scores. Furthermore, these patterns were relatively consistent across 4, 8, and 12 months. These authors concur that high levels of coordination can be construed as a form of overstimulation.

Regarding studies in which there are only two data points (better and worse outcomes in relation to some measure of contingency), Warner (1992) suggested that a limited range of values may capture only the ascending or descending arms of a U-shaped curve, leading to a linear interpretation. Linear studies that may show a piece of a wider continuum include for example Ackerman (1987), Cohn and Elmore (1988), Cohn and Tronick (1989), Crown (1991), Field, Healy, and LeBlanc (1989), Hitchcock (1991), Malatesta et al. (1989), Sander (1995), Tobias (1995), and Slade et al. (1995).

The distinctions between two poles of high intensity, overstimulating mothers and detached, underinvolved mothers, both associated with insecure attachment, are strikingly similar to the descriptions of subtypes of depressed mothers as "intrusive" versus "withdrawn" in the work of Cohn, Tronick, and Field, with the control mothers more midrange (Cohn et al., 1990; Cohn et al., 1986; Cohn & Tronick, 1989; Field et al., 1990). For adults, Warner (1992) reported a curvilinear relationship between affect and vocal rhythmicity, suggesting an optimum degree of rhythmicity in

106

social interactions, with moderately rhythmic interactions evaluated most positively.

High coordination increases the predictability of the interaction. Drawing on nonlinear dynamic systems theory indicating that rigidity is the hallmark of pathology (Gleick, 1987; Thelen & Smith, 1994), a more tightly coordinated system may be indicative of vigilance or wariness. This high degree of predictability can be construed as a coping strategy elicited by novelty, interactive challenge, or threat. At the other pole, where coordination is very low (or inhibited), the two partners are acting relatively more independently of each other, which may index withdrawal or inhibition of interpersonal monitoring. We hypothesize that midrange coordination leaves more "space," more room for uncertainty, initiative, and flexibility within the experience of correspondence and contingency. Attachment outcomes are favored when the exchange transpires in an atmosphere of somewhat looser (rather than tight or very loose) coordination, "optional rather than obligatory" contingency.

THE COCONSTRUCTION OF ATTACHMENT AND COGNITION OUTCOMES

Although "mutual regulation" or bidirectional coordination is a pivotal construct in mother-infant face-to-face interaction research, and is considered a fundamental aspect of mother-infant communication (Sander, 1977; Stern, 1985; Tronick, 1989), its value for developmental outcomes has largely been assumed rather than empirically demonstrated. Similarly, in modern systems models of development, bidirectional (reciprocal) coordinations are proposed to be the "engine" of development (e.g., Gottlieb et al., 1998), although infant data illustrating this important theory remain scarce. In this study attachment and cognition outcomes at age 12 months were predicted both by infants coordinating with adults and by adults coordinating with infants, across the group. These findings constitute a clear demonstration of the value of the mutual regulation model in conceptualizing the process of development over the 1st year, and they are consistent with the proposals of modern systems theories of development, illustrating that reciprocal coordinations between infant and adult are one method through which development proceeds. The findings also reinforce current requests for more emphasis on the infant's contribution to the interactive origins of attachment, as well as a conceptualization of development from a systems point of view, emphasizing coconstructed interaction patterns (Fox, 1994; Hinde, 1982; Pederson & Moran, 1995; Seifer & Schiller, 1995; Tarabulsy et al., 1996; van den Boom, 1997).

107

However, as important as across-group bidirectional coordination is for understanding development, the striking differences in its role in the two outcomes has led us to refine this concept. We suggest five refinements:

1. Bidirectional coordination (across-group) is not sufficient to describe our outcomes: The *degree* of coordination is essential as well. For example, *both* B and D attachment were predicted bidirectionally from the mother-infant interaction, but it was *degree* of coordination that differentiated them (midrange versus high, respectively). Our finding that different degrees of coordination predicted different attachment classifications addresses the observation of Tarabulsy et al. (1996) that the role of coordination in different types of attachment has been unclear.

2. The meaning of a particular *degree* of coordination is dependent on the outcome measure as well as partner/site condition. For example, whereas high bidirectional coordination (across-group) between stranger and infant in the lab was optimal for cognition, the same interactive pattern between mother and infant predicted disorganized attachment. The optimal set point for attachment is midrange degree of coordination, perhaps facilitating flexibility and "disruption and repair" (see Tronick, 1989), whereas the optimal set point for cognition is high coordination, indexing high response to novelty. These findings are consistent with Keller et al.'s (1999) argument that coordination per se may not carry a positive or negative value for development.

3. The nature of bidirectional coordination further differs in the two outcomes because it was the mother-infant interaction that yielded bidirectional attachment predictions, presumably describing a method of transmission of attachment, but it was the stranger-infant interaction that yielded bidirectional cognition predictions, presumably describing an interactive process that supports cognition.

4. A role for unidirectional coordination needs to be articulated, particularly for attachment (A and C types). The fact that attachment was predicted by the infant's coordination with stranger, as well as by stranger's with infant, suggests that the infant carries into the interaction with the stranger some aspect of his developing attachment security (see Flaster, 1995).

5. Different definitions of bidirectional coordination yield different kinds of information, such that only the across-group definition yielded significant age 12-months outcome predictions, whereas only the per dyad definition yielded clear age 4-months novelty findings,

particularly between mother-infant and stranger-infant. The across-group definition is continuous and uses more of the information of the system, including nonsignificant as well as significant CIT values, and unidirectional as well as bidirectional dyads, which may enhance its predictive power. The per dyad definition is categorical, dividing the dyads into bidirectional or not.

Despite the important differences between the attachment and cognition findings, the predictions nevertheless share the same predominant vocal state, switching pause CIT. This state is uniquely dyadic in the sense that it does not exist in a monologue. The switching pause is related to the turn rhythm and is interpreted as a complex regulation moment, composed of reciprocal speaker-listener role-exchange involving synchronized disengagement and reengagement. By analogy, the attachment test itself, through separation and reunion, taps the dyad's ability to disengage and recouple. The Bayley testing is also dependent on reciprocal speaker-listener turn exchange. Thus both developing cognitive and attachment processes are sensitive to the same aspect of vocal rhythm coordination, the switching pause at the moment of the turn exchange.

In sum, the role of bidirectional coordination in development is highly context-dependent. Its meaning varied by outcome measure, an example of the task specificity of the system (Gottlieb et al., 1998), as well as by novelty of partner and site.

VOCAL RHYTHMS AS PROCEDURES FOR REGULATING THE PRAGMATICS OF ADULT-INFANT DIALOGUE: IMPLICATIONS FOR REPRESENTATION

In this section we return to the question posed in the Introduction: Why would vocal rhythm coordination at age 4 months predict attachment and cognition at age 12 months? What particular timing processes might link the age 4 months and age 12 months measures?

Vocal Timing Patterns as Procedures for Regulating the Pragmatics of Social Dialogue

The six vocal parameters in the Jaffe-Feldstein model can be construed as "procedures" for negotiating the timing of face-to-face communication. These aspects are the primitives in terms of which adults and infants (presymbolically) represent the timing of ongoing vocal interactions. As noted in the Literature Review, presymbolic representation refers to expectancies of interaction sequences coded in a procedural format. The procedures include not only the rhythms of the vocal states and of turns, but also their sequencing, the activity level of vocalization-pause sequences, their degree of interpersonal coordination, and their embeddedness in the partner/site contexts of the study. Procedural memories get structured through recurrent interaction sequences, for example, high or low coordination of switching pause while interacting with mother or stranger, at home or in the lab. These procedural memories may become aspects of fundamental personality styles that are spontaneously retrieved when similar contexts recur.

This approach provides a way of understanding how the various vocal states can be used in such different ways to predict different tasks of development, as tapped by our outcome measures. In the varying patterns of vocal rhythm coordination, infant and adult are organizing procedures for when to vocalize, when to pause, and for how long; procedures for managing attention, activity level, turn taking, joining and being joined, interrupting and yielding when interrupted, and tracking and being tracked—all aspects of the timing pragmatics of dialogue. These interpersonal patterns or "moves" operate at age 4 months as procedural memories; they constitute one aspect of the relatedness pattern being jointly constructed. They are used by the infant to coordinate with his or her mother and to respond to the challenge of the stranger. They are precursors of the way the infant will later negotiate the separation and reunion of the Ainsworth test, and variations in the ways the Bayley tasks will be managed. Between ages 4 and 12 months these vocal timing procedures presumably become further coordinated and flexible as they are applied in varying interactions. But they continue to organize procedural representations of "how interactions go" in the modality of vocal timing. The logic of the argument can be summarized as follows:

1. Vocal rhythm is an index of the entire communicative package; thus, the vocal rhythm is highly correlated with other aspects of the affective exchange, such as touch or gaze rhythms.

2. Because our model parses the vocal stream into turns, coaction, pauses at the exchange of the turn, and so forth, it taps more than on/off rhythm: It gets at different kinds of *moments* in the exchange, which we call aspects of the timing pragmatics of dialogue. These procedures can regulate dialogue through the management of attention, activity level, turn taking, joining, interruption, yielding, and tracking.

3. The 4-month-old infant uses these vocal timing patterns as procedures to coordinate with his mother at home and to adapt to the

novelty of the stranger and the lab. Because these early procedures also predict outcomes at age 12 months, we infer that their interpersonal functions are precursors of the nonvocal separation and reunion patterns of the Strange Situation, as well as of patterns of tracking the stranger's movements in the Bayley test. These predictions illustrate heterotypic continuity (Sameroff, 1983) in which the interpersonal functions remain operative (e.g., turn taking), although the form differs (e.g., from face-to-face vocal rhythms to exchanges around objects during the Bayley testing). For example, the infant may construct an expectation of the duration and degree of coordination of the switching pause at the point of the turn exchange, which may continue to organize how 8 months later the infant tracks the stranger and takes a turn with the tasks in the Bayley test, or takes a communicative turn in the attachment test. Or, for another example, the approach/avoidance conflict of the 4-month-old D infant with mother (a highly coordinated distressed vocal "approach" coupled with visual-postural avoidance) can be seen as a repeated rehearsal for the analogous pattern in the reunion at age 12 months. Still another example may be found in the 4-month-old avoidant infant's inhibition of coordination with the stranger, and the inhibition of responsivity to mother in the attachment test reunion. Thus we propose that the same interpersonal timing patterns have similar functions at the two ages.

4. When we construe these various patterns of dialogic timing as procedures for managing aspects of the pragmatics of social interactions, it makes sense that they are sensitive to our social contexts (partner/site), that they are put together in rather complex ways (positive and negative correlations, and varying degrees of coordination), and that they play analogous roles at ages 4 and 12 months.

5. A similar argument can be made from the point of view of the mother as well as the stranger, who also use these patterns of vocal rhythm coordination to manage timing pragmatics. To the extent that they are processed purely procedurally, presumably these temporal patterns are largely out of awareness. Nevertheless, mothers' or strangers' own management of these dialogic moves also predicts infants' outcomes at age 12 months.

The Representation of Vocal Timing Procedures

We have previously argued that infants represent interactions in a procedural, presymbolic format (Beebe & Lachmann, 1994; Beebe et al., 1997; Beebe & Stern, 1977; see also Stern, 1985), which forms the basis for later emerging self and object representations. We have emphasized that the dynamic interactive process itself, the reciprocal interplay as each partner coordinates with the other from moment-to-moment, will be represented. The work reported here deepens this argument, specifically with respect to the dialogic timing dimension of early interactions, the importance of the concept of *degree of coordination,* the role of partner/site context in the organization of timing, particularly its bidirectional nature, and various modes of coordination of vocal rhythms. If dyad-specific patterns of coordination are represented in procedural memory by the infant (and mother), they may bias the trajectory of developing personality styles (such as joining, interrupting, vigilant tracking). The fact that the dialogic timing procedures predicted "social/cognitive" outcomes strengthens the argument that these early timing procedures are relevant to subsequent development.

Our argument that the infant represents these dialogic procedures is further enhanced by Flaster's (1995) reanalysis of this same group of 4-month-olds' dyads. From the lab (but not the home) data, the infant's degree of timing coordination with mother (M → I) predicted the infant's degree of coordination with stranger (S → I), in simultaneous moments (ISS and NSS). In this sense, when challenged by novelty, infants generalized their degree of coordination from mother to stranger. This generalization suggests that the infants indeed represented (procedurally) the degree of coordination. (We note that this generalization does not mean that the infant's degree of coordination with the stranger was the *same* as that with the mother, only that the former could be predicted from the latter). Furthermore, as a function of different attachment classifications (A, B, and D), infants at age 4 months generalized degree of coordination from mother to stranger differently, using different vocal states. This finding suggests that the developing attachment climate at age 4 months is already relevant to the way infants use their procedural representations, as they move from interacting with mother to stranger. The importance of the infant's capacity to generalize level of contingency has been noted by Tarabulsy et al. (1996) and Dunham and Dunham (1990). Similar to Papousek and Papousek (1979, 1987), Watson (1985, 1994), and Gergely and Watson (1996), Tarabulsy et al. (1996) argued that the infant's capacity to detect and use different degrees of contingency suggests that contingency detection "possesses potential as a motivational and adaptational construct, providing a process by which the infant and environment interact and leading to representations of the external world" (p. 33).

Our proposal that the infant represents these dialogic coordinations procedurally has much in common with the work of Stern (1977, 1985, 1995), who noted that ". . . subjective changes in time may provide the

112

key to how affective experiences are represented. . . . We have largely over-looked the idea that temporal contours provide the backbone that per-mits affective experiences to be represented" (1995, p. 84). He introduced the term *temporal feeling shape* to refer to the temporal contour of shifts in affect, arousal, activation, and/or motivation, which organize memory and experience and provide a basic format for representing experience. Stern emphasized that it is the small, daily, repetitive, nonverbal split-second microevents that are the stuff of early representations, and it is the repet-itiveness of events that makes them easily represented. "Repeated micro-events are assumed to be the basic building blocks of the representational world of both the infant and the parent" (Stern, 1995, p. 63). Each of the six vocal parameters of our model is such a microevent, transacted by both partners at the split-second level, repeating across the interaction, organizing, for example, whose turn it is, whether either partner is in-creasing or decreasing vocal activity, who is tracking whom, and to what degree.

Trevarthen (1979, 1993), who also argued for the central role of cor-respondences (of form, timing, and intensity) as the basis for dialogic protoconversation and intersubjectivity, maintained that timing is funda-mental to interpersonal coordination. In his view, correspondences are based on the coupling of oscillators or neural clocks. Although Tre-varthen emphasized periodic rather than nonperiodic rhythms, his formu-lation fits a procedural theory of representation and showcases the role of rhythmic coordination.

In conclusion, the dialogic nature of early procedural representation is echoed by authors in other fields. For example, the philosopher Charles Taylor (1991) has also argued for the dialogic origin of mind: "The gen-eral feature of human life that I want to evoke is its fundamentally dia-logical character. We become full human agents . . . through our acquisition of rich human languages of expression . . . in a broad sense, covering not only the words we speak but also other modes of expression . . . including the languages of art, of gesture. . . . But we are inducted into these . . . through exchanges with others who matter to us. . . . The genesis of the human mind is in this sense not 'monological,' . . . but 'dialogical' . . . the making and sustaining of our identity . . . remains dialogical through-out our lives" (pp. 34–35).

LIMITATIONS OF THE STUDY

Several limitations of the study affect its generalizability. The mothers were middle to upper-middle socioeconomic class, Caucasian, in stable relationships, and almost all were married. Linguistic considerations required that all the mothers spoke English as their first language. The results may not be applicable to subjects falling outside these categories.

Another possible limitation is that many statistical tests were conducted, and no effort was made to adjust their probability levels. We did not make this adjustment because this is the first major study of its kind and was essentially an exploration of the questions that it posed; we did not want to discard results that seemed potentially interesting and made sense theoretically. However, all statistical analyses conducted were designed prior to the project.

The generalizability of the attachment findings for the C (anxious-resistant) and D (disorganized) categories may be limited by the small numbers of subjects in these categories, although the prevalence in this study was comparable to that of other American samples. Because the D attachment category has received little research on interactive origins prior to age 12 months, it seemed particularly important to explore this category.

SUMMARY

In the mid 1980s, rhythmic coordination was theorized to be a key organizing process in early social development. But the functional advantage it might have for infant development remained vaguely defined, and predictive data demonstrating developmental outcomes were sparse. We showed that, analogous to those of conversing adults, preverbal vocal rhythms and their coordination at age 4 months carry various emotional qualities, including information about the infant's first differentiation from the original mother-infant matrix, as well as about 12-month-olds' individual differences in developing attachment and cognition. In the outcome predictions, *degree* of coordination was the operative dimension, rather its presence or absence. The 4-month-old's CIT was proposed to be one factor in the transmission of attachment security, as well as an index of the infant's novelty response relevant to cognition. Both attachment and cognition had salient bidirectional (reciprocal) prediction patterns (across the group), illustrating a proposal of general systems theories that such coordination is one engine of development.

A 4-month-old's novelty gradient from the double familiarity of mother-infant at home to the double novelty of stranger-infant in the lab organized vocal rhythms and CIT. Differences in level of vocal state activity, per dyad bidirectionality, as well as prediction of outcomes, in mother-infant versus stranger-infant interactions, provide a way of defining the infant's early differentiation from mother. The more active forms of vocal rhythm (shorter pauses) in conjunction with a constriction of the turn duration and heightened per dyad bidirectionality provide one aspect of the emotional meaning of the stranger to the infant. In contrast, the mother-infant interaction is more relaxed, in the sense that the infant's vocal rhythms are less active, with longer pauses (in conjunction with longer turns), and there is less per dyad bidirectional coordination.

The *meaning* of CIT was entirely dependent on context: partner, site, and developmental task. Midrange CIT was optimal for attachment, whereas high CIT (between stranger and infant in the lab) was optimal for cognition. A dramatic example of the contextual meaning of CIT occurred in two outcome predictions, where the same pattern, namely, bidirectional CIT in the high range, had opposite meanings: favorable for Bayley but unfavorable for attachment. High response to novelty, as seen in high stranger-infant coordination in the lab, is favorable for cognition. But midrange degree of coordination may allow more flexibility in a secure attachment climate, whereas very high coordination may index an insecure, hypervigilant process. High degrees of coordination may be the dyad's attempt to make the interaction more predictable under conditions of uncertainty, challenge, or threat.

This work further articulates and refines a coconstructed systems model of infant development, in terms of the meaning of bidirectionality at age 4 months, its role in developmental outcomes, and the neglected role of unidirectional coordination. First, our results refine the central concept of mutual (bidirectional) regulation at age 4 months, which became prominent through the work of Sander (1977), Stern (1977), and Tronick (1989). Although the concept is often used as if it referred to a particular dyad, the operational definitions have generally been *across group*. Using either definition, bidirectional CIT was far from ubiquitous at age 4 months, although the across-group definition yielded higher indices than per dyad. However, it was only the per dyad definition of bidirectionality that revealed stranger-infant in the lab to be more bidirectional than mother-infant at home. Here, greater reciprocal CIT indexed novelty: a stranger in a strange place. This finding suggests a reconceptualization of the concept of per dyad bidirectional CIT at age 4 months as a measure of interactive vigilance, such that greater interpersonal predictability is required in conditions of novelty or challenge.

Second, to see the role of bidirectional coordination in the prediction of developmental outcomes, the across-group definition was required. The per dyad definition of bidirectionality revealed information about partner/site novelty at age 4 months, but not outcomes; the across-group definition did not reveal much about novelty, but did predict outcomes. It is striking that the two definitions of bidirectionality revealed such different roles for bidirectional coordination, tapping different aspects of the system.

115

Much literature has tended to assume that bidirectional coordination is a hallmark of a well-functioning developmental process (Beebe & Lachmann, 1988; Stern, 1977, 1985; Tronick, 1989). Instead, bidirectionality must be evaluated in conjunction with its *degree*, because, for example, both secure and disorganized attachment yielded bidirectional predictions, differentiated only by *degree* of CIT. Furthermore, greater bidirectional coordination was optimal for Bayley scores, but not for attachment. Thus "more is not necessarily better," as noted by Cohn and Elmore (1988).

Finally, our results point to the importance of conceptualizing the role of unidirectional coordination, heretofore relatively neglected. At age 4 months, in the highest familiarity condition of mother and infant at home, unidirectional CIT was almost as frequent as bidirectional. In predicting outcomes, avoidant and anxious-resistant attachment classifications were predicted from unidirectional stranger-infant coordination.

Our notions of the role of rhythmic coordination in infant development have thus been refined: It does not have a single meaning, and it does not itself convey advantage or disadvantage. High CIT can be optimal or excessive, depending on developmental task. To further our understanding of coordination in infant development, it is essential to consider per dyad as well as across-group bidirectionality, the *degree* of coordination, and *unidirectional* coordination, all in relation to particular partner, site, and developmental task.

It is remarkable that completely automated scoring of 12 minutes of vocal interaction between adult and 4-month-old infant can predict the infant's outcomes on conventional tests 8 months later. Dyadic timing alone, measured here by vocal rhythms and their coordination, is a key variable that operates crossmodally and interpersonally. It can be conceptualized as a collective variable, described by Zeskind and Marshall (1991) as one that reflects the compressed activity of multiply coordinated systems. Furthermore, interpersonal theories in both development and psychoanalysis informed our systems approach to dyadic timing.

Dialogic rhythms are procedures for regulating the timing of face-to-face communication at age 4 months, and are already analogues of the social-emotional dance-to-be at age 1 year, as well as an index of the infant's novelty response relevant to cognition. These procedures get at different kinds of moments in the exchange: managing attention, activity level, turn taking, joining, interruption, yielding, and tracking. We argue that these interpersonal patterns are represented in procedural memory by mother and infant. The pragmatics of preverbal dialogue can be construed as manifesting a heterotypic continuity of timing procedures. This work further defines a fundamental dyadic timing matrix, which guides the trajectory of relatedness, informing all relational theories of development.

REFERENCES

Abelson, R. P. (1995). *Statistics as principled argument*. Hillsdale, NJ: Erlbaum.

Abrahamson, D., Brackbill, Y., Carpenter, R., & Fitzgerald, H. (1970). Interaction of stimulus and response in infant conditioning. *Psychosomatic Medicine*, **32**, 319–325.

Ackerman, M. (1987). *New variables to be considered in the prediction to attachment at one year*. Doctoral dissertation, Yeshiva University.

Ainsworth, M., Blehar, M., Waters, E., & Wall, S. (1978). *Patterns of attachment: A psychological study of the strange situation*. Hillsdale, NJ: Erlbaum.

Allen, T., Walker, K., Symonds, L., & Marcell, M. (1977). Intrasensory and intersensory perception of temporal sequences during infancy. *Developmental Psychology*, **13**, 225–229.

Als, H. (1975). *An ethological study of mother-infant interaction*. Doctoral dissertation, University of Pennsylvania.

Altmann, S. (1967). The structure of primate communication. In S. Altman (Ed.), *Social communication among primates*. Chicago: University of Chicago Press.

Anderson, B., Vietze, P., & Dokecki, P. (1977). Reciprocity in vocal interactions of mothers and infants. *Child Development*, **48**, 1676–1681.

Antonucci, T. C., & Levitt, M. J. (1984). Early prediction of attachment security: A multivariate approach. *Infant Behavior and Development*, **7**, 1–18.

Arend, R., Gove, F., & Sroufe A. (1979). Continuity of individual adaptation from infancy to kindergarten: A predictive study of ego resilience and curiosity in preschoolers. *Child Development*, **50**, 950–959.

Bahrick, I., & Watson, J. (1985). Detection of intermodal proprioceptive visual contingency as a potential basis of self-perception in infancy. *Developmental Psychology*, **21**, 963–973.

Bakeman, R., & Brown, J. (1977). Behavioral dialogues: An approach to the assessment of mother-infant interaction. *Child Development*, **48**, 195–203.

Bakeman, R., & Brown, J. V. (1980). Early interaction: Consequences for social and mental development at three years. *Child Development*, **51**, 437–447.

Bates, J. E., Maslin, A., & Frankel, M. A. (1985). Attachment security, mother-child interaction, and temperament as predictors of behavior-problem ratings at three years. In I. Bretherton & E. Waters (Eds.), *Growing points of attachment theory and research*. *Monographs of the Society for Research in Child Development*, **50**(1–2, Serial No. 2309), 167–193.

Bateson, M. C. (1971). The interpersonal context of infant vocalization. *Quarterly Progress Report of the Research Laboratory of Electronics*, **100**, 170–176.

Bateson, M. C. (1975). Mother-infant exchanges: The epigenesis of conversational interaction. In D. Aaronson & R. W. Rieber (Eds.), *Developmental psycholinguistics and* communication disorders: *Annals of the New York Academy of Sciences (Vol. 263).* New York: New York Academy of Sciences.

Bayley, N. (1969). *Manual for the Bayley Scales of Infant Development.* New York: Psychological Corporation.

Bayley, N. (1993). *Bayley Scales of Infant Development* (2nd ed.). San Antonio, TX: Psychological Corporation.

Beckwith, L. (1971a). Relationships between attributes of mothers and their infants' IQ scores. *Child Development, 42,* 1083–1097.

Beckwith, L. (1971b). Relationships between infants' vocalization and their mothers' behavior. *Merrill Palmer Quarterly, 17,* 211–226.

Beckwith, L., Cohen, S. E., Knopp, C. B., Parmalee, A. H., & Marcy, T. G. (1976). Caregiver-infant interaction and early cognitive development in preterm infants. *Child Development, 47*(3), 579–587.

Beebe, B., Alson, D., Jaffe, J., Feldstein, S., & Crown, C. (1988). Vocal congruence in mother-infant play. *Journal of Psycholinguistic Research, 17*(3), 245–259.

Beebe, B., & Gerstman, L. (1980). The "packaging" of maternal stimulation in relation to infant facial-visual engagement: A case study at four months. *Merrill-Palmer Quarterly, 26*(4), 321–339.

Beebe, B., & Jaffe, J. (1992, May). Mother-infant vocal dialogue. *ICIS Abstracts Issue. Infant Behavior and Development, 15,* 48.

Beebe, B., Jaffe, J., Feldstein, S., Mays, K., & Alson, D. (1985). Interpersonal timing: The application of an adult dialogue model to mother-infant vocal and kinesic interactions. In T. Field (Ed.), *Infant social perception.* New York: Ablex.

Beebe, B., Jaffe, J., & Lachmann, F. (1992). A dyadic systems view of communication. In N. Skolnick & S. Warshaw (Eds.), *Relational perspectives in psychoanalysis.* Hillsdale, NJ: Analytic Press.

Beebe, B., Jaffe, J., Lachmann, F., Feldstein, S., Crown, C., & Jasnow, J. (2000). Systems models in development and psychoanalysis: The case of vocal rhythm coordination and attachment. *Infant Mental Health Journal, 21*(1–2), 99–122.

Beebe, B. & Lachmann, F. (1988). The contribution of mother-infant mutual influence to the origins of self and object representations. *Psychoanalytic Psychology, 5*(4), 304–337.

Beebe, B., & Lachmann, F. (1994). Representation and internalization in infancy: Three principles of salience. *Psychoanalytic Psychology, 11*(2), 127–165.

Beebe, B., Lachmann, F., & Jaffe, J. (1997). Mother-infant interaction structures and presymbolic self and object representations. *Psychoanalytic Dialogues, 7*(2), 133–182.

Beebe, B., & Stern, D. (1977). Engagement-disengagement and early object experiences. In N. Freedman & S. Grand (Eds.), *Communicative structures and psychic structures.* New York: Plenum Press.

Beebe, B., Stern, D., & Jaffe, J. (1979). The kinesic rhythm of mother-infant interactions. In A. W. Siegman & S. Feldstein (Eds.), *Of speech and time: Temporal patterns in interpersonal contexts.* Hillsdale, NJ: Erlbaum.

Belsky, J. (1980). Mother-infant interaction at home and in the laboratory: A comparative study. *Journal of Genetic Psychology, 137,* 37–47.

Belsky, J., Rovine, M., & Taylor, D. (1984). The Pennsylvania Infant and Family Development Project, III: The origins of individual differences in infant-mother attachment: Maternal and infant contributions. *Child Development, 55,* 718–728.

Berg, C., & Sternberg, R. (1985). Response to novelty: Continuity vs. discontinuity in the developmental course of intelligence. In H. Reese (Ed.), *Advances in child development and behavior (Vol. 19).* San Diego, CA: Academic Press.

Bigelow, A. (1998). Infants'sensitivity to familiar imperfect contingencies in social interaction. *Infant Behavior and Development, 21*(1), 149–162.

Blehar, M. C., Lieberman, A. F., & Ainsworth, M. (1977). Early face-to-face interaction and its relation to later infant-mother attachment. *Child Development, 48,* 182–194.

Bloom, L. (1993). *The transition from infancy to language.* New York: Cambridge University Press.

Bloom, L. (1994). Meaning and expression. In W. Overton & D. Palermo (Eds.), *The nature and ontogenesis of meaning.* Hillsdale, NJ: Erlbaum.

Bornstein, M. (1985). Infant into adult: Unity to diversity in the development of visual categorization. In J. Mehler & R. Fox (Eds.), *Neonate cognition.* Hillsdale, NJ: Erlbaum.

Bornstein, M., & Sigman, M. D. (1986). Continuity in mental development from infancy. *Child Development, 57,* 251–274.

Bowlby, J. (1958). The nature of the child's tie to his mother. *Journal of Psychoanalysis, 39,* 350–373.

Bowlby, J. (1969). Attachment and loss. *Attachment (Vol. 1).* New York: Basic Books.

Brackbill, Y. (1975). Continuous stimulation and arousal level in infancy: Effects of stimulus intensity and stress. *Child Development, 46,* 364–369.

Brazelton, T. B., Kozlowski, B., & Main, M. (1974). The origins of reciprocity. In M. Lewis & L. Rosenblum (Eds.), *The effect of the infant on its caregiver.* New York: Elsevier.

Bruner, J. (1975). The ontogenesis of speech acts. *Journal of Child Language, 2,* 1–19.

Bruner, J. (1983). *Child's talk: Learning to use language.* New York: Norton.

Bullowa, M. (1979). *Before speech: The beginnings of human communication.* New York: Cambridge University Press.

Buros, O. K. (1978). *The eighth mental measurements yearbook.* Highland Park, NJ: The Gryphon Press.

Byers, P. (1976). Biological rhythms as information channels in communication behavior. In P. P. G. Bateson & P. H. Klopfer (Eds.), *Perspectives in ethology (Vol. 2).* New York: Plenum Press.

Cappella, J. N. (1981). Mutual influence in expressive behavior: Adult-adult and infant-adult dyadic interaction. *Psychological Bulletin, 89,* 101–132.

Cappella, J. N. (1996). Dynamic coordination of vocal and kinesic behavior in dyadic interaction. In J. Watt & C. Van Lear (Eds.), *Dynamic patterns in communication processes.* London: Sage Publications.

Cassidy, J. (1994). Emotion regulation: Influences of attachment relationships. In N. Fox (Ed.), *The development of emotion regulation. Monographs of the Society for Research in Child Development, 59*(2–3, Serial No. 240), 2228–2249.

Cassotta, L., Feldstein, S., & Jaffe, J. (1967, December). The stability and modifiability of individual vocal characteristics in stress and nonstress interviews. *Research Bulletin No. 2.* New York: The William Alanson White Institute.

Chapple, E. D. (1970). *Culture and biological man.* New York: Holt, Rinehart, & Winston.

Chapple, E. D. (1971). Toward a mathematical model of interaction: Some preliminary considerations. In P. Kay (Ed.), *Explorations in mathematical anthropology.* Cambridge, MA: MIT Press.

Cohn, J., Campbell, S. B., Matias, R., & Hopkins, J. (1990). Face-to-face interactions of depressed and non-depressed mother-infant pairs at 2 months. *Developmental Psychology, 26*(1), 15–23.

Cohn, J., Campbell, S., & Ross, S. (1992). Infant response in the still-face paradigm at 6 months predicts avoidant and secure attachment at 12 months. *Development & Psychopathology, 3,* 367–376.

Cohn, J., & Elmore, M. (1988). Effect of contingent changes in mothers' affective expression on the organization of behavior in 3-month-old infants. *Infant Behavior and Development, 11,* 493–505.

Cohn, J., Matias, R., Tronick, E., Connell, D., & Lyons-Ruth, K. (1986). Face-to-face interactions, spontaneous and structured, of mothers with depressive symptoms. In T. Field & E. Tronick (Eds.), *Maternal depression and infant disturbance. New directions for child development* (Vol. 34). San Francisco: Jossey-Bass.

Cohn, J., & Tronick, E. (1988). Mother-infant face-to-face interaction: Influence is bidirectional and unrelated to periodic cycles in either partner's behavior. *Developmental Psychology,* **24,** 386–392.

Cohn, J., & Tronick, E. (1989). Specificity of infant response to mother's affective behavior. *Journal of the American Academy of Child and Adolescent Psychiatry,* **28,** 242–248.

Collis, G. (1979). Describing the structure of social interaction in infancy. In M. Bullowa (Ed.), *Before speech: The beginning of interpersonal communication.* Cambridge: Cambridge University Press.

Colombo, J., Mitchell, D., Dodd, J., Coldren, J., & Horowitz, F. (1989). Longitudinal correlates of infant attention in the paired-comparison paradigm. *Intelligence,* **13,** 33–42.

Condon, W. S. (1979). Neonatal entrainment and enculturation. In M. Bullowa (Ed.), *Before speech: The beginnings of human communication.* London: Cambridge University Press.

Crockenberg, S. (1983). Early mother and infant antecedents of Bayley skill performance at 21 months. *Developmental Psychology,* **19,** 727–730.

Crown, C. (1991). Coordinated interpersonal timing of vision and voice as a function of interpersonal attraction. *Journal of Language and Social Psychology,* **10**(1), 29–46.

Crown, C., Feldstein, S., Jasnow, M., Beebe, B., Wagman, I., Gordon, S., Fox, H., & Jaffe, J. (1988). *The cross-modal coordination of interpersonal timing: Neonatal gaze with adult vocal behavior.* Abstract, International Conference on Infant Studies, Washington, DC.

DeCasper, A., & Carstens, A. (1980). Contingencies of stimulation: Effects on learning and emotion in neonates. *Infant Behavior and Development,* **9,** 19–36.

DeCasper, A. J., & Fifer, W. P. (1980). *Science,* **208,** 1174–1176.

Delack, J. (1976). Aspects of infant speech development in the first year of life. *Canadian Journal of Linguistics,* **21,** 17–37.

Demaney, L., McKenzie, B., & Vurpillot, E. (1977). Rhythmic perception in infancy. *Nature,* **266,** 718–719.

DeWolff, M., & van Ijzendoorn, M. (1997). Sensitivity and attachment: A meta-analysis on parental antecedents of infant attachment. *Child Development,* **68**(4), 571–591.

Dougherty, T., & Haith, M. (1997). Infant expectations and reaction time as predictors of childhood speed of processing and IQ. *Developmental Psychology,* **33,** 146–155.

Dunham, P., & Dunham, F. (1990). Effects of mother-infant social interactions on infants' subsequent contingency task performance. *Child Development,* **61,** 785–793.

Egeland, B., & Farber, E. (1984). Infant-mother attachment: Factors related to its development and changes over time. *Child Development,* **55,** 753–771.

Ellsworth, C., Muir, D., & Hains, S. (1993). Social competence and person-object differentiation: An analysis of the still-face effect. *Developmental Psychology,* **29,** 3–73.

Emde, R., Biringen, Z., Clyman, R., & Oppenheim, D. (1991). The moral self of infancy: Affective core and procedural knowledge. *Developmental Review,* **11,** 251–270.

Erickson, M., Sroufe, A., & Egeland, B. (1983). The relationship between quality of attachment and behavior problems in preschool in a high-risk sample. In I. Bretherton & E. Waters (Eds.), *Growing points in attachment theory and research. Monographs for the Society for Research in Child Development,* **50**(1–2, Serial No. 209).

Fagan, J. (1982). Infant memory. In T. Field, A. Huston, H. Quay, L. Troll, & G. Finley (Eds.), *Review of human development.* New York: Wiley.

Fagan, J., & McGrath, S. (1981). Infant recognition, memory and later intelligence. *Intelligence,* **5,** 121–130.

Fagan, J. F., & Shepherd, P. A. (1987). *The Fagan Test of Infant Intelligence Training Manual (Vol. 4).* Cleveland: Infantest Corporation.

Fagen, J. W., Morrongiello, B. A., Rovee-Collier, C., & Gekoski, M. J. (1984). Expectancies and memory retrieval in three-month-old infants. *Child Development, 55,* 936–943.

Fairbairn, W. (1952). *Psychoanalytic studies of the personality.* London: Routledge & Kegan Paul. (Original work published 1941.)

Feldman, R., & Greenbaum, C. (1997). Affect regulation and synchrony in mother-infant play as precursors to the development of symbolic competence. *Infant Mental Health Journal, 18*(1), 4–23.

Feldman, R., Greenbaum, C., Yirmiya, N., & Mayes, L. (1996). Relations between cyclicity and regulation in mother-infant interaction at 3 and 9 months and cognition at 2 years. *Journal of Applied Developmental Psychology, 17,* 347–365.

Feldstein, S. (1962). The relationship of interpersonal involvement and affectiveness of content to the verbal communication of schizophrenic patients. *Journal of Abnormal and Social Psychology, 64,* 29–45.

Feldstein, S. (1972). Temporal patterns of dialogue: Basic research and reconsiderations. In A. Siegman & B. Pope (Eds.), *Studies in dyadic communication.* New York: Pergamon Press.

Feldstein, S. (1998). Some nonobvious consequences of monitoring time in conversation. In M. Palmer & G. Barnett (Eds.), *Mutual influence in interpersonal communication: Theory and research in cognition, affect, and behavior. Progress in communication science (Vol. 14).*

Feldstein, S., Crown, C., & Jaffe, J. (1991). Expectation and extraversion: Influencing the perceived rate of tone-silence sequences. *Bulletin of the Psychonomic Society, 29*(5), 395–398.

Feldstein, S., & Jaffe, J. (1963). Language predictability as a function of psychotherapeutic interaction. *Journal of Consulting Psychology, 27*(2), 123–126.

Feldstein, S., Jaffe, J., Beebe, B., Crown, C. L., Jasnow, M., Fox, H., & Gordon, S. (1993). Coordinated timing in adult-infant vocal interactions: A cross-site replication. *Infant Behavior & Development, 16,* 455–470.

Feldstein, S., & Welkowitz, J. (1978). A chronography of conversation: In defense of an objective approach. In A. W. Siegman & S. Feldstein (Eds.), *Nonverbal behavior and communication.* Hillsdale, NJ: Erlbaum.

Field, T. (1978). The three R's of infant-adult interactions: Rhythms, repertoires, and responsivity. *Journal of Pediatric Psychology, 3*(3), 131–136.

Field, T. (1981). Infant gaze aversion and heart rate during face-to-face interactions. *Infant Behavior and Development, 4,* 307–315.

Field, T. (1994). The effects of mother's physical and emotional unavailability on emotion regulation. In N. Fox (Ed.), *The development of emotion regulation. Monographs of the Society for Research on Child Development, 59*(2–3, Serial No. 240).

Field, T., Goldstein, S., & Guthertz, M. (1990). Behavior-state matching and synchrony in mother-infant interactions of depressed and nondepressed dyads. *Developmental Psychology, 26,* 7–14.

Field, T., Healy, B., & LeBlanc, W.(1989). Matching and synchrony of behavior states and heart rate in mother-infant interactions of nondepressed versus "depressed" dyads. *Developmental Psychology, 26,* 7–14.

Fields, R. D., Eshete, F., Stevens, B., & Itoh, K. (1997). Action potential-dependent regulation of gene expression: Temporal specificity in Ca^{2+}, cAMP-responsive element binding proteins, and mitogen-activated protein kinase signaling. *Journal of Neuroscience, 17*(19), 7252–7266.

Finkelstein, N. W., & Ramey, C. T. (1977). Learning to control the environment in infancy. *Child Development, 48,* 806–819.

Flanagan, D. P., & Alphonso, V. C. (1995). A critical review of the technical characteristics of new and recently revised intelligence tests for preschool children. *Journal of Psychoeducational Assessment*, **13**, 66–90.

Flaster, C. J. (1995). *Patterns of predictability among mother-infant, stranger-infant, and mother-stranger dyads at four months distinguish infant attachment status at one year.* Unpublished doctoral dissertation, Yeshiva University, New York.

Fogel, A. (1977). Temporal organization in mother-infant face-to-face interaction. In H. R. Schaffer (Ed.), *Studies in mother-infant interaction*. London: Academic Press.

Fogel, A. (1988). Cyclicity and stability in mother-infant face-to-face interaction: A comment on Cohn and Tronick (1988). *Developmental Psychology*, **24**(3), 393–395.

Fogel, A. (1993a). *Developing through relationships*. Chicago: University of Chicago Press.

Fogel, A. (1993b). Two principles of communication: Co-regulation and framing. In J. Nadel & L. Camaioni (Eds.), *New perspectives in early communicative development*. London: Routledge.

Fox, N. (1994). The development of emotion regulation: Introduction to part 3. *Monographs of the Society for Research in Child Development*, **59**(2–3, Serial No. 240).

Frankenberg, W. K., Goldstein, A. D., & Camp, B. W. (1971). The revised Denver Developmental Screening Test: Its accuracy as a screening instrument. *Journal of Pediatrics*, **79**(6), 988–995.

Freedle, R., & Lewis, M. (1977). Prelinguistic conversations. In M. Lewis & L. A. Rosenblum (Eds.), *Interaction, conversation and the development of language*. New York: Wiley.

Gergely, G., & Watson, J. (1996). The social biofeedback theory of parental affect-mirroring: The development of emotional self-awareness and self-control in infancy. *The International Journal of Psychoanalysis*, **77**, 1181–1212.

Gianino, A., & Tronick, E. (1988). The mutual regulation model: The infant's self and interactive regulation coping and defense. In T. Field, P. McCabe, & N. Schneiderman (Eds.), *Stress and coping*. Hillsdale, NJ: Erlbaum.

Gleick, J. (1987). *Chaos: Making a new science*. New York: Penguin.

Goldberg, S. (1977). Social competence in infancy: A model of parent-infant interaction. *Merrill-Palmer Quarterly*, **23**(3), 163–177.

Gottlieb, G. (1992). *Individual development and evolution: The genesis of novel behavior*. New York: Oxford University Press.

Gottlieb, G., Wahlsten, D., & Lickliter, R. (1998). The significance of biology for human development: A developmental psychobiological systems view. In W. Damon & R. Lerner (Eds.), *Handbook of child psychology, Vol. 1* (5th ed.). New York: Wiley.

Gottman, J. M. (1979). *Marital interactions*. New York: Academic Press.

Gottman, J. M. (1981). *Time series analysis: A comprehensive introduction for social scientists*. Cambridge: Cambridge University Press.

Gottman, J., & Ringland, J. (1981). Analysis of dominance and bi-directionality in social development. *Child Development*, **52**, 393–412.

Greenberg, J., & Mitchell, S. (1983). *Object relations in psychoanalytic theory*. Cambridge, MA: Harvard University Press.

Grigsby, J., & Hartlaub, G. (1994). Procedural learning and the development and stability of character. *Perceptual Motor Skills*, **79**, 355–370.

Grossman, K., Grossman, K., Spangler, G., Seuss, G., & Unzer, L. (1985). Maternal sensitivity and newborns' orientation responses as related to quality of attachment in northern Germany. In I. Bretherton, and E. Waters (Eds.), *Monographs of the Society for Research in Child Development*, **50**(1–2, Serial No. 209).

Haith, M., Hazan, C., & Goodman, G. (1988). Expectation and anticipation of dynamic visual events by 3.5 month old babies. *Child Development*, **59**, 467–479.

Halburg, F. (1960). Temporal coordination of physiologic functions. *Symposia on Quantitative Biology*, **25**, 289–310.

Hamilton, V. (1998). John Bowlby: An ethological basis for psychoanalysis. In J. Reppen (Ed.), *Beyond Freud*. Hillsdale, NJ: Analytic Press.

Hardy-Brown, K., Plomin, R., & DeFries, J. (1981). Genetic and environmental influences on rate of communicative development in the first year of life. *Developmental Psychology*, **17**(6), 704–717.

Hedge, B. J., Everitt, B. S., & Frith, C. D. (1978). The role of gaze in dialogue. *Acta Psychologica*, **42**, 453–475.

Heller, A. (1967). Probabilistic automata and stochastic transformations. *Mathematical Systems Theory*, **1**, 197–208.

Hinde, R. A. (1982). Attachment: Some conceptual and biological issues. In C. Parkes & J. Stevenson-Hinde (Eds.), *The place of attachment in human behavior*. New York: Basic Books.

Hitchcock, D. (1992). *The regulation of attention in full-term and premature mother-toddler dyads*. Doctoral dissertation, Yeshiva University.

Hofer, M. (1994). Hidden regulators in attachment, separation and loss. In N. Fox (Ed.), *The development of emotion regulation: Biological and behavioral considerations. Monographs of the Society for Research in Child Development*, **59**(2–3, Serial No. 240).

Hollingshead, A. (1978). *Four-factor index of social status*. Unpublished manuscript, Yale University.

Iberall, A. S., & McCulloch, W. S. (1969). The organizing principle of complex living systems. *Journal of Basic Engineering*, **91**, 290–294.

Isabella, R., & Belsky, J. (1991). Interactional synchrony and the origins of infant-mother attachment: A replication study. *Child Development*, **62**, 373–384.

Izard, C., Haynes, O., Chisholm, G., & Beak, K. (1991). Emotional determinants of infant-mother attachment. *Child Development*, **62** (5), 906–917.

Jaffe, J. (1958). Language of the dyad: A method of interaction analysis in psychiatric interviews. *Psychiatry*, **21**, 249–258.

Jaffe, J. (1962). Verbal behavior analysis in psychiatric interviews with the aid of digital computers. In D. McK. Rioch & E. Weinstein (Eds.), *Disorders of communication. Proceedings of the Association of Nervous and Mental Disease, Vol. XLII*, 389–407.

Jaffe, J. (1978). Parliamentary procedure and the brain. In A. Siegman & S. Feldstein (Eds.), *Nonverbal behavior and communication*. Hillsdale, NJ: Erlbaum.

Jaffe, J., Anderson, S., & Rieber, R. (1973a). Research approaches to disorder of speech rate. *Journal of Communication Disorders*, **6**, 225–246.

Jaffe, J., Cassotta, L., & Feldstein, S. (1964). Markovian model of time patterns of speech. *Science*, **144**, 884–886.

Jaffe, J., & Feldstein, S. (1970). *Rhythms of dialogue*. New York: Academic Press.

Jaffe, J., & Norman, D. (1964). A simulation of the time patterns of dialogue (Scientific Report No. CS-4). Cambridge, MA: Harvard University Center for Cognitive Studies.

Jaffe, J., Stern, D., & Peery, C. (1973b). "Conversational" coupling of gaze behavior in prelinguistic human development. *Journal of Psycholinguistic Research*, **2**, 321–329.

Jasnow, M., Crown, C., Feldstein, S., Taylor, L., Beebe, B., & Jaffe, J. (1988). Coordinated interpersonal timing of Downs and nondelayed infants with their mothers: Evidence for a buffered mechanism of social interaction. *Biological Bulletin*, **175**, 355–360.

Jasnow, M., & Feldstein, S. (1986). Adult-like temporal characteristics of mother-infant vocal interactions. *Child Development*, **57**, 754–761.

Kaye, K. (1982). *The mental and social life of babies: How parents create persons*. Chicago: University of Chicago Press.

Kaye, K., & Wells, A. (1980). Mothers' jiggling and the burst-pause pattern in neonatal sucking. *Infant Behavior and Development*, **3**, 29–46.

Keller, H., Lohaus, A., Volker, S., Cappenberg, M., & Chasiotis, A. (1999). Temporal contingency as an independent component of parenting behavior. *Child Development*, **70**(2), 474–485.

Kiser, L., Bates, F., Maslin, C., & Bayles, K. (1986). Mother-infant play at six months as a predictor of attachment security at thirteen months. *Journal of the American Academy of Child Psychiatry*, **25**(1), 68–75.

Kobak, R., & Sceery, A. (1988). Attachment in late adolescence: Working models, affect regulation, and representation of self and others. *Child Development*, **59**, 135–146.

Kogan, J. H. (1996). Spaced training induces normal long-term memory in CREB mutant mice. *Current Biology*, **7**, 1–11.

Kohlberg, L. (1969). Stage and sequence: The cognitive developmental approach to socialization. In D. A. Goslin (Ed.), *Handbook of socialization theory and research*. Chicago: Rand-McNally.

Korner, A., & Thoman, E. B. (1972). The relative efficacy of contact and vertibular-proprioceptive stimulation in soothing neonates. *Child Development*, **43**, 443–453.

Koulomzin, M. (1993). *Attention, affect, self-comfort and subsequent attachment in four month old infants*. Unpublished doctoral dissertation, Ferkauf Graduate School, Yeshiva University.

Koulomzin, M., Beebe, B., Jaffe, J., & Feldstein, S. (1993, March). Infant self-comfort, disorganized scanning, facial distress & bodily approach in face-to-face play at 4 months discriminate "A" vs "B" attachment at one year. [Abstract] *Proceedings of the Society for Research in Child Development*, 446.

Kuhn, T. S. (1962). *The structure of scientific revolutions*. Chicago: University of Chicago Press.

Kurzweill, S. (1988). Recognition of mother from multisensory interactions in early infancy. *Infant Behavior and Development*, **11**, 235–243.

Lamb, M. E., Thompson, R. A., Gardner, W. P., Charnov, E. L., & Estes, D. (1984). Security of infantile attachment as assessed in the "strange situation": Its study and biological interpretation. *Behavioral and Brain Sciences*, **7**, 127–171.

Langhorst, B., & Fogel, A. (1982). Cross-validation of microanalytic approaches to face-to-face interaction. Paper presented at the International Conference on Infant Studies, Austin,TX.

Lashley, K. (1954). The problem of serial order in behavior. In F. A. Beach, K. O. Hebb, C. T. Morgan, & H. W. Nissen (Eds.), *The neuropsychology of Lashley*. New York: McGraw-Hill.

Lawson, K. (1980). Spatial and temporal congruity and auditory visual integration in infants. *Developmental Psychology*, **16**, 185–192.

Lenneberg, E. (1967). *Biological foundations of language*. New York: Wiley.

Lerner, R. (1998). Theories of human development: Contemporary perspectives. In W. Damon & R. Lerner (Eds.), *Handbook of child psychology, Vol. 1* (5th ed.). New York: Wiley.

Lester, B. M., Hoffman, J., & Brazelton, T. B. (1985). The rhythmic structure of mother-infant interaction in term and preterm infants. *Child Development*, **56**, 15–27.

Lester, B. M., & Seifer, R. (1990, February). Antecedants of attachment. In T. Anders, *The origins and nature of attachment in infants and mother*. Symposium conducted at the Boston Institute for the Development of Infants and Parents, Boston, MA.

Lewedag, V., Oller, D. K., & Lunch, M. (1994). Infants' vocalization patterns across home and laboratory environments. *First Language*, **14**, 49–65.

Lewin, K. (1935). *A dynamic theory of personality*. New York: McGraw-Hill.

Lewis, M., & Brooks, J. (1975). Infant's social perception: A constructivist view. In L. Cohen & P. Salapatek (Eds.), *Infant perception: From sensations to cognition (Vol. 2)*. New York: Academic Press.

Lewis, M., & Brooks-Gunn, J. (1981).Visual attention at three months as a predictor of cognitive functioning at two years of age. *Intelligence*, **5**, 131–140.

Lewis, M., & Feiring, C. (1989). Infant-mother and mother-infant interaction behavior and subsequent attachment. *Child Development*, **60**, 831–837.

Lewis, M., Feiring, C., McGuffog, C., & Jaskir, J. (1984). Predicting psychopathology in six year olds from early social relations. *Child Development*, **55**, 123–136.

Lewis, M., & Goldberg, S. (1969). Perceptual-cognitive development in infancy: A generalized expectancy model as a function of the mother-infant interaction. *Merrill-Palmer Quarterly*, **15**, 81–100.

Lewis, M., Jaskir, J., & Enright, M. (1986). The development of mental abilities in infancy. *Intelligence*, **10**, 331–354.

Lewis, M., & Rosenblum, L. (Eds.). (1974). *The effect of the infant on its caregiver*. New York: Wiley.

Lewkowicz, D. (1986). Developmental changes in infants' bisensory response to synchronous durations. *Infant Behavior and Development*, **9**, 335–353.

Lewkowicz, D. (1989). The role of temporal factors in infant behavior and development. In I. Levin & D. Zakay (Eds.), *Time and human cognition*. North-Holland: Elsevier Science Publishers.

Lewkowicz, D. (2000). The development of intersensory temporal perception: An epigenetic systems/limitations view. *Psychological Bulletin*, **126**(2), 281–308.

Leyendecker, B., Lamb, M., Fracasso, M. Scholmerich, A., & Larson, D. (1997). Playful interaction and the antecedants of attachment: A longitudinal study of Central American and Euro-American mothers and infants. *Merrill-Palmer Quarterly*, **43**(1), 24–47.

Lichtenberg, J. (1989). *Psychoanalysis and motivation*. Hillsdale, NJ: Analytic Press.

Luce, G. G. (1970). *Biological rhythms in psychiatry and medicine* (PH5 Publication No. 2088). National Clearinghouse for Mental Health Information.

Lyons-Ruth, K. (1998). Attachment disorganization: Unresolved loss, relational violence, and lapses in behavioral and attentional strategies. In J. Cassidy & P. Shaver (Eds.), *Handbook of attachment theory and research*. New York: Guilford Press.

Lyons-Ruth, K., Alpern, L., & Repacholi, B. (1993). Disorganized infant attachment: classification and maternal psychosocial problems as predictors of hostile-aggressive behavior in the preschool classroom. *Child Development*, **64**, 572–585.

Lyons-Ruth, K., Repacholi, B., McCleod, S., & Silva, E. (1991). Disorganized attachment behavior in infancy: Short-term stability and maternal and infant correlates and risk-related subtypes. *Development and Psychopathology*, **3**, 377–396.

Main, M., & Goldwyn, R. (1988/1993). Adult attachment classification system. In M. Main (Ed.), *A typology of human attachment organization: Assessed in discourse, drawings, and interviews*. Unpublished manuscript, University of California at Berkeley.

Main, M., & Hesse, E. (1990). Parents' unresolved traumatic experiences are related to infant disorganized attachment status: Is frightened and/or frightening parental behavior the linking mechanism? In M. Greenberg, D. Cicchetti, & E. Cummings (Eds.), *Attachment in the preschool years: Theory, research, and intervention*. Chicago: University of Chicago Press.

Main, M., Kaplan, N., & Cassidy, J. (1985). Security in infancy, childhood, and adulthood: A move to the level of representation. In I. Bretherton & E. Waters (Eds.), *Monographs of the Society for Research in Child Development*, **50**(1–2, Serial No. 209).

Main, M., & Solomon, J. (1990). Procedures for identifying infants as disorganized/disoriented during the Ainsworth Strange Situation. In M. Greenberg, D. Cichetti, &

E. Cummings (Eds.), *Attachment in the preschool years.* Chicago: University of Chicago Press.

Malatesta, C., Culver, C., Tesman, J., & Shepard, B. (1989). The development of emotion expression during the first two years of life. *Monographs of the Society for Research in Child Development,* **54**(1–2, Serial No. 219).

Mandler, J. M. (1992). How to build a baby: II. Conceptual primitives. *Psychological Review,* **99**, 587–604.

Martin, J. (1972). Rhythmic (hierarchical) versus serial structure in speech and other behavior. *Psychological Review,* **79**, 487–509.

Martin, J. (1981). A longitudinal study of consequences of early mother-infant interaction: A microanalytic approach. *Monographs of the Society for Research in Child Development,* **46**(3, Serial No. 190).

Martin, J., Maccoby, E., Baran, K., & Jacklin, C. (1981). The sequential analysis of mother-child interaction at 18 months: A comparison of microanalytic methods. *Developmental Psychology,* **17**, 146–157.

Masi, W., & Scott, K. (1983). Preterm and full-term infants' visual responses to mothers' and strangers' faces. In T. Field & A. Sostek (Eds.), *Infants born at risk: Physiological perceptual and cognitive processes.* New York: Grune & Stratton.

Mason, M. (1953). *Main currents of scientific thought: A history of the sciences.* New York: Henry Schuman.

Matarazzo, J., Saslow, G., & Hare, P. (1958). Factor analysis of interview interaction behavior. *Journal of Consulting Psychology,* **22**, 419–429.

Matarazzo, J., & Wiens, A. (1972). *The interview: Research on its anatomy and structure.* Chicago: Aldine-Atherton.

Mayer, N., & Tronick, E. (1985). Mother's turn-giving signals and infant turn-taking in mother-infant interaction. In T. Field & N. Fox (Eds.), *Social perception in infants.* Norwood, NJ: Ablex.

McCall, R., & Carriger, M. (1993). A meta-analysis of infant habituation and recognition memory performance as predictors of later IQ. *Child Development,* **64**, 57–79.

Messer, D., & Vietze, P. (1988). Does mutual influence occur during mother-infant social gaze? *Infant Behavior and Development,* **11**, 97–110.

Mikaye, K., Chen, S., & Campos, J. (1985). Infant temperament, mothers mode of interaction, and attachment in Japan: An interim report. *Monographs of the Society for Research in Child Development,* **50**(1–2, Serial No. 209).

Miller, G. (1954). Information theory and the study of speech. In McMillian, B., Grant, D., Fitts, P., McCulloch, W., Miller, G., & Brosin, H. (Eds.), *Current trends in information theory.* Pittsburgh, PA: University of Pittsburgh Press.

Morisset, C., Barnard, K., Greenberg, M., Booth, C., & Spieker, S. (1990). Environmental influences on early language development: The context of social risk. *Development and Psychopathology,* **2**, 127–149.

Mosteller, F. (1949). *Memorandum C: A model for speech and silence distributions.* Unpublished manuscript on the Verzeano-Finesinger Analyzer, Harvard University, Cambridge, MA.

Mounoud, P. (1995). From direct to reflexive (self-knowledge): A recursive model. In P. Rochat (Ed.), *The self in infancy.* Amsterdam: Elsevier.

Muller, U., & Overton, W. (1998). How to grow a baby: A reevaluation of image-schema and Piagetian action approaches to representation. *Human Development,* **41**, 71–111.

O'Connor, M. J., Cohen, S., & Parmalee, A. H. (1984). Infant auditory discrimination in preterm and full-term infants as a predictor of 5-year intelligence. *Developmental Psychology,* **20**, 159–165.

Ostrom, C. (1978). *Time-series analysis: Regression techniques.* Beverly Hills, CA: Sage University Papers.

Overton, W. F. (1994). Contexts of meaning: The computational and the embodied mind. In W. F. Overton & D. Palermo (Eds.), *The nature and ontogenesis of meaning.* Hillsdale, NJ: Erlbaum.

Overton, W. F. (1998). Developmental psychology: Philosophy, concepts and methodology. In R. M. Lerner (Ed.) & W. Damon (Lead Ed.), *Theoretical models of human development. Vol. 1: Handbook of child psychology* (5th ed.). New York: Wiley.

Papousek, H., & Papousek, M. (1979). Early ontogeny of human social interaction. In M. von Cranach, K. Koppa, W. Lepenies, & P. Ploog (Eds.), *Human ethology: Claims and limits of a new discipline.* Cambridge: Cambridge University Press.

Papousek, H., & Papousek, M., (1987). Intuitive parenting: A didactic counterpart to the infant's precocity in integrative capacities. In J. D. Osofsky (Ed.), *Handbook of infant development* (2nd ed.). New York: Wiley.

Papousek, M., Papousek, H., & Bornstein, M. (1985). The naturalistic vocal environment of young infants. In T. Field & N. Fox (Eds.), *Social perception in infants.* Norwood, NJ: Ablex.

Pavlidis, T. (1969). Populations of interacting oscillators and circadian rhythms. *Journal of Theoretical Biology, 22,* 418–436.

Pederson, D., & Moran, G. (1995). A categorical description of infant-mother relationships in the home and its relation to q-sort measures of infant-mother interaction. *Monographs of the Society for Research in Child Development, 60*(2–3, Serial No. 244).

Piaget, J. (1954). *The construction of reality in the child.* New York: Basic Books. (Original work published 1937.)

Piaget, J. (1995). *Sociological studies.* London: Routledge. (Originally published 1965.)

Pittendrigh, C. S. (1961). On temporal organization in living systems. In *Harvey Lecture Series, 1960–1961, (Vol. 56).* New York: Academic Press.

Ramey, R., & Ourth, L. (1971). Delayed reinforcement and vocalization rates of infants. *Child Development, 42*(1), 291–297.

Ramus, F., Hauser, M., Miller, C., Morris, D., & Mehler, J. (2000). Language discrimination by human newborns and by cotton-top tamarin monkeys. *Science, 288,* 349–351.

Reese, H., & Overton, W. (1970). Models of development and theories of development. In L. Goulet & P. Baltes (Eds.), *Life span developmental psychology: Research and theory.* New York: Academic Press.

Reiter, N. (1986). *The interpersonal accommodation of vocal behavior in the interactions of abusing mothers with abused children and their siblings.* Doctoral dissertation, University of Maryland, Baltimore County.

Richters, J., Waters, E., & Vaughn, B. (1988). Empirical classification of infant-mother relationships from interactive behavior and crying during reunion. *Child Development, 59,* 512–522.

Roe, K., Roe, A., Drivas, A., & Bronstein, R. (1990). A curvilinear relationship between maternal vocal stimulation and 3 month olds' cognitive processing. *Infant Mental Health Journal, 2,* 175–189.

Roe, K. V., McClure, A., & Roe, A. (1982). Vocal interaction at 3 months and cognitive skill at 12 years. *Developmental Psychology, 18,* 15–16.

Rose, S. A. (1989). Measuring infant intelligence: New perspectives. In M. H. Bornstein & N. A. Krasnegor (Eds.), *Stability and continuity in mental development.* Hillsdale, NJ: Erlbaum.

Rosenthal, R., & Rosnow, R. L. (1991). *Essentials of behavioral research: Methods and data analysis* (2nd ed). New York: McGraw-Hill.

Ruddy, M., & Bornstein, M. (1982). Cognitive correlates of infant attention and maternal stimulation over the first year of life. *Child Development*, **53**(1), 183–188.

Ruesch, J., & Bateson, G. (1951). *Communication: The social matrix of psychiatry*. New York: W. W. Norton.

Sagi, A., van Ijzendoorn, M., & Koren-Karie, N. (1991). Primary appraisals of the strange situation: A cross-cultural analysis of preseparation episodes. *Developmental Psychology*, **27**(4), 587–596.

Sameroff, A. (1983). Developmental systems: Contexts and evolution. In W. Kessen, (Ed.), *Mussen's Handbook of Child Psychology (Vol. 1)*. New York: Wiley.

Sander, L. (1977). The regulation of exchange in the infant-caretaker system and some aspects of the context-content relationship. In M. Lewis & L. Rosenblum (Eds.), *Interaction, conversation, and the development of language*. New York: Wiley.

Sander, L. (1995). Identity and the experience of specificity in a process of recognition. *Psychoanalytic Dialogues*, **5**(40), 579–593.

Schaffer, H. R. (1977). *Studies in mother-infant interaction*. New York: Academic Press.

Seboek, T. (Ed.). (1966). *Current trends in linguistics (Vol. 3)*. The Hague: Mouton & Co.

Seifer, R., & Schiller, M. (1995). The role of parenting sensitivity, infant temperament, and dyadic interaction in attachment theory and assessment. *Monographs of the Society for Research in Child Development*, **60**(2–3, Serial No. 244).

Serunian, S. A., & Broman, S. H. (1975). The relationship of Apgar scores and Bayley Mental and Motor scales. *Child Development*, **46**, 696–700.

Shannon, C. (1963). The mathematical theory of communication. In C. Shannon & W. Weaver (Eds.), *The mathematical theory of communication*. Urbana: University of Illinois Press.

Sherrod, L. (1979). Social cognition in infants: Attention to the human face. *Infant Behavior and Development*, **2**, 279–294.

Shields, P., & Rovee-Collier, C. (1992). Longterm memory for context-specific category information at six months. *Child Development*, **63**, 245–259.

Siegel, L. (1989). A reconceptualizaton of prediction from infant test scores. In M. Bornstein & N. Krasnegor (Eds.), *Stability and continuity in mental development: Behavioral and biological perspectives*. Hillsdale, NJ: Erlbaum.

Slade, A., Dermer, M., Gerber, J., Gibson, L., Graf, F., Siegel, N., & Tobias, K. (1995). Prenatal representation, dyadic interaction and quality of attachment. Paper presented at the Society for Research in Child Development Conference, Indianapolis, IN.

Spangler, G., & Grossman, K. (1993). Biobehavioral organization in securely and insecurely attached infants. *Child Development*, **64**, 1439–1450.

Spelke, E., & Cortelyou, A. (1981). Perceptual aspects of social knowing. In M. Lamb & L. Sherrod (Eds.), *Infant social cognition*. Hillsdale, NJ: Erlbaum.

Spitz, R. (1963). The evolution of the dialogue. In M. Schur (Ed.), *Drives, affects and behavior (Vol. 2)*. New York: IUP.

Squire, L., & Cohen, N. (1985). Human memory and amnesia. In G. Lunch, J. McGaugh, & N. Weinberger (Eds.), *Neurobiology of learning and memory*. New York: Guilford.

Sroufe, A. (1983). Infant-caregiver attachment and patterns of adaptation in the preschool: The roots of maladaptation and competence. In M. Perlmutter (Ed.), *Minnesota symposia on child psychology (Vol. 16)*. Hillsdale, NJ: Erlbaum.

Sroufe, A. (1985). Attachment classification from the perspective of infant-caregiver relationships and infant temperament. *Child Development*, **56**, 1–14.

Stayton, D., Ainsworth, M., & Main, M. (1973). Individual differences in infant responses to brief everyday separations as related to other infant and maternal behaviors. *Developmental Psychology*, **9**, 213–225.

128

Stern, D. (1971). A microanalysis of the mother-infant interaction. *Journal of the American Academy of Child Psychiatry*, **10**, 501–507.

Stern, D. (1974). Mother and infant at play: The dyadic interaction involving facial, vocal and gaze behaviors. In M. Lewis & L. Rosenblum (Eds.), *The effect of the infant on its caregiver.* New York: Wiley.

Stern, D. (1977). *The first relationship.* Cambridge, MA: Harvard University Press.

Stern, D. (1985). *The interpersonal world of the infant.* New York: Basic Books.

Stern, D. (1995). *The motherhood constellation.* New York: Basic Books.

Stern, D., Beebe, B., Jaffe, J., & Bennett, S. (1977). The infant's stimulus world during social interaction. In H. R. Schaffer (Ed.), *Studies in mother-infant interaction.* New York: Academic Press.

Stern, D., & Gibbon, J. (1979). Temporal expectancies of social behaviors in mother-infant play. In E.Thoman (Ed.), *Origins of the infant's social responsiveness.* Hillsdale, NJ: Erlbaum.

Stern, D., Hofer, L., Haft, W., & Dore, J. (1985). Affect attunement: The sharing of feeling states between mother and infant by means of intermodal fluency. In T. Field & N. Fox (Eds.), *Social perception in infants.* Norwood, NJ: Ablex.

Stern, D., Jaffe, J., Beebe, B., & Bennett, S. (1975). Vocalizing in unison and alternation: Two modes of communication within the mother-infant dyad. *Annals of the New York Academy of Sciences*, **263**, 89–100.

Stevenson, M., Verhoeve, J., Roach, M., & Leavitt, L. (1986). The beginning of conversation: Early patterns of mother-infant vocal responsiveness. *Infant Behavior and Development*, **9**, 423–440.

Stolorow, R., & Atwood, G. (1992). *Contexts of being.* Hillsdale, NJ: Analytic Press.

Sullivan, H. (1940). *Conceptions of modern psychiatry.* New York: Norton.

Tarabulsy, G., Tessier, R., & Kappas, A. (1996). Contingency detection and the contingent organization of behavior in interactions: Implications for socioemotional development in infancy. *Psychological Bulletin*, **120**(1), 25–41.

Taylor, C. (1991). *The ethics of authenticity.* Cambridge, MA: Harvard University Press.

Thelen, E. (1998, April). Presidential Address given at the International Society for Infant Studies, Atlanta, Georgia.

Thelen, E. & Smith, L. (1994). *A dynamic systems approach to the development of cognition and action.* Cambridge: MIT Press.

Thomas, E., & Martin, J. (1976). Analyses of parent-infant interaction. *Psychological Review*, **83**, 141–155.

Thomas, E. A. C., & Malone, T. W. (1979). On the dynamics of two-person interactions. *Psychological Review*, **86**(4), 331–360.

Tobias, K. (1995).*The relation between maternal attachment and patterns of mother-infant interaction at four months.* Unpublished doctoral dissertation, City University of New York.

Tononi, J., Sporns, O., & Edelman, G. (1994). A measure of forebrain complexity: Relating functional segregation and integration in the nervous system. *Proceedings of the National Academy Science*, **91**, 5033–5037.

Trevarthen, C. (1979). Communication and cooperation in early infancy: A description of primary intersubjectivity. In M. Bullowa (Ed.), *Before speech: The beginnings of human communication.* London: Cambridge University Press.

Trevarthen, C. (1993). The self born in intersubjectivity: The psychology of an infant communicating. In U. Neisser (Ed.), *Ecological and interpersonal knowledge of the self.* New York: Cambridge University Press.

Tronick, E. (1980). The primacy of social skills in infancy. In D. Sawin, R. Hawkins, L. Walker, & J. Penticuff (Eds.), *Exceptional infant (Vol. 4).* New York: Bruner Mazel.

Tronick, E. (1989). Emotions and emotional communication in infants. *American Psychologist*, **44**(2), 112–119.

Tronick, E., Als, H., Adamson, L., Wise, S., & Brazelton, T. B. (1978). The infant's response to entrapment between contradictory messages in face-to-face interaction. *American Academy of Child Psychiatry*, **17**, 1–13.

Tronick, E., Ricks, M. & Cohn, J. (1982). Maternal and infant affective exchanges: Patterns of adaptation. In T. Field & N. Fox (Eds.), *Emotion and interaction: Normal and high-risk infants*. Hillsdale, NJ: Erlbaum.

van den Boom, D. (1997). Sensitivity and attachment: Next steps for developmentalists. *Child Development*, **64**, 592–594.

van Ijzendoorn, M., Juffer, F. & Duyvesteyn, M. (1995). Breaking the intergenerational cycle of insecure attachment: A review of the effects of attachment-based interventions on maternal sensitivity and infant security. *Journal of Child Psychology & Psychiatry*, **36**(2), 225–248.

Verzeano, M. (1950). Time-patterns of speech in normal subjects. *Journal of Speech & Hearing Disorders*, **3**, 197–201.

von Bertalanffy, L. (1968). *General system theory: Foundations, development, applications*. New York: Braziller.

Warner, R. (1988). Rhythm in social interaction. In J. McGrath (Ed.), *The social psychology of time*. London: Sage.

Warner, R. (1992). Cyclicity of vocal activity increases during conversation: Support for a nonlinear systems model of dyadic social interaction. *Behavioral Science*, **37**, 128–138.

Warner, R. (1996). Coordinated cycles in behavior and physiology during face-to-face social interactions. In J. H. Watt & C. A. Van Lear (Eds.), *Dynamic patterns in communication processes*. Thousand Oaks, CA: Sage.

Warner, R., Malloy, D., Schneider, K., Knoth, R., & Wilder, B. (1987). Rhythmic organization of social interaction and observer ratings of positive affect and involvement. *Journal of Nonverbal Behavior*, **11**(2), 57–74.

Waters, E., Vaughn, B., & Egeland, B. (1980). Individual differences in infant-mother attachment relationship at age one: Antecedants in neonatal behavior in an urban, economically disadvantaged sample. *Child Development*, **51**, 203–216.

Watson, J. (1985). Contingency perception in early social development. In T. M. Field & N. A. Fox (Eds.), *Social perception in infants*. Norwood, NJ: Ablex.

Watson, J. (1994). Detection of self: The perfect algorithm. In S. Parker, R. Mitchell, & M. Boccia (Eds.), *Self-awareness in animals and humans: Developmental perspectives*. New York: Cambridge University Press.

Weinberg, K., Tronick, E., Cohn, J., & Olson, K. (1999). Gender differences in emotional expressivity and self-regulation during early infancy. *Developmental Psychology*, **35**(1), 175–188.

Weinberg, R. A. (1989). Intelligence and IQ: Landmark issues and great debates. *American Psychologist*, **44**, 98–104.

Weiss, P. (1970). Whither life science? *American Scientist*, **58**(2), 156–163.

Welkowitz, J., Bond, R., Feldman, L., & Tota, M. (1990). Conversational time patterns and mutual influence in parent-child interactions: A time-series approach. *Journal of Psycholinguistic Research*, **19**, 221–243.

Welkowitz, J., Cariffe, G., & Feldstein, S. (1976). Conversational congruence as a criterion of socialization in children. *Child Development*, **47**, 269–272.

Welkowitz, J., & Feldstein, S. (1970). Relation of experimentally manipulated interpersonal perception and psychological differentiation to the temporal patterning of conversation. *Proceedings of the 78th Annual Convention of the American Psychological Association*, **5**, 387–388.

Werner, H. (1948). *Comparative psychology of mental development.* New York: Science Editions.

Winfree, A. T. (1975). Unclocklike behaviour of biological clocks. *Nature,* **253**(5490), 315–319.

Winnicott, D. W. (1965). *The maturational processes and the facilitating environment: Studies in the theory of emotional development.* London: Hogarth Press.

Yin, J. (1995). CREB as a memory modulator: Induced expression of a dCREB2 activator isoform enhances long-term memory in drosophila. *Cell,* **81**, 107–115.

Zelner, S. (1982). *The organization of vocalization and gaze in early mother-infant interactive organization.* Doctoral dissertation, Yeshiva University, New York.

Zeskind, P. S., & Marshall, T. R. (1991). Temporal organization in neonatal arousal: Systems, oscillations and development. In M. J. S. Weiss & P. R. Zelazo (Eds.), *Newborn attention: Biological constraints and the influence of experience.* Norwood, NJ: Ablex Pub. Corp.

Zlochower, A., & Cohn, J. (1996). Vocal timing in face-to-face interaction of clinically depressed and nondepressed mother and their 4-month-old infants. *Infant Behavior and Development,* **19**, 371–374.

ACKNOWLEDGMENTS

Supported, in part, by grant NIMH41675-03; the Kohler Foundation; the American Psychoanalytic Fund; the Edward Aldwell Fund; the March of Dimes, The Daniel Principe Memorial Gift; the Clinical Research Center Grant MH30906 at NYSPI; and a Gift from Lore Kann.

We would like to thank Martha Denckla, M.D., for her enthusiasm for the project at its very inception; Alex Heller, Ph.D., for mathematics consultation; Harold Fox, M.D., for consulting on the recruitment of subjects; Sharon Gordon, Ph.D., and Samuel Anderson, Ph.D., and Lan Chin for facilitating data collection; John Gottman, Ph.D., for consulting on time-series analysis; Edward Tronick, Ph.D., for consulting on theoretical issues; Mary Jo Ward, Ph.D., for supervising attachment coding, and Judith Sirokin, Ph.D., for coding attachment; Ina Wallace, Ph.D., for supervising the scoring of the Bayley Scales; Annette Rotter, Ph.D., and Rebecca Schwartz, Ph.D., for scoring the Bayley Scales; Don Ross, Ph.D., for extensive statistical consultation; Amie Ashley Hane, M.A., for AVTA analyses; Terri Harold for editorial assistance; Sara Markese, Michael Ritter, Catherine Man, and Emma Barnstable for manuscript assistance; the graduate students who functioned as "strangers"; and the families whose generosity made this research possible.

DIALOGICAL NATURE OF COGNITION

Philippe Rochat

The overarching message of this monograph is that cognition and cognitive development are inseparable from social adaptation. Although not new, this message has often tended either to be ignored or to take a backseat in the quest for a machinelike description and explanation of cognition and its development. The report of Jaffe, Beebe, Feldstein, Crown, and Jasnow is another wake-up call to the danger of splitting the cognitive from the social.

The complex and careful observations reported in this monograph demonstrate that from the origins of development children do not construe the world in independence of the process by which they establish relationships with other individuals. After reading the report of this research, one should be convinced that the study of cognitive processes (thinking, reasoning, problem solving, concept formation, etc.) cannot and should not be divorced from social processes that allow the individual to commune with others, to manage social proximity, and to search for intimacy.

There are two parts to my commentary. First, to complement Jaffe and collaborators' findings I offer some considerations regarding important developmental changes marking the 1st year of life. My point is that we should avoid the temptation to reduce infants to a fixed quantity of intelligence or interpersonal skills that would explain long-term predictions and stability of behavioral outcome, whether IQ or attachment patterns. In fact, the story is much more complex, involving major developmental transitions and changes between birth and age 12 months.

In the second part of this commentary, I make a theoretical plea for the socially grounded nature of cognition. This plea is inspired by the remarkable findings compiled in this monograph. These findings demonstrate the reliable link between interpersonal (vocal) coregulation at age 4 months and attachment patterns as well as cognitive abilities at age 12 months. Particularly remarkable is the fact that the assessment of cognition was based on test items that are not obviously social. These were items originally designed to be purely cognitive, involving for the most part physical objects such as stacking blocks or looking for hidden objects (Bayley, 1969).

Social-Cognitive Development in the 1st Year

There is a danger that the general picture of the infant that emerges from the findings of Jaffe and collaborators will suggest to some that the infant exhibits potentially "innate" interpersonal sophistication and a sophisticated information processing capacity, along with a stability of behavior that extends across the 1st year of life. Such nondevelopmental conclusions, however, are not warranted. By comparing infants at ages 4 and 12 months, the monograph skips over major behavioral reorganizations that occur during the 1st year of life. My first goal in this commentary is to provide a reminder of those developments.

The monograph affirms the view that 4-month-old infants are full-fledged participants in bidirectional exchanges with social partners. The way they coregulate their vocal exchanges is, in some respect, analogous to the way adults interact. Jaffe et al. show in minute detail that, "aspects of adult dialogic structure are already in place at age 4 months." They show, for example, that infants tend to match switching pause duration, pausing for periods comparable to those of the adult before taking their turn in vocal exchanges. As Jaffe et al. remind us, this is a well-documented fact found in the literature on the pragmatics of conversation among adults (Crown, 1991; Jaffe & Feldstein, 1970; cited by Jaffe et al. in their monograph).

The early ability of infants to coconstruct rhythms of vocal exchanges with adults is combined with an exquisite sensitivity to context. The monograph demonstrates very convincingly that not only do 4-month-olds coregulate their vocal exchanges in an adult manner, but this sophisticated coregulation is modulated by the degree of novelty of the social partner. The research suggests that, as for adults (Crown, 1991), tighter conversational coordinations are expressed when conversing with a novel compared to a familiar person. Furthermore, this phenomenon is compound with the novelty of the location where the conversation takes place (i.e., laboratory as opposed to home).

Jaffe et al. reveal that 4-month-old infants engaging in protoconversation are not merely passive responders to adults' solicitations; rather, they are active participants exploring and discriminating social partners in situ. Infants at this age already manifest timing aspects characterizing the pragmatics of mature social exchanges that are potentially the basis of procedural memories associated with specific individuals. As suggested by the authors, these representations of "timing pragmatics" could be the basis of social discrimination by the young infant (e.g., mother vs. stranger) and apparently are the source of developing patterns of attachment. But what is the origin of this remarkable social sophistication?

Based on Jaffe et al.'s findings, there is the danger of jumping too quickly to the conclusion that this interpersonal sophistication may be "innate" or "hard wired" into the biology of the neonate (see, e.g., Trevarthen, 1979). This conclusion, however, would overlook the major developmental achievements that occur in the first few weeks of postnatal life, which lead infants toward the interpersonal and communicative skills so well captured in this monograph. In fact, a great deal happens prior to age 4 months in terms of socialization and mental growth. What follows is a reminder that the younger infants studied by Jaffe et al. are already the product of marked behavioral transformations and important experiential changes. I will later turn to a consideration of developmental changes that occur between age 4 months and age 12 months when the infants were retested.

Age 2 Months: Revolution With a Social Smile

Between birth and age 4 months, significant development changes take place both in the way infants enter into relationships with others and in the way they interact with physical objects. Until the 2nd month, the behavior of the healthy term infant in many ways resembles the behavior of the healthy fetus in the last 2 to 3 months of pregnancy. Ultrasonic techniques allowing for fine analysis of fetal behavior reveal the unquestionable continuity between pre- and postnatal behavior (De Vries, Visser, & Prechtl, 1982; Prechtl, 1984). Until approximately 6 weeks outside the womb, infants behave essentially as externalized fetuses (Rochat & Striano, 1999a). Their wake-sleep cycle is comparable, many of their patterns of sensory motor coordination are similar to that expressed in the womb, and each demonstrates a capacity for learning by habituation and dishabituation to novel multimodal events (De Casper & Fifer, 1980; DeCasper et al., 1994; Marlier, Schaal, & Soussignan, 1998).

By approximately age 6 weeks, infants appear to wake up to the world. Their state regulation shifts markedly. By this age, there is a dramatic increase in the amount of time infants spend in an awake and alert state, the state in which infants appear to process new information and explore their environment (Wolff, 1987). Accompanying this state regulation change, infants manifest for the first time socially elicited smiling in face-to-face interaction with a social partner. This is an unmistakable and crucial event

135

recognized with delight by parents and caretakers who typically discover a person in their infant.

The emergence of externally elicited smiling marks the beginning of an explicit bidirectional sense of shared experience between infants and the people surrounding them. It is, in many ways, the true beginning of intersubjectivity, the beginning of a long conversation with others, a psychological birth that follows by a few weeks the biological birth of the infant. The timing of this psychological birth appears to be remarkably robust, regardless of the variety of care-giving practices surrounding the infant (Barr, Bakeman, Konner, & Adamson, 1987).

From age 2 months on, infants interact with people and objects in new ways. There are changes in what guides the infant's attention, changes in the infant's preferences, changes in the process of scanning objects, and, most important, changes in the way the infant interacts with other persons. From being discriminative, the infant's social stance becomes reciprocal and conversational (Rochat, 2001a).

The developmental change in social stance is particularly important in that it opens new possibilities for rapid developments. The entry into reciprocal exchanges with others involves the kind of bidirectional vocal transactions depicted in the present monograph, along with eye exchanges, facial expressions, and postural, tactual, and tonic transactions. All of these contribute to a transformation not only of the infants' construal of the others with whom they enter into relationships, but also of their way of construing and acting on *physical* objects in the world as indexed by the Bayley test.

From the time they smile at other persons, and up to age 4 months and beyond, infants develop social expectancies and begin to explore systematically the consequences of their own actions on objects (Rochat, 2001b; Rochat, Querido, & Striano, 1999; Rochat & Striano, 1999b). They become deliberate agents expecting both reciprocity from others and efficacy in their action on objects. In short, there is a long and marked development leading infants to become the sophisticated 4-month-old communicators depicted by Jaffe and collaborators. Often, much of this development is unrecognized, and its mechanisms remain largely unknown.

Age 9 Months Revolution: Triangulation Between Self, Objects, and People

The developmental predictions reported in this monograph, although real, might also give the illusion of a general behavioral stability between ages 4 and 12 months. As with the period between birth and age 4 months, the period from age 4 months to age 12 months is marked by major developments in the way infants construe the world, particularly in the way they relate to other persons. By age 6 months, the primacy of face-to-face exchanges tends to decrease as infants become increasingly infatuated with the exploration of physical objects. Research in my own lab has shown over and over again that between ages 4 and 6 months there is a very robust decrease in the relative amount of visual attention paid by the infant to a soliciting social partner (e.g., Rochat, Striano, & Blatt, in press, 2001). From a stage dominated by an interest in person, infants move to a stage dominated by an interest in objects. Postural development and the emergence of independent locomotion, generally by 9 to 12 months of age, support infants' propensity to explore ever larger areas of their physical environment (Campos, J. J., Anderson, D. I., Barbu-Roth, M. A., Hubbard, E. M., Hertenstein, M. J., and Witherington, D. (2000), Travel Broadens the Mind, *Infancy*, 1 (2), 149–219). Interestingly, it is also at around this age that infants begin to exhibit stranger anxiety, or what is sometime labeled as the "8th month anguish" (Spitz, 1965). Stranger anxiety and the increased fear of separation from primary caretaker(s) is probably closely related to infants' ever-expanding object exploration that leads them away from the immediate proximity of mother, whom however they still need as secure base.

In fact, infants at about this age face a major dilemma. They are pulled by two contradictory forces: the drive to explore increasingly larger portions of the object world and the drive to remain close and maintain contact with primary caretakers (Rochat, 2001a). This fundamental dilemma, which I believe to be universal and a major source of progress for the infant, is somehow resolved when, beginning at age 9 months, the infant begins to incorporate others into his or her exploration of the physical world via joint engagement.

From age 9 months, infants make efforts to incorporate other people in their foray into the world of objects. They begin to display joint attention, social referencing, and imperative gestures such as pointing. They also begin to comprehend symbolic gestures and they utter their first words to communicate with others about specific events and things occurring in an environment that is explicitly shared (Carpenter, Nagell, & Tomasello, 1998; Tomasello, 1995a, 1999).

Just as by age 2 months infants show first unambiguous signs of shared experience via smiling (so-called "primary" intersubjectivity; Trevarthen, 1979), by age 9 to 12 months infants bring intersubjectivity to a dramatically new level, the level of a referential triangle between the self, objects, and people.

The developments briefly outlined here serve as a reminder of the major transformations that occur in the 1st year of life, but they do not diminish the remarkable predictive findings reported by Jaffe and collaborators in their monograph. On the contrary, these developmental transformations make the Jaffee et al. findings all the more striking. Indeed, a major question is how the stability and apparent order found in this monograph are possible in the face of so many profound developmental changes. It appears that for the authors, what remains stable is the temporal information processing ability of the infant—specifically the general capacity to parse temporal events that are coconstructed with a social partner as well as the general capacity to respond to novelty.

This mediating mechanism is put forth by Jaffe et al. to account for both interpersonal transmission of style with respect to attachment at age 12 months, and the infant's mental status at the same age as measured by the Bayley test. However, as noted by the authors, the Bayley test is both a measure of cognitive and social abilities requiring infants to process the pragmatics of the communicative exchange as the test is administered, as well as the object of the test itself. Obviously, a test is never *purely* cognitive, particularly at age 12 months. It is always part of a complex social exchange between individuals adopting specific roles, either the role of tester or tested, with all the authority and submission attached to each. Therefore, it is indeed reasonable that the predictions of attachment pattern and mental ability at age 12 months have a common social-cognitive denominator, in particular the ability to process and sequence temporal events that are coconstructed in interaction with others.

Next, I would like to push this idea further by suggesting that cognition is ontogenetically rooted in social exchanges, whether real as depicted in this monograph, or virtual as in private dialogical thinking emerging later in older children and adults. The general idea is that an essential aspect of thinking and reasoning as higher functions is their framing in the ongoing dialogues we carry on with others, and that we also constantly carry on with ourselves (Fernyhough, 1996; Vygotsky, 1962, 1978; Wertsch, 1991).

Thinking as Real and Virtual Dialogues

Thinking is both private and public. We solve problems in interaction with others as well as on our own. Thinking alone and thinking with others are, in fact, strikingly analogous situations. In both cases we tend to engage in dialogues, whether real or virtual. In thinking—for example, trying to solve a problem, build a theory, or defend a case—we are constantly playing devil's advocate to test our construct. For an adult, it is hard to imagine any problem-solving situation without such real or virtual role taking. As a case in point, overt monologues while thinking are not uncommon, and they are even uncontrollable for many. This is not abnormal behavior. Rather, it appears to be the expression of a real and highly meaningful phenomenon, namely the fact that, at least for adults, private thoughts are framed as virtual social exchanges involving virtual interlocutors.

This idea is certainly not new (see Bakhtin, 1981, in relation to literature; Cole, 1985; Fernyhough, 1996; Vygotsky, 1962, 1978; and Wertsch, 1991, in relation to psychology and developmental cognition in particular; and Fridlund, 1994, in relation to the expression of emotion and real or virtual audience effects). However, relatively few systematic efforts have been made by contemporary researchers to conceptualize thinking, problem solving, reasoning, or even social cognition in these dialogical terms. This is remarkable considering that we can all agree that at least part of our conscious interpersonal and thought processes entails inner dialogues that closely resemble brainstorming with real people.

Thinking as virtual dialogues is a major avenue of cognitive progress, and consequently it is a major avenue of knowledge acquisition and the process by which knowledge is redescribed to become more explicit (Karmiloff-Smith, 1992; Tomasello, 1999). Virtual dialogues are analogous to and, in fact, modeled after the process by which one gains knowledge via tutoring and problem solving in interaction with real interlocutors. It is obvious that virtual dialogues are not available from the beginning of language, and thinking itself requires a good deal of development before these dialogues become available. Specifically, symbolic functioning and some basic ability to switch perspectives and adopt different virtual roles or "voices" (i.e., the acquisition of a "theory of mind") are necessary prerequisite abilities. The first evidence of virtual dialogues in children seems to occur at around 2 to 3 years of age when they first begin to engage in pretend play (Harris, 1994; Tomasello, 1999). Role taking in the form of virtual dialogues is the hallmark of early pretend play, which in turn is the hallmark of childhood.

The artifacts that surround children, such as toys and other miniature replicas of real things, nourish the propensity to pretend, to adopt roles, and ultimately to create virtual dialogues. Parental culture is very systematic in nurturing this propensity by surrounding the child with pretend opportunities via manufactured toys and games. Note however that this cultural scaffolding is especially prominently promoted in the industrialized West, although toys probably exist in all cultures, at least in higher social classes.

Thinking via the process of virtual dialogues opens several developmental opportunities to the child. As in tutoring and learning via interaction with someone else, it is a major source of knowledge and problem resolution. When discussing issues or problems with someone else or in a group, whether in casual conversations or in more formal settings (e.g., the classroom), there is always on-line tutoring and mutual consolidation of thoughts and ideas. Coconstructing ideas and resolving problems in negotiation with others allow individuals to bypass their own cognitive limitations. I believe that such social-cognitive dialectic or instructive social exchanges are re-created in virtual dialogues as a source of cognitive progress for the individual. This idea was formulated many years ago by Vygotsky (1962, 1978) in relation to children's internalization of culture and language expressed in internal speech.

Language is not a prerequisite for children to experience the basic benefit of conversing with others. As clearly demonstrated in this monograph, infants at age 4 months are already actively engaged in coordinating their interpersonal exchanges. From such coordination they gain the experience of rhythms of vocal and turn states as well as the coconstruction of novel sequencing or temporal parsing of auditory events. In fact, such exchanges enhance temporal parsing. It scaffolds the infant in breaking the flow of perceptual events into analyzable units that can be represented as organized procedural or pragmatic memories, as suggested by Jaffe et al. In other words, *protoconversation provides infants with the unique opportunity to parse and represent perceptual events.* This is probably an important aspect of the ontogenetic roots of collaborative thinking and future thinking as virtual dialogues.

When infants begin to coregulate their transactions with others, they are actually inducted into the realm of instruction and collaboration and are engaged in the coconstruction of experience. This is the source of intersubjectivity or shared experience, but also the origin of thinking as virtual dialogue.

It is worth noting that the parent-infant engagement in extended face-to-face exchanges is a particularly human activity. Nonhuman primates, although they engage in grooming and display much affectionate care for their progeny, do not seem to engage in coconstructed face-to-face dialogues to the same extent that human mothers and infants do, regardless of culture or social status. It is thus reasonable to assume that there is something uniquely human in the instructional and collaborative model offered to infants in face-to-face dialogues. This may be a partial mechanism for the developmental emergence of uniquely human cocognitive adaptations such as language and explicit thinking in the form of real as well as virtual social dialogues.

Others in Mind and the Emergence of Coawareness

The dialogical nature of cognition finds strong support in the fact that beyond infancy, and in particular by the 2nd year, children begin to manifest explicit social coawareness. It is by this time that children begin to express self-consciousness in mirrors and other reflecting devices (Bertenthal & Fisher, 1978; Lewis & Brooks-Gunn, 1979). In identifying themselves, children actually become aware of how others perceive or, more precisely, how others might perceive them. This explains why children beginning to manifest mirror self-recognition also often manifest embarrassment (Lewis, 1992). What children start to manifest is a sense of the self that is exposed to the public eye. This novel awareness shapes children's cognition and cognitive progress. It also determines their behavior in general. This phenomenon is concisely captured in the following passage:

> There is a thing that happens with children: If no one is watching them, nothing is really happening to them. It is not some philosophical conundrum like the one about the tree falling in the forest and no one hearing it: that is a puzzler for college freshmen. No. If you are very small, you actually understand that there is no point in jumping into the swimming pool unless *they* see you do it. The child crying, "Watch me, watch me," is not begging for attention; he is pleading for existence itself. (M. R. Montgomery, *Saying Goodbye: A Memoir of Two Fathers*, cited by Tomasello, 1995b, p. 449).

By their 2nd year, healthy children (as opposed to children who eventually develop relational impairments such as autism) progress increasingly with others and virtual others in mind. For example, we have recently found that a means-ends problem-solving task (a Piagetian task of pulling a blanket to bring an attractive object within reach) that is easily solved at 9 months of age is not as easily solved by 18-month-old children, who tend to place their effort in requesting help from the experimenter rather than in solving the problem on their own (Goubet, Maire-LeBlond, Poss, & Rochat, 2001).

A simple task typically resolved alone at age 8 months is transformed 10 months later into the primarily social task of including others in its resolution. At the purely surface level of performance, this is a regression. At a deeper level of competence, it is the sign of a big step toward teaching and instruction, two major engines of human cognitive growth.

In conclusion, the intriguing data reported by Jaffe et al. stimulate the revival of radical views on development and the dialogical nature of cognition that I have tried to articulate in the latter part of this commentary. They provide strong empirical vindication to the radical intuitions of previous theorists like Lev Vygotsky who proposed that

> All higher psychological functions are internalized relationships of the social kind, and constitute the social structure of personality. Their composition, genetic structure, ways of functioning—in one word—all their nature is social. Even when they have become psychological processes, their nature remains quasi-social. The human being who is alone also retains the functions of interaction. (Vygotsky, 1960; cited in Valsiner, 1997, p. 154).

141

This view should inspire more developmental research capturing in systematic ways the dialogical and social nature of cognition as it unfolds in development. This monograph shows how stimulating such research can be, from the outset of development.

References

Bakhtin, M. M. (1981). *The dialogic imagination*. Austin: University of Texas Press.

Barr, R., Bakeman, R., Konner, M., & Adamson, L. (1987). Crying in !Kung infants: A test of the cultural specificity hypothesis. *Pediatrics Research*, **21**, 178A

Bayley, N. (1969). *Manual for the Bayley Scales of Infant Development*. New York: Psychological Corporation.

Bertenthal, B. I., & Fisher, K. W. (1978). Development of self-recognition in the infant. *Developmental Psychology*, **14**, 44–50.

Campos, J. J., Anderson, D. I., Barbu-Roth, M. A., Hubbard, E. M., Hertenstein, M. J., & Witherington, D. (2000). Travel broadens the mind. *Infancy*, **1**(2) 149–220.

Carpenter, M., Nagell, K., & Tomasello, M. (1998). Social cognition, joint attention, and communicative competence from 9 to 15 months of age. *Monograph of the Society for Research in Child Development*, **63**(4), 1–143.

Cole, M. (1985). The zone of proximal development: Where culture and cognition create each other. In J. V. Wertsch (Ed.), *Culture, communication, and cognition: Vygotskian perspectives*. Cambridge, UK: Cambridge University Press.

Crown, C. (1991). Coordinated interpersonal timing of vision and voice as a function of interpersonal attraction. *Journal of Language and Social Psychology*, **10**(1), 29–46.

DeCasper, A. J., & Fifer, W. P. (1980). Of human bonding: Newborns prefer their mothers' voices. *Science*, **208**(4448), 1174–1176.

DeCasper, A. J., Lecanuet, J.-P., Busnel, M.-C., Granier-Deferre, C. (1994). Fetal reactions to recurrent maternal speech. *Infant Behavior & Development*, **17**(2), 159–164.

De Vries, P. I. P., Visser, G. H. A., & Prechtl, H. F. R. (1984). Fetal motility in the first half of pregnancy. In H. F. R. Prechtl (Ed.), *Continuity of neural functions from prenatal to postnatal life*. Spastics International Medical Publications. Oxford: Blackwell Scientific Publications Ltd.

Fernyhough, C. (1996). The dialogic mind: A dialogic approach to the higher mental functions. *New Ideas in Psychology*, **14**, 47–62.

Fridlund, A. J. (1994). *Human facial expression*. San Diego: Academic Press.

Goubet, N., Maire-Leblond, C., Poss, S., & Rochat, P. (2001). Emerging collaborative stance by 9-18 month-old infants. Poster presented at the meeting of the Society for Research in Child Development, Minneapolis, April 2001.

Harris, P. L. (1994). Understanding pretence. In C. Lewis & P. Mitchell (Eds), *Children's early understanding of mind*. Hillsdale, NJ: Erlbaum.

Jaffe, J., & Feldstein, S. (1970). *Rhythms of dialogue*. New York: Academic Press.

Karmiloff-Smith, A. (1992). *Beyond modularity: A developmental perspective on cognitive science*. Cambridge, MA: MIT Press.

Lewis, M. (1992). *Shame: The exposed self*. New York: Free Press.

Lewis, M., & Brooks-Gunn, J. (1979). *Social cognition and the acquisition self*. New York: Plenum Press.

Marlier, L., Schaal, B., & Soussignan, R. (1998). Neonatal responsiveness to the odor of amniotic and lacteal fluids: A test of perinatal chemosensory continuity. *Child Development*, **69**(3), 611–623.

Prechtl, H. F. R. (1984). *Continuity of neural functions: From prenatal to postnatal life.* Spastics International Medical Publications. Oxford: Blackwell Scientific Publications Ltd.

Rochat, P. (2001a). *The infant's world.* Cambridge, MA: Harvard University Press.

Rochat, P. (in press, 2001b). Social contingency detection and infant development. *Menninger Bulletin.*

Rochat, P., Querido, J. G., & Striano, T. (1999). Emerging sensitivity to the timing and structure of protoconversation in early infancy. *Developmental Psychology, 35*(4), 950–957.

Rochat, P., & Striano, T. (1999a). Social-cognitive development in the first year. In P. Rochat (Ed.), *Early social cognition: Understanding others in the first months of life.* Mahwah, NJ: Erlbaum.

Rochat, P., & Striano, T. (1999b). Emerging self-exploration by 2-month-old infants. *Developmental Science, 2,* 206–218.

Rochat, P. Striano, T., & Blatt, L. (in press, 2001). Differential effects of happy, neutral, and sad still-faces on 2-, 4-, and 6-month-old infants. *Infant and Child Development.*

Spitz, R. A. (1965). *The first year of life: A psychoanalytic study of normal and deviant development of object relations.* New York: Basic Books.

Tomasello, M. (1995a). Joint attention as social cognition. In C. D. P. J. Moore (Ed.), *Joint attention: Its origins and role in development.* Hillsdale, NJ: Erlbaum.

Tomasello, M. (1995b). Understanding the self as social agent. In P. Rochat (Ed.), *The self in infancy: Theory and research. Advances in psychology, 112.* Amsterdam: North-Holland/ Elsevier Science Publishers.

Tomasello, M. (1999). *The cultural origins of human cognition.* Cambridge, MA: Harvard University Press.

Trevarthen, C. (1979). Communication and cooperation in early infancy: A description of primary intersubjectivity. In M. M. Bullowa (Ed.), *Before speech: The beginning of interpersonal communication.* New York: Cambridge University Press.

Valsiner, J. (1997). *Culture and the development of children's action.* New York: Wiley.

Vygotsky, L. S. (1962). *Thought and language.* Cambridge, MA: MIT Press.

Vygotsky, L. S. (1978). In M. Cole (Ed.), *Mind in society: The development of higher psychological processes.* Cambridge, MA: Harvard University Press.

Wertsch, J. V. (1991). *Voices of the mind.* Cambridge, MA: Harvard University Press.

Wolff, P. H. (1987). *The development of behavioral states and the expression of emotions in early infancy: New proposals for investigation.* Chicago: University of Chicago Press.

FACE-TO-FACE PLAY: ITS TEMPORAL STRUCTURE AS PREDICTOR
OF SOCIOAFFECTIVE DEVELOPMENT

Daniel N. Stern

The authors of this monograph take what at first glance is a small piece of behavior, the on/off timing of adults and 4-month-old infants vocalizing to each other. They describe and analyze it with state-of-the-art methods. They argue convincingly that the resulting timing patterns reflect basic features of the social interaction—as they put it, the "pragmatics" of interpersonal dialogue. They set their findings within a systems theory view of the coconstructed nature of development. Then they go on to show that these early-established dialogic patterns predict later attachment and cognitive outcomes.

I would like to take up some issues that particularly interested me. But first there are several aspects of this monograph worth emphasizing as a guide to further studies in this area:

- The Automated Vocal Transaction Analyzer (AVTA) system provides a method of examining a fundamental feature of social interaction that is very fast, relatively cheap for what it does, extremely precise, and not labor intensive.

- The distinction between "coupling" and "coordination" is crucial to a deeper understanding of this material and to any other similar dialogic interactive material collected elsewhere and in other ways.

- The analysis of individual dyads as well as group data is also critical and should be adopted when possible.

- The literature review fully sets the problem in its historical context and clearly indicates the current frontier. It shows where to go, both methodologically and conceptually.

Besides these clear virtues, there are several issues that intrigued me particularly, and which I will develop further.

What Is Involved in Playing With Someone? Or What Are the Many Features of the Quality of Play That May Be Predictive?

The situation studied was one of face-to-face play, which almost all agree may be the most central experience at age 4 months for learning how to be with another, socially. Remember, the infant is not yet proficient in reaching or grasping objects. He is not yet captivated by objects to manipulate, and his world is still confined to, designed for, and geared to interact with the "sound and light show" that is his parent's vocal and gestural behavior. One would think that the quality of face-to-face play with the mother at home would predict later attachment patterns even better than they did. The story the authors found was not so simple. I will try to simplify it.

The study searches for mother-infant rhythmic coupling and bidirectional coordination in the face-to-face play situation. Yet play requires a certain level of openness that does not permit high predictability. These considerations bear on three intriguing findings of the research. First, when mother and infant are at home in a doubly familiar context (mother in home vs. stranger in the lab) the degree of bidirectional coordination is less. The authors suggest that the stranger in the lab is a situation of novelty that carries uncertainty, challenge, or threat. To adapt to those circumstances, interpersonal predictability in timing is increased. At least you know when and for how long the other is going to do whatever he or she is going to do, relative to your own behavior, and vice versa. In the home base setting with mother, there is less need for vigilance, and the temporal patterns do not need to be as constrictive or predictive. Mother and infant can relax together. I would add that their relaxing is an active and necessary condition for play, not just the release from pressure.

The second finding is that under these conditions the degree of bidirectional coordination is relatively less and the unidirectional coordination is increased. The third finding is that when examining the coordination between mother and infant, it was only the scores of bidirectional coordination in the midrange that distinguished 12-month-olds' secure attachment patterns from the disorganized classification, which fell in the high range of bidirectional coordination.

When we consider the special conditions needed for playing, these three findings taken together make sense. Playing can only occur in a setting where there is a feeling of ease, of security, of not having to be vigilant, being free of other pressing needs. Only in such a setting can some of the basic aspects and requirements for play appear, such as a loose frame that permits spontaneity and unpredictability; the incorporation of accidents, errors, and rule violations; the momentary uncoupling from the other to explore and adjust inside yourself and then rejoin the partner; sometimes fiddling with the very timing of interactions and expectations so as to create variations and pleasurable violations; and other such nonlinear and frame-breaking features that enhance creativity.

Accordingly, during mother-infant play at home, we would expect a midrange of bidirectional coordination, a roughly equal proportion of uni- and bidirectional coordination (which is partially dependent on the former), and evidence of the extent of "relaxation" into the relationship, as the authors describe it. This last measure could be, for example, the difference between the degree of bidirectional coordination in the doubly novel condition (stranger, lab) minus that pertaining in the doubly familiar condition (mother, home). Might these three criteria of quality of play, taken together, better predict the attachment outcomes? The study, as a systematic descriptive effort, has examined the predictive power of each variable. With that done, one can return to the basic question of whether there is heterotypic continuity from quality of face-to-face play with mother at home to quality of attachment at age 12 months. I still imagine that face-to-face play with mother at home should be the most predictive for all patterns of attachment—after all, that is where most of social affective life gets lived at age 4 months. Being unwilling just yet to give up this idea, it may be necessary to independently describe clinically different qualities of face-to-face play to see which clusters of timing variables are correlated. Then the validated grouping of timing variables can be used to predict later attachment behavior.

Stated otherwise, to enhance predictability and to make even more clinical sense of this approach, one may have to move in the direction that attachment research did early in its history, namely, grouping variables to arrive at categories that will be better predictors than any variables alone. The findings of this monograph indicate how to start doing that. Perhaps the slower 20–30 s interactive rhythms could be helpful here too, as a possible additional criterion for quality of play. I suggest this because it often happens in face-to-face play that these longer cycles reflect the success in bringing the interaction to stretches of high excitement/activation, followed by stretches of cooling off and recuperation. This is a sign of interactive success.

Chunking, and the Psychological "Present Moment" for an Infant

We are all interested in infant's subjective life, even if we cannot do much to elucidate it. Nevertheless, certain data suggest inferences. The idea of a "present moment" has been circulating in psychology for a long time. Such an idea is necessary when we consider that life is directly experienced only in the present moment. There is no other time when life is lived. The phenomenological present moment has gone by several names: the "sensible present" (James, 1891), the "perceived present" or "psychological present" (Fraise, 1964), the "actual present" (Koffka, 1935), and the "personal present" (W. Stern, 1930). The concept is a crucial entity in the phenomenology of perception (Merleau-Ponty, 1962). All capture slightly different aspects of this subjective experience. And, currently, the neurosciences have taken up this notion in exploring the neurological mapping of subjective experience and in particular consciousness (including "simple" awareness or primary consciousness).

The basic idea of a present moment is that the flow of experience is not subjectively continuous but is parsed into groupings that have some kind of coherence. A musical phrase is a good example. It is the whole phrase as a global unit that is parsed and occupies an extended subjective present while it is being heard; in other words, it is a present with a duration. This is the basic unit of heard music. The individual notes are registered but passed over to capture the phrase. The same applies to the spoken phrase, where the individual phonemes and words that compose it are passed over to capture the sense of the larger unit, its meaning, which unfolds during an extended present moment.

Data from various sources show that for adults, an average musical phrase, line of spoken poetry, spoken sentence, breath cycle, and many communicative movements and gestural groupings last 2–7 s (e.g., Fraise, 1964, 1978; Trevarthen, 1999/2000; Stern, in preparation). This appears to be a fairly ubiquitous duration in which the presently unfolding events are grouped into coherent meaningful wholes. (The duration needed to chunk is dependent, in part, on the nature and frequency of the events. The duration of the subjective present is thus variable, but within limits.)

Data from this monograph may bear on these questions in infancy. Are there units of awareness? Does the infant parse the flow of experience into bounded present moments, as adults do, making his subjective world partially discontinuous? Are such units the units of "meaning" or sense, such as the sense of a dialogue of pragmatics?

The authors find that in the condition of an infant interacting with mother at home, the average maternal vocalization plus switching pause is 1.29 s + .91 s = 2.20 s, and the average maternal vocalization plus nonswitching pause is 2.24 s (Table 2). In comparison, when the mother is talking to an adult stranger at home, her vocalization plus switching pause averages 2.38 s, and her vocalization plus nonswitching pause averages 2.37 s. The difference between the durations directed to the infant, as against those directed to the adult, are not very large. In one case,

147

vocalizing to the infant, we are talking about music. In vocalizing to the adult, we are talking about speech. Either way, the chunks within the total flow fall into that range of 2 to 7 s.

Is the infant's ability to parse human events into meaningful wholes that occupy a "psychological present" being formed or entrained? Or are infants born with a temporal predisposition to chunk into units with durations of roughly several seconds? Did evolution create in parallel a temporal disposition in the infant, and a range of durations of meaningful human sound and movement? Or do infants just learn it, given their extraordinarily precocious timing capacities?

The infants themselves produce chunks (vocalization plus pause) of 1.51 s or 1.69 s when interacting with mother, a little less than a second shorter than hers. Is this a question of temporal limitations in parsing (a psychological issue) or shortness of the breath cycle (a physiological issue)? Or, does self-parsing have different parameters than parsing the behavior of others and the infant must simply learn to become more effectively communicative? Many such questions are lying in this very rich data.

Representing the Pragmatics of Dialogue

The discussion of the infant's representation of the "pragmatics of dialogue" is most valuable and of clear clinical importance. Representing such pragmatics raises several questions. Clearly the time parameters are represented. There are two kinds of time involved: filled time (vocalizations) and empty time (pauses). In experimental situations, the mind treats them differently (Fraise, 1978). Granted, pauses can be filled with anticipation and other silent internal state shifts. And they are very likely to be so filled in this situation. So the represented unit could be, and probably must be, the vocalization + pause unit. I would imagine that the vocalizations are remembered and represented (implicitly) both in terms of what fills the durations as well as the duration itself. If what fills the duration (including the pauses) is viewed as a "temporal feeling shape" or "vitality affect" (D. N. Stern, 1985, 1995, 1998; D. N. Stern, Hover, Haft, & Dore, 1984), then the temporal parameter is perceived and represented as part of a pragmatic event that is bounded by the arc of an intention. The pieces are then in place for a representation of the pragmatics of dialogue.

One could go on. The solidity and richness of this work invites speculation and inspires further experimentation.

References

Fraise, P. (1964). *The psychology of time.* (Translated from the original, *La Psychologie du Temps*, 1963, by Jennifer Leith.). London: Eyre & Spottiswoode Ltd.

Fraise, P. (1978). Time and rhythm perception. In E. C. Carterette & M. P. Friedman (Eds.), *Handbook of Perception: Vol 8*. New York: Academic Press.

James, W. (1891). *Principles of psychology*. London: Macmillan.

Koffka, K. (1935). *Principles of Gestalt psychology*. New York: Harcourt.

Merleau-Ponty, M. (1962). *The phenomenology of perception*. London: Routledge.

Stern, D. N. (1985). *The interpersonal world of the infant*. New York: Basic Books.

Stern, D. N. (1995). *The motherhood constellation*. New York: Basic Books.

Stern, D. N. (1999). "Vitality Contours": The temporal contour of feelings as a basic unit for constructing the infant's social experience. In P. Rochat (Ed.), *Early social cognition*. Hillsdale, NJ: Erlbaum.

Stern, D. N., Hofer, L., Haft,.W., & Dore, J. (1984). Affect attunement: The sharing of feeling states between mother and infant by means of intermodal fluency. In T. Field & N. Fox (Eds.), *Social perception in infants*. Norwood, NJ: Ablex.

Stern, W. (1930). William Stern. In C. Murchison (Ed.), *A History of Psychology in Autobiography (Vol.I)*. Worcester, MA: Clark University Press.

Trevarthen, C. (1999/2000). Musicality and the intrinsic motive pulse: Evidence from human psychobiology and infant communication. Musicae Scientiae: Special Issue, *Rhythm, Musical Narrative, and Origin of Human Communication*.

CONTRIBUTORS

Joseph Jaffe (M.D., 1947, New York University) is professor of clinical psychiatry (in neurosurgery), College of Physicians & Surgeons, Columbia University and chief, Communication Sciences, N.Y.S. Psychiatric Institute. His interests include neuroscience and theoretical biology. With Stanley Feldstein he is author of *Rhythms of Dialogue*, Academic Press, 1970; with Clay Dahlberg, he is author of *Stroke: A Doctor's Personal Story of His Recovery*, Norton, 1977.

Beatrice Beebe (Ph.D., 1973, Columbia University) is associate clinical professor of psychology (in psychiatry), College of Physicians & Surgeons, Columbia University and in the department of Communication Sciences, N.Y.S. Psychiatric Institute. She is faculty at the N.Y.U. Postdoctoral Program in Psychotherapy and Psychoanalysis, the Institute for the Psychoanalytic Study of Subjectivity, the Columbia University Psychoanalytic Center, and the Columbia Psychoanalytic Center Parent-Infant Program. With Frank Lachmann, she is the author of *Infant Research and Adult Treatment: Co-Constructing Interactions*, Analytic Press, 2001.

Stanley Feldstein (Ph.D., 1961, Columbia University) is professor and associate chair of psychology at the University of Maryland, Baltimore County and lecturer in the Department of Psychiatry of Columbia University. His research interests focus on adult-adult and adult-infant interactions as well as the influence of speech rate on interpersonal perception. He is the co-author (with Joseph Jaffe) of *Rhythms of Dialogue* (1970) and coeditor (with Aron W. Siegman) of *Nonverbal Behavior and Communication* (1987), *Of Speech and Time* (1979), and *Multichannel Integrations of Nonverbal Behavior* (1985).

Cynthia L. Crown (Ph.D., 1984, University of Delaware) is a professor of psychology at Xavier University in Cincinnati, Ohio. Her teaching is in the area of social psychology and research design and analysis. Research interests include interaction chronography, positive psychology, and program evaluation. She is a consulting editor of the Journal of Social Psychology.

Michael D. Jasnow (Ph.D., 1983, George Washington University) is assistant professor at the Center for Professional Psychology, George Washington University and teaching analyst at the Baltimore-Washington Institute for Psychoanalysis. His interests include psychoanalysis and neuroscience.

Philippe Rochat (Ph.D., 1984, University of Geneva) is professor of psychology at Emory University in Atlanta. His research interests focus on the development of a sense of self in infancy, social and emotional development in the first year, symbolic functioning in infants, young children, and nonhuman primates. He is the editor of *The Self in Infancy* (1995) and *Early Social Cognition* (1999), and is the author of *The Infant's World* (2001).

Daniel N. Stern (M.D., 1960, Albert Einstein College of Medicine) is Professor of Psychology at the University of Geneva and Adjunct Professor of Psychiatry at Cornell University Medical School, New York City.

STATEMENT OF EDITORIAL POLICY

The *Monographs* series is devoted to publishing developmental research that generates authoritative new findings and uses these to foster fresh, better integrated, or more coherent perspectives on major developmental issues, problems, and controversies. The significance of the work in extending developmental theory and contributing definitive empirical information in support of a major conceptual advance is the most critical editorial consideration. Along with advancing knowledge on specialized topics, the series aims to enhance cross-fertilization among developmental disciplines and developmental subfields. Therefore, clarity of the links between the specific issues under study and questions relating to general developmental processes is important. These links, as well as the manuscript as a whole, must be as clear to the general reader as to the specialist. The selection of manuscripts for editorial consideration, and the shaping of manuscripts through reviews-and-revisions, are processes dedicated to actualizing these ideals as closely as possible.

Typically *Monographs* entail programmatic large-scale investigations; sets of programmatic interlocking studies; or—in some cases—smaller studies with highly definitive and theoretically significant empirical findings. Multi-authored sets of studies that center on the same underlying question can also be appropriate; a critical requirement here is that all studies address common issues, and that the contribution arising from the set as a whole be unique, substantial, and well integrated. The needs of integration preclude having individual chapters identified by individual authors. In general, irrespective of how it may be framed, any work that is judged to significantly extend developmental thinking will be taken under editorial consideration.

To be considered, submissions should meet the editorial goals of *Monographs* and should be no briefer than a minimum of 80 pages (including references and tables). There is an upper limit of 150–175 pages. Only in exceptional circumstances will this upper limit be modified (please submit four copies). Because a *Monograph* is inevitably lengthy and usually substantively complex, it is particularly important that the text be well organized and written in clear, precise, and literate English. Note, however, that authors from non-English-speaking countries should not be put off by this stricture. In accordance with the general aims of SRCD, this series is actively interested in promoting international exchange of developmental research. Neither membership in the Society nor affiliation with the academic discipline of psychology is relevant in considering a *Monographs* submission.

The corresponding author for any manuscript must, in the submission letter, warrant that all coauthors are in agreement with the content of the manuscript. The corresponding author also is responsible for informing all coauthors, in a timely manner, of manuscript submission, editorial decisions, reviews received, and any revisions recommended. Before publication, the corresponding author also must warrant in the submission letter that the study has been conducted according to the ethical guidelines of the Society for Research in Child Development.

Potential authors who may be unsure whether the manuscript they are planning would make an appropriate submission are invited to draft an outline of what they propose, and send it to the Editor for assessment. This mechanism, as well as a more detailed description of all editorial policies, evaluation processes, and format requirements, can be found at the Editorial Office web site (http://astro.temple.edu/~overton/monosrcd.html) or by contacting the Editor, Willis F. Overton, Temple University–Psychology, 1701 North 13th St.—Rm. 567, Philadelphia, PA 19122-6085 (e-mail: monosrcd@blue.vm.temple.edu) (telephone: 1-215-204-7718).

Monographs of the Society for Research in Child Development (ISSN 0037-976X), one of three publications of the Society for Research in Child Development, is published four times a year by Blackwell Publishers, Inc., with offices at 350 Main Street, Malden, MA 02148, USA, and 108 Cowley Road, Oxford OX4 1JF, UK. Call US 1-800-835-6770, fax: (781) 388-8232, or e-mail: subscrip@blackwellpub.com. A subscription to *Monographs of the SRCD* comes with a subscription to *Child Development* (published six times a year in February, April, June, August, October, and December). A combined package rate is also available with the third SRCD publication, *Child Development Abstracts and Bibliography*, published three times a year.

INFORMATION FOR SUBSCRIBERS   For new orders, renewals, sample copy requests, claims, change of address, and all other subscription correspondence, please contact the Journals Subscription Department at the publisher's Malden office.

INSTITUTIONAL SUBSCRIPTION RATES FOR MONOGRAPHS OF THE SRCD/CHILD DEVELOPMENT 2001   The Americas $293, Rest of World £192. All orders must be paid by credit card, business check, or money order. Checks and money orders should be made payable to Blackwell Publishers. Canadian residents please add 7% GST.

INSTITUTIONAL SUBSCRIPTION RATES FOR MONOGRAPHS OF THE SRCD/CHILD DEVELOPMENT/CHILD DEVELOPMENT ABSTRACTS AND BIBLIOGRAPHY 2001   The Americas $369, Rest of World £246. All orders must be paid by credit card, business check, or money order. Checks and money orders should be made payable to Blackwell Publishers. Canadian residents please add 7% GST.

BACK ISSUES   Back issues are available from the publisher's Malden office.

MICROFORM   The journal is available on microfilm. For microfilm service, address inquiries to Bell and Howell Information and Learning, 300 North Zeeb Road, Ann Arbor, MI 48106-1346, USA. Bell and Howell Serials Customer Service Department: 1-800-521-0600 ×2873.

POSTMASTER   Periodicals class postage paid at Boston, MA, and additional offices. Send address changes to Blackwell Publishers, 350 Main Street, Malden, MA 02148, USA.

CURRENT